Racing to the Brink:

The End Game for Race and Capitalism

by

Vernon Turner

Dedication

This book, my last non-fiction effort, is dedicated to all my loyal and true friends, family and colleagues who have helped me get through bouts with cancer with patience, love and encouragement. My wife, Elaine and my friend Molly Wingate have been instrumental in keeping my work as sharp and focused as possible. To them, especially, I owe unbridled thanks.

Other books by Vernon Turner

The Voter's Guide to National Salvation

A Worm in the Apple: The Inside Story of Public Education

Killing the Dream: America's Flirtation With Third World Status

Table of Contents

Foreword

Beginning...

Part I: Capitalism and the Battle for Economic Purity

Chapter 1:   How Did We Get Here?

Chapter 2:   Honor, Compromise and Sound Government

Chapter 3:   The Dilemma of Economic Theories

Chapter 4:   Don't Blame Capitalism

Chapter 5:   Wall Street's Homer Simpson Moment

Chapter 6:   Consider a Hybrid System of Economics

Chapter 7:   The Deregulation Scam

Chapter 8:   The Failure of Extremism

Chapter 9:   Slavery and the Modern Capitalist

Chapter 10: Capitalism and Neo-liberal Libertarianism Cannot Co-exist

Chapter 11: The Sounds of Familiarity

Part II: How Our Failed Models Keep Destroying our Greatness

Chapter 12: It's Hard to Watch

Chapter 13: Spinning the Moral Compass

Chapter 14: Backwards to Yesteryear

Chapter 15: Grover's Groove

Chapter 16: Unraveling Democracy

Chapter 17: Is Anyone Thinking Correctly?

Chapter 18: Mandatory Laws

Chapter 19: Why Republican Models Fail Every Test

Chapter 20: The GOP Money Game

Chapter 21: No Longer the Land of Opportunity

Chapter 22: I'm Your Friend – Really!

Chapter 23: The Time for Lying is Now

Part III: Public Education

Chapter 24:   The Evolution of Learning and Teaching

Chapter 25:   Education in America: The Beginning of Greatness

Chapter 26:   The Real Value of Teachers

Chapter 27:   The Death of Learning

Chapter 28:   Where We Went Wrong and How to Fix It

Chapter 29:   The "Super" Who Gets It

Chapter 30:   How Long Can We Do it This Way?

Chapter 31:   The Kids are All Right

Chapter 32:   Fixing and Changing the Education Paradigm

Part IV: Race in America: Consequences of Institutionalized Hate

Chapter 33:   Lincoln's Second Inaugural

Chapter 34:   Has It All Been for Nothing?

Chapter 35:   Pink Palms

Chapter 36:   Slavery and the Modern Capitalist

Chapter 37:   Unavoidable Conclusions

Chapter 38:   A Failure in the Republic

Chapter 39:   Capitalists Unchained

Chapter 40:   The Accurate Obama

Chapter 41:   Nothing to Offer

Part V: Guns and the American Way

Chapter 42:   Is It Our Right to be Slaughtered?

Chapter 43:   The Second Amendment: Beginnings and Present

Chapter 44:   The Tyranny of Fear

Chapter 45:   Who Are We?

Part VI: Resetting the American Idea

Chapter 46:   Understanding Ourselves

Chapter 47:   The Wages of Disagreement

Chapter 48:   Where Are We Headed?

Chapter 49:   What's Really Important? Hint: It Isn't Ultra-conservatism

Chapter 50:   The Echo Chamber

Chapter 51:   Forgetting Democracy

Chapter 52:   The Assault on Women

Chapter 53:   Changing Minds and Habits

Chapter 54:   The Koch Archipelago

Chapter 55:   The Outrage of the Corporatocracy

Chapter 56:   War and Veterans

Chapter 57:   Rediscovering the Art of Governance

Chapter 58:   The Trap of Unlimited Progress

Chapter 59:   Let Freedom Ring

Chapter 60:   Accentuating the Positive

Chapter 61:   Outside the Box

Chapter 62:   Grid Level Electron Storage

Chapter 63:   The Twenty-eighth Amendment

Afterword

Acknowledged Sources

Forward

North and South America were populated by humans who migrated from Asia, across the *Beringia* land bridge and/or down the coast of the Americas by some sort of water craft. Archaeologists and anthropologists measure this "invasion" at between 35,000 and 16,000 years depending on what artifacts one is using, where they are found and how they are dated. Nevertheless, the "original" Americans settled the land a very long time ago compared to current, written, Western history.

It was merely 1,000 years ago that the first intrepid explorers from Scandinavian Europe visited the "New World" by establishing rude settlements in what are now the maritime provinces of Canada. Their success was very limited and they abandoned North America after some very bad winters. It took another 300 years for a "civilized" European nation to rediscover the western hemisphere by beginning colonies in the Caribbean islands. From that time forward, a pattern of imperialistic conquest and exploitation from the major European nations has proceeded unimpeded by anything.

Colonization may be used as a modern euphemism for capitalism's need for market expansion and wealth creation for those who own the mechanisms for economic growth and expansion. Trade has been with the human condition ever since we discovered commodities, over-production of goods and the ability to barter. Before those discoveries, humans hoarded and fought each other at the tribal level to gather MORE resources for survival including human slaves and gene pool fresheners, aka, women and children from other tribes. When Western explorers first saw native Americans, these behaviors were still very much in practice among those tribes and shocked them with their similarities to the same sorts of behaviors in Europe and Asia over the centuries preceding "civilization" and church dogma. The only conclusion left us is to assume that colonization, plunder, rape and combat between groups is a normal part of our human behavior suite. How we manage it and control it determines how civilized we are today and how we construct our moral and ethical systems to honor behaviors that actually share largesse, despise wanton killing and war and promote a "love thy neighbor" attitude. When these things outweigh the primitive side of human nature, we create civil obedience, community relations that actually benefit all members of that community and actions that prepare our children for survival and success in their adulthood. That's the idea for most civilizations in modern times.

The last 500-600 years of history in the Americas has seen the complete abrogation of the original residents' rights, lands and ways of life by the irresistible wave of European technology, greed, voraciousness for resources and markets and the imposition of western religion on peoples who had developed their own for thousands of years. Yes, many "pilgrims" were escaping one form of repression or another in Europe. The Spanish, Portuguese, Dutch, French, British and, to a lesser extent, Russian merchants/explorers invaded the Americas at their leisure and swept aside native resistance with their guns, diseases and deceit. As you will discover in following chapters, the advent of the sugar, rice, tobacco and cotton industries set the bar for what European merchants and their influence on their national leaders would do to exploit, use up and discard both material and human resources. The ancient concept of slavery was brought to the New World by the very descendants of those Europeans and Asians who used slaves to expand their economic systems.

Slavery itself was not thought to be immoral until certain sects of Christianity began pressuring western governments to take human chattel out of the economics picture. Even though the British, Dutch and French were all involved with the slave trade in the New World, it fell to the United States to endure the greatest blood-letting in the known history of North and South America before the shock of this human immorality was fully appreciated. Still today, however, the echoes and scabs of slavery persist with the racism, prejudice, bigotry and hatefulness that drives wedges between people in every country on both continents.

Once the European explorers fulfilled their governments' edicts and "claimed" portions of the two continents, the exploitation began and the fates of the aboriginal peoples' fates were sealed. The grinding maw of unregulated capitalism forced the moves by the colonists into the forests, the rivers, the mountains and the prairies to begin the wholesale exploitation of furs, people and land. When more sophisticated technology developed, new mineral resources were required, discovered and used. Gold, of course, began the mindless exploitation of ancient cultures in Central and South America by the Spanish and Portuguese. They used guns to terrorize the populace and take what they wanted, while unwittingly leaving the disease germs of Europe to decimate the aboriginal populations; not a great bargain.

7

In North America, the sweep west took only about 200 years until European descendants had defeated the native tribes and placed them in hopelessness-ridden reservations, just short of genocide. The history of the "manifest destiny" of the United States is fraught with abuse, murder, disease and outright slaughter of our native peoples. Today, the lust for oil, gas and coal continues that exploitation and road to extinction with the destruction of the land, rivers and air support systems that supported these tribes for thousands of years. I can't help but pause every so often, and take stock of the incredible arrogance our European ancestors harbored as they mindlessly swept westward, northward and southward to extract a new country without regard for the residents of the old country they were taking over.

Then, I am using the metric of morality and decency I was taught regarding my fellow man when I use strong language condemning what our American colonists did to not only forge a new nation, break from the governmental colonization of Great Britain but to ignore our own lessons regarding those who were here before us. It is incumbent on all of us to remember that we, as a species, are about 200,000 years old. But it is only in the last 10,000 years, or so, that we have discovered agriculture, economics and capitalism. These concepts and practices are immensely sophisticated compared to the previous 190 centuries of hunter-gatherer-tribal organisms who barely clung to survival by their wits and abilities to make weapons and tools.

The point is, of course, that we are a very sophisticated social organism still carrying the very basic instincts and emotions of a very ancient organism whose brain is still hard-wired to survive at any cost; humans are the most adaptable organism to walk the planet. The final determination of our continued success on this planet depends on how we continue to break ourselves away from ancient ways and forge an entirely new path toward controlling our urges, our economics and our propensity for self-destruction.

We waste, we discover more resources and we use them up. We then move to another place where we can use up those resources, lay waste to the environment and move on. We need only look at how we are investigating the objects in outer space to get a hint that there are those among us who already are looking outside our Earth for mineral resources to keep the all-consuming economic engine of growth and exploitation alive and well. Meanwhile, we refuse to consider that we have over-populated the planet to the point where our exponential consumption growth per human will literally eat us out of house and home.

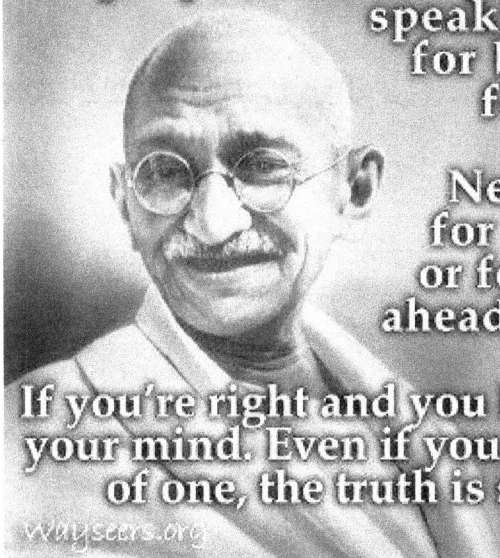

"Many people, especially ignorant people, want to punish you for speaking the truth, for being correct, for being you.

Never apologize for being correct, or for being years ahead of your time.

If you're right and you know it, speak your mind. Even if you are a minority of one, the truth is still the truth."

~ Gandhi

Wayseers.org

Part I

Capitalism and the Battle for Economic Purity

Capitalism is the extraordinary belief that the nastiest of men for the nastiest of motives will somehow work for the benefit of all.

- John Maynard Keynes

We are not in the business to save lives, but to make money.

- Executive for Roche Laboratories

We may have democracy, or we may have wealth concentrated in the hands of the few, but we cannot have both.

- Supreme Court Justice Louis Brandeis

Beginning...

The little boy pressed his nose to the cold glass of his dad's car and watched the rivulets of rain slide effortlessly downward until they disappeared into the door. He often wondered where the water went until he saw it dripping out the bottom of the door on another car being washed by his neighbor. The boy was curious like this about everything.

He would ask his dad unusual questions like why they called a spark plug a "plug". "Did it hold sparks in?" The father was often patient, then, equally impatient with the boy's curiosity. Sometimes the father was highly enthused about being a father to this curious boy and would charge ahead with lessons on things that certainly no other 9 or 10 year old boy would see. The father showed the boy how to read complex blueprints as if to trick him into being confused. But the boy understood how the lines and dimensions and the logic of the different views worked and understood the perception of seeing in his mind the transformation of two-dimensional drawings into 3-dimensional objects. He could see the grooves and flanges and the hidden holes just by looking at the drawings. The father showed him how to calculate the dimensions and made up little problems for the boy to solve. The boy learned about decimals before he learned them in school and showed off to his teacher how he could turn a fraction into a decimal number. He was a smart boy, a curious boy who didn't mind learning….anything.

This day, however, was not the day to learn about drawings and numbers and decimals. This day the father decided to take the boy down to skid row, the slums of Cleveland, Ohio. This chilly, gray, rainy day seemed most appropriate for the boy to learn about the dark side of town, so the father decided in his limited social experience. The father was just 33 years old, but had endured the sacrifices of World War II on the home front. The father worked in a factory making airplane engine valves for all the warplanes the allies used to fight and win that war. Everyone including the father wore their sacrifices like badges of honor and filled their mantels with mementos of those times. The father's mantel held the one-millionth engine valve produced at his factory. The father once told the boy that he had worked 11 months without a day off. The factory produced many more millions of valves before the war finally ended.

The father thought that this day would be a good day to teach the boy his first lesson in what he perceived as social issues. They were headed for the infamous Hough Avenue neighborhood near East 55th St., the heart of the Cleveland ghetto. They didn't call it a ghetto then. The Yiddish word had not yet made it into the lexicon of American cities in 1952; it still belonged to Warsaw and the other cities of death in Europe. In Cleveland it was merely "the slums". In New York it was "the tenements". The people all looked alike if you went to see them in the different cities. In Chicago it was "the South Side". In St. Louis it was East St. Louis, but that was across the river in Illinois, a natural barrier from the "other" part of town.

As the nearly new 1951 Mercury eased its way down the trash-lined streets, it crossed St. Clair Avenue and headed toward Euclid. The boy looked out the window at row after row of apartment buildings rising 4 or 5 stories above the street. The backs of the buildings all had wooden balconies that were connected from one floor to the next by rickety looking staircases, some with railings some without. It seemed to the boy that these structures clung to the buildings like gray skeletons waiting for the occupants of the buildings to walk on their bones. The dark gray sky gave the scene a kind of hopeless feeling to the boy even before he lowered his eyes and saw the people there.

The people.... They were not like him in any way except that they had the requisite number of limbs and a head. They all had dark skin. He'd never seen a person with dark skin before. Their clothes were kind of worn looking and, of course, wet. Still, they played a kind of faux baseball in the streets using what looked like broom handles and an old tennis ball. When the Mercury cruised into view, they all stopped and stared at it looking at the boy and wondering who he was and why was he "down here". The boy stared back and felt as if he'd left his world for another. He had.

The father broke the spell by beginning a lecture about how he, the boy, could end up in a place like this if he didn't study hard in school and pay attention to the rules and obey the laws. The father did mention that these people were poor, that they'd always been poor and they would remain poor forever, because "they" had no ambition to improve themselves. "That's the difference between them and us," the father said. "They don't want to improve themselves, but we do. I didn't get a chance to finish high school or go to college, but, by God, you're going to so you don't end up like this. No son of mine is going to end up on skid row. Do you understand?!"

This sudden burst of admonition caught the boy off guard. He felt as if he'd done something wrong already and started to feel as if he would cry. The father, sensing that he may have come on too strongly, changed the subject and pointed out a black man wearing a red suit while an overly dressed young woman, also black, held an umbrella over him. Upon seeing the Mercury slowly cruise the streets, the man in the red suit ambled in their direction using that peculiar style of walking known as the *pimp roll* where the hips and shoulders of the walker preceded and followed each other to a unique rhythm of the streets. The father pointed to the man in the red suit and told the boy that he was a pimp.

The boy didn't ask what a pimp was for a while and the father didn't offer any further explanation. Finally, the boy asked, "What's a pimp? And who was that lady holding the umbrella for him?"

"That 'lady' was a whore (he pronounced it: "Whooer") and the pimp is the guy who finds her customers."

"Customers? What kind of customers, dad?"

"Customers for sex", the father mumbled realizing he had ventured into unintentional territory that would require more explanation than he felt like providing.

The boy, sensing that this was a kind of moral minefield he had only barely heard of said, "Oh."

The drive back home to East Cleveland took about 20 minutes, but seemed like an eternity for the boy. He leaped out of the car and ran to his room and closed the door. The sensory overload had pushed him to wanting quiet, quiet where no fear, anxiety, guilt or sadness could find its way into his place just then. The cascade of things he had just seen that day flew by his mind's eye like someone flipping a tablet cartoon movie, each scene being a page, each page being another emotion. He didn't even take off his jacket. He just sat on the edge of his bed and wondered why his father had taken him to that awful place just to tell him that he'd better be a good boy.

The father didn't understand that the bluntness of his introduction of his son to a lifestyle he himself was only barely familiar with was as dramatic and impressionable as it was on the boy. He sensed that the boy had come home with a new appreciation for something, but wasn't sure what that was. He would soon find out, because the boy would spend the rest of his life discovering what it was that made "those people" so hopeless and what could be done to make it different. At the end of this day, the boy was helpless to come to any conclusion except to wonder again why his father took him to such a place and what he'd done wrong to be punished so.

Chapter 1:   How Did We Get Here?

It began with sugar, of course. Sugar, that sweet-to-the-taste substance that oozes from the stalks of a grass known as *cane*, was a seductive sensation from Indonesia, discovered by Westerners in the 15th century. It became a prized trading substance and was anointed "for royals only" from the Arabian peninsula to the ornate palaces of Europe for almost 100 years before somebody figured out how to grow it and refine it for commercial value. Once tasted by the general public everywhere, it became such a hot commodity that new sugar cane plantations had to be built to allow this new business to flourish and for huge profits to be made by those owning the plantations and the infrastructure necessary to bring it to market.

None other than Christopher Columbus planted the first sugar cane in the western world, on the island of *Hispaniola*. What he and the eager businessmen discovered was that growing, harvesting and processing sugar cane was difficult, dirty, hot and dangerous work. European laborers, being mostly free men, found other ways to destroy their bodies and minds and refused to work on sugar plantations such that profits could be realized. Enter the concept of "indentured servitude", aka slavery for the new world. It didn't take long for European businessmen to discover that the continent of Africa was teeming with labor potential; in fact a whole new industry emerged from the need to profit from sugar: The Slave Trade.

Deals were struck between slave merchants and African tribal leaders who had prisons filled with old enemies and/or a surplus of people of their own to sell. The slave traders eagerly purchased these people and shipped them to the Americas to feed the maw of the sugar industry. With the explosive growth of the sugar business, the pressure for more slaves became so strong that the kidnapping and shipping of people from Africa to the Americas became as equally important as the bartering with tribes for human chattel.

The sugar business gave rise to the rum and molasses businesses along the way requiring more infrastructure and labor to support the profits generated by those enterprises. For over 200 years, this exploitation of man and land in the "New World" fed the sweet tooth and alcoholism of the European societies. As the new British colonies in North America began producing other crops, in addition to sugar, like tobacco and cotton for European consumption and trade, slavery was merely extended there to bolster the concept of the cheapest labor available on the planet.

These centuries of exploiting black and brown people for their free labor to fill the coffers of businessmen around the world became the "normal" condition for the Western hemisphere well into the 18th century before some activists realized the immorality of these conditions. In a rare burst of righteousness, certain Christian churches in Europe deemed slavery to be immoral and convinced politicians to cease and desist in participating in the slave trade between Africa and the Americas. This didn't stop slavery from keeping the economy booming, but merely transferred the effort from transporting slaves to creating slave "farms" in the Americas.

As the United States fought for and won its independence from Great Britain, slavery was incorporated into the original Constitution in order to keep the southern colonies "in the fold" of the new nation. Slavery was, after all, the cheapest labor on Earth and the Southern economy was basically agrarian and competitive with foreign markets *because* of the cheap labor. To abolish slavery would have been a paradigm shift causing great bankruptcy and disruption of this economy.

The anti-slavery zeal found its way to the United States, but primarily in the Northern tier of states where the most self-righteous, big money people and political influence resided. Abolition, the anti-slavery movement, became the wedge of the 19th century that drove itself between the people of North and South such that a war was inevitable. That war – some say it was America's penance for adopting slavery from the nation's inception – was the most horrific conflict the nation endured before or since. Nearly 700,000 Americans were either directly or indirectly killed during that four-year horror.

President Lincoln's assassination at war's end allowed any ordered, moral and legal reconstruction of the nation's wounds to go glimmering. White "carpetbaggers" from the North exploited the prostrate South and created as much enmity as profit from the people left from the war. Meanwhile, the Southern resentment extended to the black people recently freed by the 14th Amendment put in place by the Lincoln administration. The result of this festering humiliation and frustration by Southerners created the "Jim Crow" laws of the 19th and 20th centuries.

"Separate and unequal" was the order of the day in the "old Confederacy". Black people were still treated like slaves and any attempts they made to join the country were thwarted by the states rights laws of the South. Even though rights like voting and public schools were protected by the Constitution, Jim Crow made it very difficult for black people to vote and their schools were much poorer and less funded than those for white children.

Even though the 13th, 14th and 15th Amendments to the Constitution gave black people all the rights of everyone else, it took the Civil Rights legislation of the 1960s to finally break the Jim Crow grip on Southern blacks. These new laws did not come cheaply as much agitation, murder and blood were necessary to get the attention of enough people to provide the political support to get these laws passed and enforced by Congress.

Fast-forward to 2008 and the Presidential election season... The Democratic candidate turned out to be a man of color; a man of a Kenyan-born father and an American Caucasian woman. This man, Barack Obama, was raised mostly by his mother and grandparents in the Midwest. He was born in Hawaii and lived in Indonesia with his mother for a time while still a child. His accomplishments academically were of the first order of excellence including grading *magna cum laude* from the prestigious Harvard Law School.

He was elected President and was inaugurated on 20 January 2009. Barack Obama openly stated that he wanted and needed to work with ALL Americans to repair the disaster left him by his predecessor. He said these things in the spirit of Lincoln's "bind up our wounds" speech. Merely weeks after Obama became President, the leader of the Senate Republicans, Mitch McConnell (R-Kentucky), stated that the number one priority of the Republican Party was to make Barack Obama a one-term President. Now, why would he say that?

The country was embroiled in two wars of choice, jobs were allowed to leave to Asia, Africa and South America faster than ever before, the deficit was skyrocketing, banks were collapsing from their own greed, the national infrastructure was crumbling, the auto industry was teetering on collapse and the Great Recession was upon the land like a plague of locusts born of Wall St. Yet, the spokesperson for the opposition party was more interested in getting Barack Obama out of office as quickly as possible.

This stroll down history's halls and memory lane sets the stage for this book's theme and message. It is an expose' about a nation losing its mind and its way to and not binding up its wounds, not fixing its roads and bridges, not re-energizing its schools and not returning privacy to its citizens while not fighting back against the creeping resurgence of those same forces that embraced slavery and the oppression of black people 200 years ago. How does any rational person explain the mishandling of our priorities to wit: With failing schools, 20 million starving children, 50 million people living in poverty, crumbling roads, an unwillingness to provide health care for its people, pressure to suppress voting rights, the highest incarceration rate and volume in the world and a grossly unfair tax code, how do we justify spending the majority of our treasure on our military? What, exactly, are we defending if not the well-being of our people, and thus our nation?

Let's begin here with this question: What exactly are we defending that causes us to be so war-like and so backward toward the well-being of our people? This book will examine many of the aspects of our recent history and how we do things and the results of action, inaction, brilliance and abject stupidity. Few punches are pulled and little objective history is ignored.

Chapter 2:   Honor, Compromise and Sound Government

My friend and colleague, Mr. Steve Love coined some wonderful thoughts about our state of the nation and the machinations between our political differences. I will set his words in italics or bold when he uses italics.

"We mutually pledge to each other our Lives, our Fortunes and our sacred Honor" *is how the Declaration of Independence ends.* These are words written by men faced with the real possibility that they were signing their own death warrants. The signatories of this document knew that they were committing the American colonies to the pursuit of freedom from the yoke of British imperialism. They knew it would be war and that it would test the resolve of every American citizen to the utmost whether they were loyalists or revolutionaries. The full measure of that commitment would be paid by some of the signers and some would go on to eventually write the Constitution. They didn't know whether they would be successful, but they knew they had to try.

As we look back at those Founders, we must understand that their commitment was to each other! It was not made to a nation, for none existed at the time; or to a deity, though they put their trust in "divine Providence." It was a pledge of fidelity by a small compact of men devoted to a common cause becoming aware of the price they might be asked to pay to achieve their goal...that for America to come into existence they might have to sacrifice their lives, fortunes and sacred honor.

Today, this sort of commitment and value structure seems lost on our current population of elected officials who presume to govern. *Conservatives seem to have linked faithfulness of their convictions to their sense of honor so that if they hold out for their convictions, even at the price of losing their seat in the next election, they will maintain their honor. It is this conviction that sets them in opposition to all forms of compromise. To compromise – in their way of thinking - is to lose their honor. Such was not how Lincoln or the Founders thought.*

This conceptual conflict is the precise difference between the Founders and today's so-called conservatives. *The Founders understood that majority rule arrived at through compromise is the only way that a society ... can exist. Lincoln wrote in his First Inaugural;* **"If the minority will not acquiesce, the majority must, or the government must cease."** The choices we faced at that moment, March 4, 1861, were between the despotism of minority rule, anarchy with no discernible government or majority rule *with the price to be paid for majority rule being the willingness of those with* *minority opinions to be submissive to the decisions of the majority.* This idea required a definition of honor that assumed the devotion to country over self-service; a commitment to civil order trumping special, individual interests. The southern politicians of that time could not accept that view of honor and thus triggered the bloodiest war in our history – STILL!

The question remains for today's conservatives that they understand majority rule and join with Lincoln and the Founders in sacrificing their "sacred honor" to find a middle ground where our democracy is preserved and the domestic tranquility of our nation is restored. If they are willing to meet at that middle ground with liberals and progressives on those issues that benefit the majority of the people and thus the country, we may yet avoid another schism of great upset while proving to the world and ourselves that our form of democracy can work in the worst of times as well as in the best of times.

Compromise is not a dirty word. It is the word that defines democracy and majority rule. One has to wonder why we lost that commitment in government. In my opinion it has to do with the money. And not just money by itself, but with those who have it and are using it to corrupt the ideals upon which this country was founded. The word for these people doing the corrupting is *plutocrats.*

The plutocrats are those who have allowed money and their ability to acquire it to morph into a self-image of power broker. It is a condition that is not unusual to humans no matter their status or relative wealth. But when there are only a few who have SO MUCH money and SO MUCH lust for power that Lincoln's idealism for compromise goes out the window, our democracy is in jeopardy.

The continuing attempts to buy government by Charles and David Koch are the perfect examples of how corruption of democracy works. The pandering to power brokers like the Kochs by our U.S. Supreme Court's *Citizens United v. FEC* decision is also a perfect example of how far into the halls of government the plutocrats have reached. As someone who took the pledge to defend this country against all enemies foreign and domestic, this corruption shakes me to my core that our democracy of compromise will be replaced by minority rule in the persons of the moneyed elite who are already despots in their own right, but call themselves businessmen. They are not. They used business and money to buy power and influence. That's how despots gain control of countries. History is filled with these examples.

The outcomes from despotic governments are always brutal, short-lived and destructive. We have the power to overcome this corruption. We the people still have the power to send people to our governments who are NOT corrupt, willing to compromise and humble enough to accept majority rule. We must overturn *Citizens United* and send a message to the plutocrats that the people of the United States are still in charge. Let them spend their money on innovation, technology, education and job creation instead of investing in the siren songs of corruption and power.

Chapter 3:   The Dilemma of Economic Theories

There are many gloom and doom artists out there writing about the demise of our world resulting from conflicts in economics and social behaviors. I quote several books, articles and authors in various chapters who either offer a solution or redefine the problem. Some even go so far as to define the cause of our dilemma centered on the unequal distribution of goods, services, food, water and freedom from disease as a disconnect between rates of biological and sociological evolution (*The Watchman's Rattle* – Rebecca Costa). Others derive today's Western version of capitalism from the 16th-19th century loot-and-plunder tactics of Europeans against indigenous populations also known as *imperialism.*

The following three quotes define, I think, why economic systems associated with capitalism are so easily perverted from their original intent. Economic theory either resists or ignores the natural intention of humans to fend for themselves first, fend for the tribe next and to acquire, by whatever means possible, those resources that will ensure the survival of the tribe and the individual. By extension, this means a better chance of perpetuating those genes to subsequent generations. A truly socialistic society, theoretically, cannot therefore exist.

"The problem of social organization is how to set up an arrangement under which greed will do the least harm; capitalism is that kind of system". – Milton Friedman

"Capitalism is the astounding belief that the most wickedest of men will do the most wickedest of things for the greatest good of everyone". – John Maynard Keynes.

"Unregulated capitalism will destroy itself from within". - paraphrased from Karl Marx (*Das Kapital*).

Obviously, history has shown that these three statements have been, to varying degrees, accurate. It is how they are balanced during any given period that determines how well or how poorly the society does while operating under capitalism. When there is sufficient money circulating, more people do well. When the money is being hoarded or moved to offshore banks, fewer people do well and only the wealthiest get richer.

The dilemma that neither Friedman nor Keynes anticipated was created by the voraciousness of capitalism. Because, during their time, there were still resources to exploit; indeed they seemed endless and new ones were discovered all the time. The driving motive for profit made people ceaseless innovators to not only increase profits through invention and innovation, but to make products faster and cheaper in order to continually increase profits. Now those resources – including cheap human labor - are drying up. We've roamed the entire planet looking for more oil and gas, for example, while the sun continues to provide 10,000 times more free energy than we can use while being sufficient to run dozens of Earths every day. We continue to ignore the magnitude that solar energy applications can have on our energy use mostly because it doesn't show short-term profit under today's version of capitalism.

Today's investors are only interested in *growing* businesses that show *growing* profits. I recently listened to an "analyst" say that investors were losing interest in Apple because it showed little growth lately and indicated slow near-future growth. "Oh, Apple is still hugely profitable, but investors need to see growth before they will risk their money", he said.

If this is true throughout the world of investment, finance and stockholding, then good and great companies that don't grow will see their stock value decline, thus reducing their new investments, even though they are making lots of money. How is this possible?

It's the greed thing. Greed is the element of survival for humans. We developed it consciously when we learned how to stash food and resources during lean times in order to survive them. More must be better. Greed has evolved into a necessity of living in today's world of wealth. Now, wealth MUST grow, or the wealthy person doesn't feel so wealthy and thus insecure. So, what is wealth?

Is wealth the assurance of longer life? Sort of. If you are wealthy you can afford the finest in private medical care, food and protection while those of less wealth may not be able to afford that same quality – in the United States, anyway. We're still struggling with the concept of universal health care that the rest of the world has realized improves their entire society. In those countries, money is spent on the general population instead of on just the few who want to control wealth, and who get to be wealthy. Denmark and Germany (recently) have lifted the tuition fees for higher education while American students "graduate" into six-figure indebtedness and no good-paying jobs by which to relieve that debt.

This supports the model of Milton Friedman's model for a stratified society economic plan: Supply-side economics. This idea to control wealth by having the wealthy control it instead of the government regulating it has been tried a couple times in our own history and resulted in catastrophic economic failure each time – except for the wealthy. When Friedman and friends were hired by nations like Chile, Bolivia, Poland and even China to employ this system, social chaos, disruption, corruption, despotism and ruination for the working classes and the poor was the result each time. Naomi Klein's disturbing book, *Shock Doctrine* chronicles this Frankenstein monster of economic plans, aka *Reaganomics*.

The citizenry in these countries eventually rebelled and the government was once again "allowed" to regulate wealth distribution and even make programs that kept people from starving to death or fomenting another revolution. And this was in the 20th century! The cries for small U.S. government, mostly from the Republican Party, resulted in an even bigger government with a Congress pretty much bought and paid for by the wealthy – presumably to do the bidding of those "contributors".

Here is the dilemma in a nutshell. We are running out of familiar resources. We are loath to invest in renewable energy resources because they aren't immediately profitable. Yes, the profit motive creates innovation for new ways to become more profitable and for more people to become richer, but the lords of finance have to decide there is a market. Supply-side economics stifles innovation because it ignores the greed of those controlling and hoarding capital, thus removing it from the overall economy. Take away the fuel and the engine dies. The Keynes approach allows government to stimulate growth both in job creation and available capital so that more citizens can improve their lives through gainful employment, taxes, etc. It keeps money circulating – lots of it. When we all do well, we all do well.

Finally, Marx and Engels floated too much idealism while ignoring the hoarding, greedy nature of humans actually working and sharing their society with one another. Communism stifles innovation and makes despotism too easy to form. It also tries to control the simpler socialistic instincts of people still living and thinking like it was 50,000 B.C.

Now that we've identified the dilemma, what do we do about it?

Chapter 4:   Don't Blame Capitalism

Ray Carey is the author of *Democratic Capitalism: The Way to a World of Peace and Plenty.* He wrote a very illuminating essay (#26) that we all should take care to read and understand before we let the angels of our more reactive nature mislead us into making fools of ourselves. He said that we have been wrong to blame the current economic disaster on capitalism. Instead, we should point to the misdeeds of the money managers and traders who used the peoples' capital to speculate. He correctly points out that these people are and were not capitalists and they perverted capitalism for short-term and individual gains. What he didn't mention was that the overturning of the Glass-Steagall Act of 1933 by the Gingrich Congress of 1999 allowed them to do that.

Carey also points out that capitalism is the peoples' trillions of dollars invested in companies that produce and distribute goods and services while creating jobs. He says, "Wall Street deflected this capital away from job growth exactly as Adam Smith warned that the 'prodigals and projectors' would do".

We the people should be furious with ourselves for electing those who allowed this perversion of capitalism and who promote the duplicity involved with giving trillions of dollars to the banks for even more speculation instead of requiring the investment in real capitalism in the form of jobs, goods and services. The Federal Reserve actually provided over $7 trillion dollars instead of the stated $700 billion TARP money to the banks. The banks "borrowed" this money from the FED at rates as low as .01% while raking in $13 billion (so far) by "investing" in government bonds. Meanwhile, student education loans from the U.S. government charge 6% interest.

The real scandal is that for about 25 years, "shareholder capitalism" has sacrificed job-growth programs for the price of stock, thereby building up enormous cash surplus from job layoffs. There is $1 trillion of corporate cash surplus in the domestic economy, with another $1 trillion abroad, about $3 trillion left in 401 (k) savings, and $1 trillion above required reserves sitting idle in the banks for lack of borrowers, or perhaps lack of lending motive.

Carey concludes: "If our government had applied some of the energy and creativity in putting people back to work that they applied in putting the Wall Street speculators back in business, our economic crisis would be over. With a few changes in tax law, money could be moved out of Wall Street into infrastructure repair bonds, investment in growth programs, and additions to consumer demand from dividends.

"Libertarians have hated the Federal Reserve forever, and these events may help explain why. I think it is a deeper, more sinister reason, or reasons, that we are currently experiencing this global financial upheaval that threatens the very concepts of capitalism and global economy. Beginning in the early 1980s (the Reagan era) the political movements to deregulate everything gained a foothold in the psyche of politicians and began the great "investment" in career politicians who supported corporate/banking America."

From that period to today, lobbying grew like fetid pond scum such that now our "elected" officials depend on and are beholden to the cash that comes from PACs and other groups that fund their elections and reelections. Finally, the 2010 Supreme Court's *Citizens United* decision allowed corporations and banks to fund elections and candidates with no constraints, thus opening up the vaults to literally buy influence and politicians. Before that final blow to the power of the people to choose their representatives, there was the creeping deregulation of business, industry and banking. One by one, the watchdog agencies were cut and compromised so that the financiers could have their way with investor money.

Someone has said that there is nothing new under the sun. Well, people have been trying to steal things from other people for as long as history reports. Now, however, there are 7 billion of us on Earth and stealing has become very sophisticated indeed. Legalized speculation with other peoples' money and without their permission is stealing on a global scale, and we let it happen.

Perhaps we will regain our senses soon and replace this government of Wall Street employees with people who choose to represent "We the people" instead.

UPDATE: It didn't happen in 2014. Two-thirds of American voters stayed home and allowed the extreme (in every sense of the word) minority vote in those who will do the most harm to the general public.

Chapter 5:   Wall Street's Homer Simpson Moment

Did you see where the stock markets took a dip the other day? It seems the *Barons of the Bull Market* got jittery because consumer spending wasn't up to expectations and oil prices (2015) continue to be as low as they were ten years ago. Yes, it's true. Americans just aren't spending what the 1% wants them to spend. Why this is so?

This may sound like just another trip down the memory lane of so-called "conservative" economics, but *Prosperity Lane* has morphed into a muddy path strewn with the rocks and roots of broken philosophies and just plain capitalistic incompetence.

In the 1920s, the top income tax bracket was around 25%. After the infamous George W. Bush tax cuts for the rich in 2001 and 2004, the rate was around 35%, the lowest since the Great Depression. Not only did the tax rates get lowered, but other loopholes were added to the tax code to allow corporations and wealthy individuals to pay even LESS taxes. Those cuts have recently expired and are now a little over 39%. Republican economics say that low taxes equate to jobs creation. Well, in 1929 and 2007, coincident with the tax cuts, the American jobs environment cratered and millions of American workers (note: These are not "takers".) became unemployed, some permanently. One could say it's just coincidence if it weren't for the similarities in the government's approach to minding the store for the "general welfare of the people".

Both of these eras were saddled with the "something for nothing" thinking of politicians who listened to the wrong economics "experts". They said that the free market would take care of all ills. They said that low taxes on the wealthy would create more jobs for the working classes. Neither of these "ideas" proved valid. Finally, the *savior of capitalism*, Franklin Roosevelt, did what was needed to create long-term stability and prosperity for the vast majority of the American citizenry; he brought forth the *New Deal* and all of its controls on capital, banking and investing that prevented what happened in the 1920s and the early 2000s. It's ironic that a liberal Democrat would actually show the capitalists how to save themselves from themselves.

We can trace our recent problems back to the 1971 memo by corporate attorney Lewis Powell to the U.S. Chamber of Commerce (another delicious irony) that called for corporate/banking America to purchase the U.S. Congress in order to get the laws changed to favor business and banking without those annoying restrictions like the Glass-Steagall Act. This great law prevented commercial and investment banks from merging and blowing everyone's money at the crap tables of "free market" enterprise. So, naturally, when Republicans controlled the House in 1999 they repealed this act and forced the politically crippled Bill Clinton to sign it into law. Clinton also foolishly promoted and signed into law the North American Free Trade Agreement that rewarded corporate America for sending our jobs to cheaper labor markets. Another part of NAFTA allowed us to ship our surplus corn to Mexico which raised prices in the U.S. and put many Mexican farmers out of work. These two actions are most responsible for the economic fragility which the American economy finds itself enduring today. The other significant drain on our domestic capital is allowing corporations to avoid paying taxes and allowing the rich to hide trillions of dollars in off-shore banks. General Electric, for example, hasn't paid ANY taxes for years. How is that fair or even possible, and why should their tax responsibility avoidance be shifted to those who can afford it the least?

The outcome of eight years of the Bushites' actions on de-regulating banks and providing more tax loopholes added to the almost six years of the Obama administration screwing up their political advantages by having to negotiate with a brick wall, aka the Republicans in Congress. The result is nothing is happening that benefits the majority of citizens. This is economic stagnation with the slow-growth, and cheapening of the consumer classes. While the rich get richer, the consuming classes consume less.

First, the American consumer used credit cards to keep consuming and ran up huge personal debt. Then those who did own homes were allowed to refinance them and use the equity for consuming goods and services. Well, now both those chickens have come home to roost and the droppings being left are destroying households and, slowly, the ability of our economy to respond to perturbations.

Is Wall St. finally figuring out that it screwed up again? Are the investors finally getting it that sending good jobs overseas and fighting against living wages for those 30-year olds working in fast food might be reducing consumer spending? Are they finally getting it that there might be a problem that the greatest consumer nation in history is not able to consume at an ever increasing rate, thus limiting profit growth? Does Wall St., the Republican Party and the lobbyists that support it finally see that austerity and squeezing money OUT of the system is the wrong thing to do to grow the economy? Is this their Homer Simpson moment when they slap their foreheads and utter that famous groan of understanding that unregulated capitalism will consume itself from within – just as their arch-enemy Karl Marx predicted it would? Will the movers and shakers of American finance finally get it that the American worker in the 21st century needs to be well-educated and employed in a good paying job in order for *any* economic stability to exist?

As long as the moneyed interests in this country keep K St. awash with lobbyists to do their specific bidding in Congress, nothing will change. The poor will keep getting poorer, the middle (consumer) class will vanish and another dramatic series of events will occur that will make the Great Depression look like a walk in the park. Why, because there are now 315 million of us instead of the 125 million as in 1929. That's a lot more angry and hungry mouths for the 1% to ignore this time.

Chapter 6:   Consider a Hybrid System of Economics

In Chris Hedges' informative and important book, *The Death of the Liberal Class*, he defines how liberals basically took the money and disappeared from the scene after 1975, allowed supply-side economics to hand over the country to the plutocrats and sat there wringing their hands while the Republicans shifted far to the right. This apathy from the so-called liberals allowed "business" to offshore everything, including their incorporation status for the sake of higher profits while taxable revenue went to foreign banks to avoid taxes. NAFTA rewards companies for sending work to other countries. The repeal of Glass-Steagall allowed banks to speculate with depositor money. Why weren't there protests against these thefts of wealth? Just enough money was passed out to the "liberals" to keep them quiet while the big money went to the top 2%, or less, that's why. Today (2014) we see corporations who have become extremely rich and successful trying to re-incorporate in other nations (inversion) to avoid paying U.S. taxes. This is the most craven example of how profit overwhelms ethics and reason to say nothing of patriotism and gratitude for the nation that allowed them to get rich.

In re-reading Howard Zinn's book, *A People's History of the United States*, I discovered that the disparity between top incomes and low incomes was always great before and since the Civil War. There has always been the fight between working classes and ruling classes. Despite what anyone tries to tell you, it's ALWAYS been a class war in this country. The so-called conservatives have ALWAYS wanted the cheapest labor they can get. Slavery, of course, is the ultimate ideal for capitalism's labor environment.

Working classes and President Teddy Roosevelt fought like hell to keep the earnings gap as narrow as possible. Now, the gap is so wide that the working class - which has devolved into a minimum wage class - has pretty much quit trying to get a fair share of the pie. Business has helped solve that problem by sending so much work to cheaper labor markets and eliminating labor unions. I wonder what will happen once those cheap labor markets recapitulate our labor struggles of the 20th century. Where will the capitalists go from there? Maybe that's why they've stashed $30 trillion and change in offshore banks. Maybe they think they can capitalize a whole new world.

Now, we're in a pickle of having a political "conversation" about deficits that never worried anybody until Barack Obama became President. Now, we have a schism in government between the extreme right and people who actually still want this country to operate. That's called gridlock, and it is one of the major indicators that our country/society is approaching the point of imminent collapse. How inconvenient it is for Republicans that our deficit is half of 2008's and we've experienced 50-some consecutive months of positive job growth – as of this writing.

In Rebecca Costa's book, *The Watchman's Rattle*, she describes other great societies that have followed the path we are now on. Her main point is that we have evolved much more quickly sociologically than we have biologically. That means that we are still, as individuals, operated by our primitive nature of hoarding and violent defense of our "stuff", territory and resources, while the complexities of morals, economics, religion and other threads of societal cohesiveness tug us in the opposite direction. To me this means that liberalism is an attempt to strengthen the threads of community cohesiveness, while so-called conservative dogma tries to operate as a modern day society of Lords v. Serfs. Strip away the silk suits, the glass and steel skyscrapers and the limousines and that's what we are. The buildings and the Armani suits are today's versions of castles and fine needlework. The profit motive, the largest burning candle in the capitalist's chandelier outshines everything else to the demise of everything else. Capitalists are *compelled* to worship profit; it is their very nature.

Chapter 7:   The Deregulation Scam

Paul Buchheit wrote a scathing piece citing why the great lie of deregulation is destroying our economy. Below is my summary of his points and citations that make his point one fo the more chilling realization for those of us who actually want our nation to succeed for a while longer.

1. The taxes avoided by one "business"-man would have covered the salary of 30,000 nurses.

The lack of regulation in the financial industry allowed hedge fund manager John Paulson to conspire with Goldman Sachs in a plan to create packages of risky subprime mortgages...then short-sell (bet against) the sure-to-fail financial instruments. The ploy paid him $3.7 billion. Deregulation in the tax code allowed him to call his income "carried interest" which is taxed at a 15% rate. More deregulation allowed him to defer his profits indefinitely.

The lost taxes of $1.3 billion (35% of $3.7 billion) would cover the salaries of 30,000 LPNs. Instead, one clever businessman took it all.

2. The TEN richest Americans made enough money to feed virtually every hungry person on Earth for a year, or maybe just half that number for two years.

The richest 10 Americans increased their wealth by over $50 billion in one year. That's enough, according to estimates (2008) by the Food and Agriculture Organization and the UN's World Food Program to feed the 870 million starving people in the world.

But should anyone be blamed for this imbalance? Didn't the rich people EARN their money through hard work and innovation? Sixty percent of the income from the Forbes 400 came from capital gains. A lot more of it came from other forms of deregulatory subterfuge like carried interest, performance-related pay, stock options and deferred compensation.

3. Taxes not paid via loopholes would pay off the deficit or create 20 million jobs. Take your pick.

The backlash against government regulation has led to tax abuses that cost us almost a trillion dollars a year.

Corporations doubled their profits to $1.9 trillion in less than ten years, but since 2008 they've reduced their tax payments from a twenty-year average of 22% to just 10%. That's a drop-off of over $225 billion.

The Tax Justice Network estimated that up to $32 trillion is hidden offshore, untaxed. With Americans making up 40% of the world's Ultra High New Worth Individuals and with a historical stock market return of 6%, $750 billion of income is lost to the U.S. every year, resulting in a tax loss of about $260 billion.

Finally, the IRS estimates that 17 percent of taxes owed were not paid, leaving an underpayment of $450 billion.

The deficit could be covered but *because of lax or non-existing regulations that allow wealthy individuals and corporations to avoid their tax responsibilities, it persists.*

4.   Unregulated trading industries prevent another $350 billion per year in tax revenues.

For a $10 purchase of children's clothing, mothers pay up to a dollar in sales tax. For a $10 purchase of financial instruments, investors refuse to pay one cent.

We had a financial transaction tax from 1914 to 1966, but it was repealed in a surge of Congressional deregulation. Now, it is estimated that $350 billion could be generated every year, enough for almost ten million teachers or nurses or firefighters of medical technicians.

5.   Wealth distribution to the top few percent is destroying entrepreneurship in the United States.

Because of financial deregulation, our country's income and wealth keep moving to the top while the middle class shrinks. Entrepreneurship is going down with it.

Studies reveal that relatively few business startups are initiated by the very wealthy. Only three percent of the CEOs, upper management and financial professionals were entrepreneurs in 2005, even though they made up about 60% of the richest 0.1% of Americans. Instead, they invest over 90% of their assets in a combination of low-risk bonds, the stock market and real estate.

Entrepreneurs come from risk-takers in the middle class, but with financial deregulation causing redistribution toward the top, the money has been taken out of the hands of middle-class innovators resulting in a 53% decrease in entrepreneurs since 1977.

In the recent past, venture capitalists invested in a variety of ideas that could pay off big. The entrepreneur spirit created risk takers. Often, a venture capitalist only "hit" on 25% of his/her investments, but when they hit, the losses from the "misses" were easily absorbed. That kind of support for progress and innovation is what made us a great nation, not fiddling regulations to benefit the few.

Without the hyperbole these data scream for, it must be clear to everyone what is meant by "deregulation" in the world of finance. The lies coming from the Republicans about tax cuts and deregulation creating jobs are not getting sufficient attention. Why not?

PEOPLE!! They are stealing your money and your country.

Try finding venture capital today. You'll have to visit the Cayman Islands or Switzerland, because that's where the money went. Risk aversion is the order of the day for investors.

Without operating revenue, our services decline in quality and quantity. That's why Republicans insist on destroying the New Deal programs that actually assist citizens in need. They want the money for themselves and their *patrons* on Wall Street and in corporate board rooms…at least those who are not yet sitting in them. This is what Karl Marx meant when he said that unregulated capitalism will destroy itself from within.

Welcome to "within". Senator Elizabeth Warren eloquently states: "The system is rigged!" Yes, it is. The "riggers" intended to rig the system so they could become ever richer and presumably more powerful. Why? What has power to do with a nation collapsing? Costa suggests that our primitive instincts remain even as our societies become increasingly "sophisticated" and complex. The question remains: Why do we do these things that defy our best interests?

Why do we ignore the point that regulations are necessary? Somewhere along the way the regulations WERE necessary. Well, using the theorem of simplicity, regulations became necessary because somebody was trying to screw somebody else unfairly to create an unfair advantage, a monopoly or a suffocation of fair market trading. Imagine that. Why would anyone do that? Well, it's because that's who and what we are as an organism. It's what got us to be successful in terms of tribal survival against hunger, thirst, other tribes and predation.

The regulations are in place to ensure our survival within the system we've created. Not all of the regulations are perfect, but most of them are necessary. Ask the magic 400 wealthiest Americans about that. Then, ask the guy living out of dumpsters in some inner-city slum and you'll have your answer.

Clearly, more deregulation means less money for goods and services for those who need them, the so-called consumers. So, how do the magic 400 expect to keep getting richer if they are cutting off the sources of their own revenue stream by their lust and rush for more unseemly wealth? Do they think they can get away with this forever? I'll bet they do, or just don't care.

Chapter 8:   The Failure of Extremism

There is something drastically and terribly wrong in America when the same political party that tries to take away voting, civil, human, social and Constitutional rights encourages people to take up arms in the fear that a tyrannical government is taking away our rights. That "wrong" is called propaganda based on manufactured lies. This is right out of the Joseph Goebbels School of mind control.

For the last few years, world politics has been fraught with extremists pulling and tugging at one another for some sort of dominance and control over money, religion, people and government. History shows us that there is a thread of connection between today's extremism and earlier times. An entire book is necessary to cover all the topics in adequate detail, so this piece will look at two schools of economics and their results.

The *neoliberal* school of economics is the invention of Milton Friedman and his University of Chicago School of Economics brethren. This school of thought embraces total free-market societies where the corporation/business is king. There are no regulations to speak of in Friedman's world, nor are there labor unions. There is no government safety net for the citizens; they are on their own. Schools are privately owned. Health care is strictly private. Government spending on infrastructure is only by absolute necessity and taxes – especially on business – are low or non-existent. The government owns and regulates virtually nothing including banks which are left to manage the currency and monetary policies of a nation with impunity. In short, this is ultimate capitalism.

This particular form of extremism, aka, *Supply-side* or *trickle-down* economics is predicated on the corporation creating the jobs and wages necessary to compete in every marketplace no matter how large or small. The results of this "philosophy" are consistent and exhibit some disturbing outcomes.

In partnership with the CIA, the IMF and the World Bank, the "shock doctrine", necessary to overturn economic practices in governments, was engineered by the above groups to not only overthrow duly elected governments, but to create enough social instability such that these draconian measures of change (Supply-side economics) could be put in place without the general citizenry having any say in the matter. This seems more than a little egregious since the implementation of "supply-side" strictures virtually destroys the working classes' hopes and dreams. At the same time, the bureaucrats bought up the previously federalized businesses and industries and made huge profits selling them to others "investors"from other countries. The elite classes of the effected countries did very well, while everyone else fell into abject poverty. Any social support or retirement services were banned and the cash distributed to the new "governors".

Naomi Klein's book, *Shock Doctrine,* uses many illustrations for the above summary. She highlights, how Friedman's trained advocates at the University of Chicago (and himself) pushed this doctrine in Chile (Pinochet's coup), Argentina, Brazil, Poland, South Africa, China and even Russia after the collapse of the Soviet Union. In each case, major "shocking" social upheavals or events created the opening for governments to employ the "Chicago Boys' " methods to make a few people very rich. It was especially egregious in Poland and South Africa where so much idealistic revolutionary promise went glimmering due to the leverage from international money "managers" at the IMF and World Bank. In the end, the rich got richer and the poor suffered worse deprivations than before from the extremist economic policies of Milton Friedman (Nobel Prize in Economics).

In view of the number of people affected negatively by this activity, I would seem that this scheme failed. It didn't fail for the banks, the corporatists or the rich investors. It failed for the people of those nations who didn't pay enough attention to what was being done to them. Sound familiar? Even Margaret Thatcher was able to cut deeply into the social services fabric of Great Britain while conducting the Falkland Islands war. Clever those conservative politicians...

The opposite extreme from neoliberal economics is *Communism*. The biggest complaint about communism is that it doesn't allow rich people to stay rich and limits the wealth of those in power. Karl Marx created this philosophy, but also included warnings. He warned against a perpetual governing state too; his utopia was having the human population act as a giant collective to support everyone including freedom from want, easy access to health care and education, and purposeful, dignified work for everyone. As with many of Marx's theories, this ideal didn't work out too well. He also predicted that capitalism would destroy itself from within if it became unregulated. Clearly, Marx's idea of communism has failed. No communist country every approached the ultimate goal of government of and by the proletariat.

There is a common thread between these two extremes: Dictatorships. In each case mentioned in Latin America, the Soviet Union and Mao's China, a dictator or small, strong central government (aka, an oligarchy) was necessary to implement and maintain either of these two economic extremes. History continues to show us that these extreme economic philosophies fail, mostly because too many people are so negatively affected by the extremism itself.

Today, in the United States, there is a continuing battle of extremes, or more correctly, a battle between one political entity that is becoming increasingly extreme and continuing its gravitation toward the Friedman school of thought, and the opposing force of moderation and balance between social services, taxation and favorable business climates. As the Republican Party keeps sliding to the right, it drags the rest of the ideologues to the right also. That's why the middle class of the United States has been reduced so greatly in recent decades. Ever since the Reagan administration embraced *supply-side economics*, the middle class, unions, social services and public education have been under assault by our politicians. Add to that the curious desire to privatize Social Security and you have a virtual blueprint for the Friedman-esque extremism that has failed around the world.

I think capitalists just can't help it. That's why there MUST be regulations on greed. Deregulate a banking system (1999 repeal of Glass-Steagall) and bankers gamble with everyone's money. Destroy a labor union and workers no longer can afford the consumer goods that keep a consumer economy going strong. Cut education funding and the quality of educators, curriculum and, ultimately, the workers plummets.

There simply must be a moderated approach to wealth, the ability to gain it and at the same time more respect for the people in society who tried to be great.

Chapter 9:   Slavery and the Modern Capitalist

In April of 2012, Joshua Freeman and Steve Fraser wrote a lengthy piece (from which I quote in italics and paraphrase extensively) describing a new kind of slavery conducted by corporate America's capitalist spirit. They begin with:

"All told, nearly a million prisoners are now making office furniture, working in call centers, fabricating body armor, taking hotel reservations, working in slaughterhouses, or manufacturing textiles, shoes, and clothing, while getting paid somewhere between 93 cents and $4.73 per day."

The writers call this "sweatshop labor", but research shows that it is something more sinister than that *birth-of-the-industrial-revolution* horror show. *Penitentiaries have become a niche market for such work. The privatization of prisons in recent years has meant the creation of a small army of workers too coerced and right-less to complain.*

Prisoners still don't have a legitimate place in today's American economy. Their ranks are increasing to the point where the United States leads the world in actual and per capita incarceration. This situation provides a huge labor base for those who desire to pay very low to no wages. As the prison system becomes more commercialized with companies like *The Corrections Corporation of America* or *G4S (formerly Wackenhut)* who sell inmate labor at sub-minimum wages to Fortune 500 companies like Chevron, B of A, AT & T and IBM.

These companies can, in most states, lease factories inside prisons or hire out prisoners to work on the outside. All told, nearly a million prisoners are now making office furniture, working in call centers, fabricating body armor, taking hotel reservations, working in slaughterhouses, or manufacturing textiles, shoes, and clothing, while getting paid somewhere between 93 cents and $4.73 per day.

It's hard to imagine a more compliant labor force where the worker has no rights of any sort, can be disciplined at the whim of the "supervisor" and be excluded from all other labor laws of the land. This emulates a 19th century model where convict labor was "normal" for confinement at "hard labor". This situation repeats a time when, similar to today's economy, capitalists thought that capital accumulation was a top priority crisis.

Some historians call the span between 1870s – 1890s "the long Depression" caused, in part by frequent investment panics and slumps, mass bankruptcies, deflation and self-destructive competition among businesses that were specially designed to depress labor costs. Sound familiar? The political pressure to commit austerity instead of capital investment is specifically designed today to shrink the society's wages for the working classes. There is no capital problem today, except that it isn't working capital. It is sitting in a variety of banks to avoid taxation. This is the new capitalism of the 21st century.

Convict labor is once again an appealing way for business to address their overwhelming desire to cut wages and benefits. The taxpayer, ultimately, pays the wages of the prisoner-based labor force. Penal servitude may now seem like a barbaric throwback to some long-lost time that preceded the industrial revolution, but that is incorrect. From its first appearance in this country, it has been associated with modern capitalist industry and large-scale agriculture.

That is only the first of many misconceptions about this peculiar institution. Infamous for the brutality with which prison laborers were once treated, indelibly linked in popular memory (and popular culture) with images of the black chain gang in the American South, it is usually assumed to be a Southern invention. So apparently atavistic, it seems to fit naturally with the retrograde nature of Southern life and labor, its economic and cultural underdevelopment, its racial caste system, and its desperate attachment to the "lost cause."

As it happens, penal servitude -- the leasing out of prisoners to private enterprise, either within prison walls or in outside workshops, factories, and fields -- was originally known as a Yankee invention.

First used at Auburn prison in New York State in the 1820s, the system spread widely and quickly throughout the North, the Midwest, and later the West. It developed alongside state-run prison workshops that produced goods for the public sector and sometimes the open market.

A few Southern states also joined in. Prisoners there, however, were mainly white men, since slave masters, with a free hand to deal with the "infractions" of their chattel, had little need for prison. The Thirteenth Amendment abolishing slavery would make an exception for penal servitude precisely because it had become the dominant form of punishment throughout the non-slave states.

Those men AND women sentenced to "confinement at hard labor" were not restricted to digging ditches or other unskilled work. Prisoners were employed in a broad range of tasks from rope- and wagon-making to carpet, hat, and clothing manufacturing (where women prisoners were sometimes put to work), as well as coal mining, carpentry, barrel-making, shoe production, house-building, and even the manufacture of rifles. The range of small and larger workshops where the felons served made up the heart of the new American economy.

While observing free-labor textile and convict-labor mills, during a visit to the United States, novelist Charles Dickens couldn't tell the difference between them.

State governments used the rental revenue garnered from their prisoners to meet budget needs, while entrepreneurs made outsized profits either by working the prisoners themselves or subleasing them to other businessmen.

After the Civil War, the convict-lease system metamorphosed. In the South, one of several grim methods, including the black codes, debt peonage, the crop-lien system, lifetime labor contracts, and vigilante terror, were used to control and fix in place the newly emancipated slave. Those "freedmen" were eager to pursue their new liberty either by setting up as small farmers or by exercising the right to move out of the region at will or from job to job as "free wage labor", but were thwarted in this by imposed constraints on their movements.

It is inaccurate to assume that the convict-lease system was exclusively the brainchild of the apartheid, all-white "Redeemer" governments that overthrew the Radical Republican regimes (which first ran the defeated Confederacy during Reconstruction) and who used their power to introduce Jim Crow to Dixie. In Georgia, for example, the Radical Republican state government took the convict-lease initiative soon after the war ended. They did this because the convict-lease system was tied to the modernizing sectors of the post-war economy throughout Dixie.

Convicts were leased to coal-mining, iron-forging, steel-making, and railroad companies, including Tennessee Coal and Iron (TC&I, a major producer across the South), especially in the booming region around Birmingham, Alabama. More than a quarter of the coal coming out of Birmingham's pits was mined by prisoners. By the turn of the century, TC&I had been folded into J.P. Morgan's United States Steel complex, which also relied heavily on prison laborers.

All the main extractive industries of the South were, in fact, wedded to this system. Turpentine and lumber camps deep in the fetid swamps and vast forests of Georgia, Florida, and Louisiana commonly worked their convicts until they dropped dead from overwork or disease. The region's plantation monocultures in cotton and sugar made regular use of imprisoned former slaves, including women. Among the leading families of Atlanta, Birmingham, and other "New South" metropolises were businessmen whose fortunes originated from the dank coal pits, malarial marshes and isolated forests in which their *un-free* peons worked, lived, and died.

The Southern system also stood out for the intimate collusion among industrial, commercial, and agricultural enterprises and every level of Southern law enforcement as well as the judicial system. Sheriffs, local justices of the peace, state police, judges, and state governments conspired to keep the convict-lease business humming. Indeed, local law officers depended on the leasing system for a substantial part of their income. They pocketed the fines and fees associated with the "convictions," a repayable sum that would be added on to the amount of time at "hard labor" demanded of the prisoner.

The arrest cycle was synchronized with the business cycle, timed to the rise and fall of the demand for fresh labor. County and state treasuries similarly counted on such revenues, since the post-war South was so capital-starved that only renting out convicts assured that prisons could be built and maintained. It was a kind of self-fulfilling business enterprise; capitalism with almost zero labor expense.

There was, then, every incentive to concoct charges or send people to jail for the most trivial offenses: vagrancy, gambling, drinking, partying, and hopping a freight car, tarrying too long in town. A "pig law" in Mississippi assured you of five years as a prison laborer if you stole a farm animal worth more than $10. Theft of a fence rail could result in the same.

In the North, where 80% of all U.S. prison labor was employed after the Civil War, and which accounted for over $35 billion in output (in current dollars), the system was reconfigured to meet the needs of modern industry and the pressures of "the long Depression." Convict labor was increasingly leased out only to a handful of major manufacturers in each state. These textile mills, oven makers, mining operations, hat and shoe factories -- one in Wisconsin leased that state's entire population of convicted felons -- were then installing the kind of mass production methods becoming standard in much of American industry. As organized markets for prison labor grew increasingly oligopolistic (like the rest of the economy), the Depression of 1873 and subsequent depressions in the following decades wiped out many smaller businesses that had once depended on convict labor.

Companies leasing convicts enjoyed authority to dispose of their rented labor power as they saw fit. Workers were compelled to labor in total silence. Even hand gestures and eye contact were prohibited for the purpose of creating "silent and insulated working machines."

Supervision of prison labor was often shared by employers and the prison authorities alike. Many businesses continued to conduct their operations within prison walls where they supplied the materials, power, and machinery, while the state provided guards, workshops, food, clothing, and what passed for medical care. As one observer put it, "Felons are mere machines held to labor by the dark cell and the scourge."

Free market industrial capitalism, then and now, invariably draws on the aid of the state. This might be shocking to the Hayek/Friedman school of economists, but in that convict labor system's formative phases, the state regularly used its coercive powers of taxation, expropriation, and incarceration to free up natural and human resources lying outside the orbit of capitalism proper.

In both the North and the South, the contracting out of convict labor was one way in which that state-assisted mechanism of capital accumulation arose. Contracts with the government assured employers that their labor force would be replenished anytime a worker got sick, was disabled, died, or simply became too worn out to continue.

Penal institutions all over the country became auxiliary arms of capitalist industry and commerce. Two-thirds of all prisoners worked for private enterprise.

Even today, government is once again providing subsidies and tax incentives as well as facilities, utilities, and free space for corporations making use of this same category of convict labor. A principal objective in using prison labor is to undermine efforts to unionize.

Opposition to convict labor arose from workingmen's associations, labor-oriented political parties, journeymen unions, and other groups, which considered the system an insult to the moral codes of egalitarian republicanism nurtured by the American Revolution. The specter of proletarian dependency haunted the lives of the country's self-reliant handicraftsmen who watched apprehensively as shops employing slave-wage labor began popping up across the country. Much of the early agitation by unions was aimed at the use of prisoners to replace skilled workers while unskilled prison labor was initially largely ignored.

It was bad enough for craftsmen to see their livelihoods and standards of living put in jeopardy by "free" wage labor, but is was worse still watching unfree labor do the same thing. At the time, employers were turning to that captive prison population to combat attempts by aggrieved workers to organize and defend themselves. On the eve of the Civil War, for example, an iron-molding contractor in Spuyten Duyvil, north of Manhattan in the Bronx, locked out his unionized workers and then moved his operation to Sing Sing penitentiary, where a laborer cost 40 cents per day, $2.60 less than the going day rate. It worked, and Local 11 of the Union of Iron Workers quickly died away.

The workingman's movement of the Jacksonian era was deeply alarmed by the prospect of "wage slavery," a condition conflicting with their sense of self as citizens of a republic of independent producers. Prison labor was a sub-species of that dreaded "slavery"; a caricature of it.

Throughout the Gilded Age of the 1890s, convict labor served as a magnet for capitalists trying to get the cheapest labor possible. But prisoner rebellions became ever more common, particularly in the North where many prisoners turned out to be Civil War veterans and dispossessed working people who already knew something about fighting for freedom and against oppression. Major penitentiaries like Sing Sing became sites of repeated strikes and riots; a strike in 1877 even took on the transplanted Spuyten Duyvil iron-molding company.

Above and below the Mason Dixon line, political platforms, protest rallies, petition campaigns, legislative investigations, union strikes, and boycotts by farm organizations like the Farmers Alliance and Grange cried out for the abolition of the convict-lease system, or at least for its rigorous regulation. Over the 19th century's last two decades, more than 20 coal-mine strikes broke out because of the use of convict miners.

The Knights of Labor, that era's most audacious labor movement, was particularly involved. During the Coal Creek Wars in eastern Tennessee in the early 1890s, for instance, TC&I tried to use prisoners to break a miners' strike. The company's vice president noted that it was "an effective club to hold over the heads of free laborers."

Strikers and their allies affiliated with the Knights, the United Mine Workers, and the Farmers Alliance launched guerilla attacks on the prisoner stockade, sending the convicts they freed to Knoxville. When the governor insisted on shipping them back, the workers released them into the surrounding hills and countryside. Gun battles followed.

In the North, the prison labor abolition movement went viral, embracing not only workers' organizations, sympathetic rural insurgents, and prisoners, but also widening circles of middle-class reformers. The newly created American Federation of Labor denounced the system as "contract slavery." It also demanded the banning of any imports from abroad made with convict labor and the exclusion from the open market of goods produced domestically by prisoners, whether in state-run or private workshops. In Chicago, the construction unions refused to work with materials made by prisoners.

By the latter part of the 19th century, state after state pushed penal servitude toward extinction. New York state, where the "industry" was born and largest, killed it by the late 1880s. The tariff of 1890 prohibited the sale of convict-made wares from abroad. Private leasing of convict labor continued in the North, but under increasingly restrictive conditions, including Federal legislation passed during the New Deal in the 1930s. By World War II, it was virtually extinct.

Convict labor even ended in Tennessee, Louisiana, Georgia, and Mississippi by the turn of the 20th century. Higher political calculations were at work in these states. Established elites were eager to break the inter-racial alliances that had formed over abolishing convict leasing by abolishing the hated system itself. Too often it ended in name only.

What replaced it was the state-run chain gang, although some Southern states like Alabama and Florida continued private leasing well into the 1920s. Inmates were set to work building roads and other infrastructure projects vital to the flourishing of a mature market economy and to the continuing process of capital accumulation. In the North, the system of "hard labor" was replaced by a system of "hard time," that numbing, brutalizing idleness where masses of people extruded from the mainstream economy are pooled into mass penal colonies. The historic link between labor, punishment, and economic development was severed, and remained so... until now.

"Now," means our second Gilded Age and its aftermath. In these years, the system of leasing out convicts to private enterprise was reborn. This was a perverse triumph for the law of supply and demand in an era infatuated with the charms of the free market. On the supply side, the U.S. holds captive 25% of all the prisoners on the planet: 2.3 million people. It has the highest incarceration rate in the world as well, a figure that began skyrocketing in 1980 with Ronald Reagan's election as president. Since the 1970s American industrial corporations have found it increasingly unprofitable to invest in domestic production. Instead, they have sought out the hundreds of millions of people abroad who are willing to, or can be pressed into, working for far less than American workers.

Consequently, American workers -- disproportionately African-American -- found themselves living in economic exile, scrabbling to get by. They began showing up in similarly disproportionate numbers in the country's rapidly expanding prison archipelago. It didn't take long for corporate America to come to view this as another potential foreign country, full of cheap, local and subservient labor.

What began in the 1970s as an end run around the laws prohibiting convict leasing by private interests now became an industrial sector in its own right: employing more people than any Fortune 500 corporation and operating in 37 states. The ultimate irony is that our ancestors found convict labor obnoxious in part because it seemed to prefigure a new and more universal form of enslavement. Could its rebirth foreshadow a future ever more unnervingly like those past nightmares?

Today, we are being reassured by the president, the mainstream media, and economic experts that the Great Recession is over, that we are in "recovery" even though unemployment is still too high and American businesses still refuse to invest in new technologies and their subsequent job expansion. Today, "recovery" means that the mega-banks are no longer on the brink of bankruptcy, the stock market has made up lost ground, corporate profits have achieved record levels, and notoriously unreliable employment numbers have improved by several percent.

What accounts for this peculiarly narrow view of recovery, however, is that the general costs of doing business are falling off a cliff as the economy eats itself alive. The current celebrated recovery owes thanks to local, state, and Federal austerity budgets, the starving of the social welfare system and public services, rampant anti-union campaigns in the public and private sector, the spread of sweatshop labor, the coercion of desperate, unemployed or underemployed workers who accept lower wages, part-time work, and temporary work, as well as relinquishing healthcare benefits and a financially secure retirement. In sum, the contract between American labor and business is broken with the attendant loss of hope and incentive to work toward a future success.

This downward spiral of the working classes toward becoming an underclass begins to look much like the prison labor environment of decades gone by. The question really becomes: How long will the American worker and free person put up with this spiral before committing to outright rebellion?

Chapter 10: Capitalism and Neo-liberal Libertarianism Cannot Co-exist

After listening to Grover Norquist talk about small government, the elimination of taxes, the slashing of regulations and the destruction of social services that many people around the world and in this country have come to accept as the universal truth of a prosperous democracy, I started counting the things that would collapse should he get his wish. While combining this list with other lists that show where the United States currently ranks among the world's most advanced nations, I heard an ominous rumble from the fractured logic of *supply-side economics* cross my consciousness.

As I understand the Libertarian/neo-liberal mantra, no public services, or regulations on the "free" market plus few or no taxes on anything that would hinder the ideal Ayn Rand utopia of civilization. The scam here is that the working classes, even with reduced wages, no benefits and no unionization, would be required to pick up the tax tab in order to keep the strong military, police and other necessities going. I don't understand why these supposedly intelligent people don't get it that Ayn Rand wrote FICTION. Well, anyone can dream.... The problem I see with this ideal lies with the system of economics this country embraces: *CAPITALISM.* More specifically: Neo-Liberal capitalism as invented and espoused by the troll of modern economics, Milton Friedman.

Neo-Liberal Capitalism desires two things: freedom from any controls that reduce profit and the freedom to exploit physical and human resources to their exhaustion without constraint. So far, that sounds like a perfect match for the Libertarian mindset, but wait....

What if there were no public schools? The poor would not become educated and the "good" jobs would only be available to those who could afford schooling. What if there were no taxpayer funded highway departments? Then, only the richest would be able to afford to pave their streets while the rest of the nation dealt with muddy tracks. What if there was no FDA, OSHA or EPA? Well, maybe only the rich could afford to test their incoming groceries for contamination, but everybody else would be at the mercy of the grower, harvester and shipper of those food products. Safety in the workplace would be at the behest of the profiteers. To me this is so Dickensian as to be spooky.

This is where capitalism and Libertarianism go awry. The schools, being all private, would become the propaganda mills for corporations. After all, those who fund them would be the employees who were paid enough to send their children to these schools. It would be a "1984" scenario in the 21st century. The "investor" would naturally want the curriculum to align with their ideas and philosophies for creating more profit centers. What about the food producer? He/she wouldn't want to spend the extra money to inspect foods, because that would take away from profits.

If OSHA and the EPA were non-existent in Norquist's world industrial/farming injuries would not cause liability suits because there would be no regulations to guard against unsafe working conditions and therefore no responsibility for the employer to do anything to protect workers. Medical malpractice would not be subject to law suits for incompetence that cost lives. The same "thinking" applies to the air and water surrounding the industrial bases. No regulations of waste products means no profit-sucking controls on poisoning the environment. When the land, water and air were destroyed, the corporate entity would just move on and exploit another plot of the Earth until it too was destroyed....all for profit. Note that nobody in Libertarian circles is asking about the time when we run out of places to go that are safe. Oh, and the people who were injured, maimed or poisoned in or around the workplace would be on their own for medical assistance since there would be no Medicare or company sponsored insurance. Texas has a "voluntary" environmental control policy for businesses and the result is that Texas also has the most polluted air and water in the nation. Texas is yet again another laboratory experiment in how not to do things for the benefit of its citizens. I guess the spikes in cancers downwind from the refineries don't matter to those "volunteering" to make the air and water safe.

I haven't even begun to talk about retirement plans. In a Libertarian world there would be no such thing from government and since corporations would be under no obligation to provide retirement plans, the workers are, once again, on their own. After all, pensions take away from profits, no matter the interest earned against them. The Enron fiasco illustrated how eager corporate moguls are to pirate pensions for securing more profit – legal or illegal, it doesn't matter.

What is the final outcome from this scenario of a Libertarian/Neo-Liberal Capitalism society? Well, it's been tried before in just about every other country that tried to overcome some major upheaval in their society, either induced by outside sources like the IMF, or from just a power struggle among the controlling elites. The outcome from exploiting the land and the people, forming economic barriers to class strata and basically ignoring the needs of the people in general by government created the environment for rebellion and revolution. All one has to do is examine how much fun the crowned heads of Europe had with rebellions over the last 2,000 years, before they figured it out.

But this is 2014, not 1014, or even 1974. The United States, in spite of all its exceptionality chest thumping ranks 49th in life expectancy, 73rd in infant mortality, 27th in math knowledge and skills, 22nd in science and leads the world in only three things: The percentage of its population incarcerated, the percent of people who believe angels and bigfoot are real and the amount spent on the military/security apparatus. We spend more on "defense" than the next 26 nations *combined* and 25 of them are our friends. We used to be number one in all the good stuff.

My previous books (*The Voter's Guide to National Salvation* and *Killing the Dream: America's Flirtation With Third World Status*) explain how we got to these levels in historical detail.   It would help everyone to stop listening to intellectual dwarfs like Norquist and Newt Gingrich and start paying attention to serious economists like Paul Krugman who know what they're talking about and have no political agenda. Our politics are a shambles right now, so anything coming from that corner of the room where the employees of corporate America reside is worthless. We have plenty of smart, ethical, honest and honorable thinkers around the country. They are the ones who everyone should be listening to, instead of the screamers in the tabloid, right wing media.

Chapter 11:   The Sounds of Familiarity

Someone I know recently sent me a summary of characteristics (*The 14 Characteristics of Fascism* by Dr. Lawrence Britt published in *Free Inquiry*, Spring 2003) that smacks me as pertinent in today's Western governments, especially in the United States since 1981. Read them and draw your own conclusions. Mine follow the list.

Dr. Britt, is a political scientist, studied the fascist regimes of Hitler (Germany), Mussolini (Italy), Franco (Spain), Suharto (Indonesia), and Pinochet (Chile). He found the regimes all had14 things in common, and he calls these the identifying characteristics of fascism.

1. **Powerful and Continuing Nationalism** -- Fascist regimes tend to make constant use of patriotic mottos, slogans, symbols, flag waving, songs, and other paraphernalia.

2. **Disdain for the Recognition of Human Rights** -- Because of fear of enemies and the need for security, the people in fascist regimes are persuaded that human rights can be ignored in certain cases because of "need." The people tend to 'look the other way' or even approve of torture, summary executions, assassinations, long incarcerations of prisoners, etc.

3. **Identification of Enemies/Scapegoats as a Unifying Cause** -- The people are rallied into a unifying patriotic frenzy over the need to eliminate a perceived common threat or foe: racial, ethnic or religious minorities; liberals; communists; socialists, terrorists, etc.

4. **Supremacy of the Military** -- Even when there are widespread domestic problems, the military is given a disproportionate amount of government funding, and the domestic agenda is neglected. Soldiers and military service are glamorized.

5. **Rampant Sexism** -- The governments of fascist nations tend to be almost exclusively male-dominated. Under fascist regimes, traditional gender roles are made more rigid. Opposition to abortion is high, as is homophobia and anti-gay...national policy.

6. **Controlled Mass Media** -- ... the media is directly controlled by the government, (or may be) is indirectly controlled by government regulation, or through sympathetic media spokespeople and executives. Censorship, especially in wartime, is very common.

7. **Obsession with National Security** -- Fear is used as a motivational tool by the government over the masses.

8. **Religion and Government are Intertwined** -- Governments in fascist nations tend to use the most common religion in the nation as a tool to manipulate public opinion. Religious rhetoric and terminology is common from government leaders, even when the major tenets of the religion are diametrically opposed to the government's policies or actions.

9. **Corporate Power is Protected** -- The industrial and business aristocracy of a fascist nation often are the ones who put the government leaders into power, creating a mutually beneficial business/government relationship and power elite. *(Citizens United vs. FEC, for example)*

10. **Labor Power is Suppressed** -- Because the organizing power of labor is the only real threat to a fascist government, labor unions are either eliminated entirely or are severely suppressed.

11. **Disdain for Intellectuals and the Arts** -- Fascist nations tend to promote and tolerate open hostility to higher education, and academia. It is not uncommon for professors and other academics to be censored or even arrested. Free expression in the arts is openly attacked, and governments often refuse to fund the arts.

12. **Obsession with Crime and Punishment** -- ... the police are given almost limitless power to enforce laws. The people are often willing to overlook police abuses, and even forego civil liberties, in the name of patriotism. There is often a national police force with virtually unlimited power in fascist nations.

13. **Rampant Cronyism and Corruption** -- Fascist regimes almost always are governed by groups of friends and associates who appoint each other to government positions, and who use governmental power and authority to protect their friends from accountability *(the revolving door of lobbyists, for example)*. It is not uncommon in fascist regimes for national resources and even treasures to be appropriated or even outright stolen by government leaders.

14. **Fraudulent Elections** -- Sometimes elections in fascist nations are a complete sham. Other times elections are manipulated by smear campaigns against (or even the assassination of) opposition candidates, the use of legislation to control voting numbers or political district boundaries, and the manipulation of the media. Fascist

nations also typically use their judiciaries to manipulate or control elections.

It should also be noted that Dr. Britt has been discredited by many of his colleagues, so the reader is left to his/her own conclusions about defining fascism in our country or individual states.

I don't think we are exactly ready to strap on the Sam Browne belts and jackboots, but I see the United States trending this way with some areas more strongly leaning than others. We still have the arts more or less separated from the government, but there is still political pressure to abandon government funding of artistic free expression.

The systematic destruction of public education, however, is the scariest item; we've almost always lived with a strong military and been militant as a nation throughout most of our history. The most recent exception being our draw down across the board after WW I. We've also suppressed minority populations, even committing near genocide to aboriginal Americans. Perhaps the most specious of these 14 items is the attack on fair elections by the Supreme Court. The new voter-suppression laws in Southern and "conservative" states tells us much about where the seat of American fascism resides. In Texas, for example, there have been FOUR (4) cases of suspected voter fraud in the last TEN (10) years. The American Association of Republican Attorneys points out that the known voter fraud in the last decades amounts to about $1/10,000^{th}$ of one percent.

One should also note that it is the Republican platform and that of its red-headed stepchild, the Tea Party that most closely follow these 14 traits of fascism. For absolutists it is tough to see the United States without some fascism, socialism, communism, democracy (there's still quite a bit left) and capitalism entwined in the dance for future control. So far, we've been able to keep one or another of these "isms" from dominating, but ever since the Reagan administration every Republican regime has shifted us toward more fascist behavior than toward any other.

We the people have much world and national history to show us what happens when one ideology dominates all the others. Not only are we a blend of various peoples, we are a blend of many ideologies. These have historically been our strengths as has strong government that keeps single ideologies at bay...so far. By the way, when the majority of the eligible voters vote, trends tend to balance out over time. When they don't vote, anarchy and revolution allow fascism to replace democracy.

Part II

How Our Failed Models Keep Destroying our Greatness

The test of our progress is not whether we add more to the abundance of those who have much; it is whether we provide enough for those who have little.

- Franklin Delano Roosevelt

My Dream is of a place and a time where America will once again be seen as the last best hope of Earth.

- Abraham Lincoln

There is a bad joke that deals with the repetition of errors. It begins with a man walking down the street whereupon he sees another man beating his head against a wall. The first man tends to his errands and walks past the same man still beating his head against the wall. He stops and asks the man why he keeps doing this. The man in question answers by saying, "Because it feels so good when I stop."

Chapter 12:   It's Hard to Watch

Watching news television is getting more difficult every day. The objectivity factor is diluted greatly by pundits from both sides trying to sell air time about candidates and politicians who insist on looking and sounding foolish, extremist and cheap. It is an ugly, vulgar display of disinformation and a throwback to the days of McCarthyism and what it brought to the American history books.

McCarthy's fear mongering about communists fed the rhetoric of the early Cold War, but even after he was debunked and vilified, the fears remained. Those fears also fed unfounded theories like the "Domino Theory" of nations falling to communism. The French wanted to reconstitute its colony in Indo-China after World War II. They failed because the Vietnamese wanted to be a sovereign nation instead of lackeys of France. We felt obliged to help out our old allies and then were stuck with the mess after the French were defeated on the battlefield and pulled out of Viet Nam. We decided that Ho Chi Minh was a communist and must not be allowed to take over his own country.

Presidents, Eisenhower, Kennedy, Johnson and Nixon were each complicit in responding to the domino theory fears. They were all wrong. Worse, they didn't listen to the experts who had lived and served in Asia for decades. No, it was all about defeating the Communist bogeyman. We had just finished "defeating" communism in Korea and were determined to defeat it in Viet Nam, even if it meant lying to the American people to make it happen. The Gulf of Tonkin Resolution was Johnson's contrivance to allow us to enter a ground war in Asia. Once in, it was a tar baby we couldn't get out of for another 10 years and 58,000 American lives. This is what fear and lies create.

As it happened, Ho Chi Minh and his successors, though communists philosophically, were nationalists first and eventually created a stable, national government and society. Viet Nam is now a growing economic success and one of our best trading partners. Our fears were unfounded and we looked foolish to the world for following those fears into war. Yes, hindsight is a luxury, but it is also a teacher.

We are now experiencing fear mongering by Republican politicians and right wing talk show hosts (see Fox News anytime) about Muslims and their religious takeover of our country. They are directing this nonsense at our President who has a most unusual name. That name alone justifies their fear mongering. Meanwhile corporate America works hard at funding the election of their favorite candidate because they are allowed to. The Koch brothers recently (January, 2015) pledged over $900 million to buy the 2016 Presidential election for the Republicans.

The real fear here is having our democracy hijacked by a profit-motivated plutocracy that cares nothing about anything else *except* profits, least of all the quality of life for the majority of people in the United States of America.

The Republicans are falling all over themselves to complete the shift/lurch to the right of the political spectrum in order to garner favor and money from the plutocrats. The right wing of the GOP seems to be the overarching influence to their platform, rhetoric and public outbursts. It's getting so bizarre that the Tea Party appears to be more like the event thrown by the Mad Hatter than a movement predicated on a famous historical event. This right wing lurch is, of course, funded and promoted by corporate/banking America led by the infamous Koch brothers and their fellow richest 400.

A major question arises: How will the GOP manage to come back toward the center of the spectrum when the candidate they pick will have to find the centrist voters and independents that will end up electing the next President?

But wait! There are the voter disenfranchisement movements around the country. The fear mongering about voter fraud has been used to get the state legislatures controlled by Republicans to rush laws into place that make it much more difficult for certain constituencies to vote. The poor (read: most brown people) or the elderly who don't drive cars and thus have no picture ID as a driver's license are two groups targeted for preventing voter fraud. College students will not be allowed to register to vote outside their home districts. Early voting and absentee ballots are being assaulted as well. All of this is to prevent voter fraud.

Except there is no voter fraud anywhere that even tickles the meter. A study by Republican lawyers found that the cases of voter fraud amount to about 0.0001% of all votes cast across the country in the last ten years. The one visible case of voter fraud is attributed to the attorney general of the state of Indiana who was convicted on six counts of felony election tampering. He's a Republican, of course. So, why are the Republicans jumping through these hoops to prevent something that isn't occurring?

The Karl Rove style of thinking is that if the margin of victory is only a few percentage points in certain states, by preventing citizen groups who tend to vote for Democrats from voting, the Republicans can overcome that margin and actually win all the electoral votes for President and put more of their kind in Congress, the White House and state legislatures. Pretty slick..... Where I come from, this is called rigging elections. So, which is worse, a 0.0001% of voter fraud occurrences or disenfranchising maybe 5-8% of eligible voters from performing their constitutionally guaranteed right?

Chapter 13:   Spinning the Moral Compass

My wife and I reminisced about our long lives, the other day. We shared comments about the stories we heard first-hand from our grandparents about their days in America. We compared our degree of luxury and freedom from want to theirs and the relative efforts, both physical and intellectual, that we invested. Physically, we did much, much less to achieve what we could in our productive lifetimes. Since my wife and I are both well-educated, we invested our intellectual capital to achieve comfortable lives with few regrets.

Then we ventured into larger scopes of history and the events that spanned those three generations where we enjoyed first-hand knowledge. From the covered wagons that got people to Texas from elsewhere to us driving around in a comfortable car, from the hand-dug wells to being just a phone call away from having a rig punch holes in the yard to tap a working aquifer.

Extending that example made me think about the first oil well drilled in Pennsylvania in the mid 19th century. Today's grandchildren will likely see the exhaustion of oil in the entire world during their lifetimes. By understanding that what took nearly 300 million years to make will be used up in only 300 years by a species that has only lived for 200,000 years, is reflective of our rapaciousness.

From covered wagons to Chevrolets in 100 years is humbling in itself, but we also fought a long, seemingly endless series of mechanized wars that gobbled up and wasted huge portions of those trillions of gallons of oil and millions of lives. Meantime, we went to the moon and back. Then, plastic became a major part of everything we touch in our lives. We behave like oil will be around forever. Never mind the chemical residues that may affect our long-term health; we are committed to convenience…and to cheap.

Today, oil is still cheap whether or not the prices are in line with other economic factors. Plastic is made from oil and is cheaper than any other kind of packaging or container material. Is anyone preparing their grandchildren for the next sea change in energy, materials or convenience? How will they clean up the pollution and waste left to them? Perhaps examining ourselves a little more closely will provide an answer or two.

I recently read an article that estimated a cool $32 trillion of American-made money sits in banks all over the world except ours. This money was accrued over several decades as the result of just a few very wealthy people and corporations hiding their money to avoid paying taxes to the government that allowed them the freedoms and the opportunities to accrue that wealth in the first place. My wife and I agreed that it was an obscene amount of money to be sitting idle and serving no purpose except to make a few hundred people even richer....at least in terms of dollars and cents. Their moral wealth remains in question in light of how the money was created and to what use it is put.

While the general population of the United States lives in relative comfort compared to second and third world nations, the vigor of the working classes has been squelched and its opportunities for individuals to grow better existences has been all but cancelled by this flow of wealth out of the country and into bank accounts overseas. No jobs are created, and the 15% of the chronically poor are ignored. So why do these rich people clamor for still more tax breaks when they can't spend all they have now? Who first floated the great lie that the rich would trickle down their wealth to the lower classes thus floating all boats? It was Milton Friedman who invented and maintained this great lie. The neoliberal economics theory lie is the single most important factor that keeps the moral compass of capitalism and the political system of the United States spinning without finding a truth to which it can align.

Jesus' Sermon on the Mount set and summarized many moral standards for adherents of all faiths, yet there are those adherents to Christianity who maintain that letting "those people" eat cake while they eat steak is how the world is ordered and how God ordained it. The "richest" country in the history of the world is among the poorest at taking care of its citizens when one considers the available resources. The moral compass spinning out of control in America is that of greed, selfishness, hypocrisy and wastefulness. Why aren't those advocates of those astoundingly simple, human survival standards and morals practicing them to the benefit of all? Are the standards false? Do we just deny our community spirit whenever it suits us and let the others go to rot?

There is much social and political angst regarding illegal immigration in this country. Well, the people involved are NOT a burden on our precious resources and society. We have $32 trillion in the bank, remember? These people work whenever and wherever they can, and do jobs that most "real" Americans wouldn't touch. And they send 75% of their below-minimum wage salaries home to their families in poorer countries. Now, who among us can say our moral compass is better than theirs? Why don't we, the citizens of the land of silk and money step up and appreciate how many billions of dollars those "illegal" workers are saving our businesses who hire them outside the law? The compass is spinning quite rapidly here.

In 2014 thousands of Central Americans came alone or sent their children north to our border with Mexico. Why? They were fleeing for their

56

lives from drug gangs and certain slaughter at the hands of the gangsters. Our response? Screaming demonstrators demanding their return to certain death while THEIR children bought and used the drugs that fuel the horror show south of our borders. Texas deployed National Guardsmen to the border as a show of force to these destitute, frightened people. Where is the "good Christian" value of charity? Where is the compassion for those in serious trouble? Have we forgotten that most of us are here because our ancestors escaped some form of oppression too? I guess so. In the Texas run by Republicans none of this matters. Texas would rather waste millions of dollars on a military face at the border than spend a few thousand helping these people survive their ordeal.

The natural instincts to hoard affect everyone, but in quite different ways. People who earn in the neighborhood of $70,000 per year are, according to several studies, among the happiest people. Those who make less than this feel stress of need and the associated anxiety more often. Those making more than $70,000 start feeling more stress and unhappiness because they worry about their ability to keep hoarding and/or buying the things they desire to make their lives even more comfortable. There is truth to the "poor little rich girl" or "living in a gilded cage" situations.

The real question for me in my twilight years is what will my generation's legacy be to those that follow? Have we done the right things often enough to say that we fulfilled our moral obligations to our country, our fellow citizens and whatever else we believe in? Each of us must make that final inventory some day. The sum of those inventories will report to history for as long as there are beings who can read it.

Chapter 14:   Backwards to Yesteryear

It took me a while and a few pinches to realize that I was actually reading a document created in 2012 after looking at the platform for the Texas Republican Party. The walls rippled and the floor trembled as I pored over the 16 points listed by the dominant political force in the great state. I thought I heard the madly howling ghost of Molly Ivins and the horse laugh of Jim Hightower as this list of incredulousness unfolded. The first question: Who in their right mind...?, couldn't be completed. It was moot. The second question is: Are all the states' GOP platforms like this?

Rereading the list of "planks" hurt more than the first read, because I know some Republicans who are actually rational and are currently living in the 21st century. How embarrassing it must be for them to have their party of choice don the miters and hoods of the 16th century and conjure up this ode to regression, disrespect, ignorance, selfishness and hypocrisy. If I hadn't read it myself I would never have believed that anything this absurd, ridiculous and wretchedly stupid could have come from ANY group in our fair state. But there it was in all its ignominy.

The sixteen planks (Italics) follow with my comments:

1. *"We urge that the Voter Rights Act of 1965 codified and updated in 1973 be repealed and not reauthorized."* I guess Jim Crow-style poll taxes and minority citizen voter suppression are still on the plate. The SCOTUS answered the bell when they vacated the key parts of this law (section 5) allowing the "suspect" 12 states to make any voting laws they wanted. Justice Scalia blithely noted that racism no longer existed. He needs to get out more.

2. *"We oppose sale and use of the dangerous "Morning After Pill."* I guess the FDA saying it is safe is heresy. Nobody mentions how will we feed all those new hungry mouths when food stamps and government assistance go away too?

3. *"We also urge the Texas Legislature and the U.S. Congress to enact legislation prohibiting any judicial jurisdiction from allowing any substitute or parallel system of Law, specifically foreign Law (including Sharia Law), which is not in accordance with the U.S. or Texas Constitutions."* I guess our Constitutions' articles aren't good enough to protect us from other laws by themselves. This must come from the GOP's department of redundancy department.

4. *"We oppose the teaching of Higher Order Thinking Skills (HOTS) (values clarification), critical thinking skills and similar programs that are simply a*

relabeling of Outcome-Based Education (OBE) (mastery learning) which focus on behavior modification and have the purpose of challenging the student's fixed beliefs and undermining parental authority." What about those kids who have felons for parents, or no parents? How will these kids be able to decide whether to buy a lemon or an egg? Anyone sane must find this an incredulous statement until one realizes that this sort of action is going on in every state where Republicans control the school boards. They must think that having little robots running around with no thinking skills is a good thing. I think Adolf Hitler tried this with the German youth of the 1930s. We all saw how well that worked out.

5. "We support the return to the time tested precious metal standard for the U.S. dollar." Sure. This will make OUR currency a slave to the world-wide gold market and its constant perturbations. Brilliant. Let's bring back steam locomotives too, so we can burn more coal. Too bad the gold standard caused a global economic collapse 120 years ago. Did we not learn from that?

6. "Further, we urge Congress to withhold Supreme Court jurisdiction in cases involving abortion, religious freedom, and the Bill of Rights." And these guys are afraid of Sharia law... Do they even understand the concept of law at all? This is another whack at trying to employ states rights. We fought our bloodiest war over this subject. Texas still has a strong secessionist movement. Maybe the U.S. government should just let it go.

7. "We support the withdrawal of the United States from the United Nations and the removal of U.N. headquarters from U.S. soil." Why not? Then let's bring the rest of the global economy, our overseas military and our offshore bank accounts down into the isolationist hole with us. This sort of backward thinking is what got us into World War II and fomented the creation of the United Nations.

8. "We strongly support women who choose to devote their lives to their families and raising their children. We recognize their sacrifice and deplore the liberal assault on the family." Who is doing the assaulting here? I thought that women's rights included all these things guaranteed by the Constitution for all citizens. Does this mean they do not support the millions of single mothers who are working two jobs to feed their children and keep a roof over their heads? Isn't this the same political party that talks about "legitimate rape"? And these guys are afraid of Sharia Law... Queue the Scarecrow song...(from the Wizard of Oz)

9. "All adult citizens should have the legal right to conscientiously choose which vaccines are administered to themselves or their minor children without penalty for refusing a vaccine." Right. The CDC doesn't understand communicable diseases, but Texas Republicans sure do. We are now seeing a resurgence of childhood diseases in those children whose parents opted out of

vaccination. Can we vaccinate against backwardness and abject, selfish stupidity?

10. *"We recommend that local school boards and classroom teachers be given more authority to deal with disciplinary problems. Corporal punishment is effective and legal in Texas."* Sure. Let's beat them until they break. Then we can just wait until those kids start beating their kids. This "idea" flies in the face of virtually all the research dealing with child behavior and how it influences their adult behavior.

But wait. There's even more backwardness…

11. *"We recommend repeal of the Sixteenth Amendment of the U.S. Constitution, with the goal of abolishing the I.R.S and replacing it with a national sales tax collected by the States."* Great. Typical Texas. Let's employ the most regressive tax possible so those who earn the least will pay the largest share of their income in taxes. What if there are no jobs because we've become totally isolationist and nobody has any money to buy anything? Uh oh. No taxes. Perfect.

12. *"We strongly oppose all efforts of the extreme* (they fail to note which groups are extreme and which are moderate) *environmental groups that stymie legitimate business interests. We strongly oppose those efforts that attempt to use the environmental causes to purposefully disrupt and stop those interests within the oil and gas industry. We strongly support the immediate repeal of the Endangered Species Act….We believe the Environmental Protection Agency should be abolished."* Oh, hell yes! Let's just keep pouring our wastes into the water and air until we can see all the air we try to breath and have our kids glow in the dark. Besides, who needs all those other critters anyway? We can't do anything to get in the way of business. When the workers die of pollution poisoning, we'll just hire new ones…or import them…or something. This is the most short-sighted and naked sop to business special interests in the nation. This is Texas after all, and everything is bigger in Texas including backward-thinking ideas like this.

13. *"We support the definition of marriage as a God-ordained, legal and moral commitment only between a natural man and a natural woman, which is the foundational unit of a healthy society, and we oppose the assault on marriage by judicial activists."* Whew. I'm sure every biologist cringes at the prospect of unnatural men and women. How can our society be healthy when we have over 50 million people living in poverty and 25 million children being food insecure? Texas has the highest percentage of its citizens in these categories of any of the 50 states. From recent court rulings by "activist" judges, the concept of marriage is being *promoted*, not denied. Oh right. It's about those

"unnatural" people trying to exercise their Constitutional and God-given rights to love one another and make personal commitments.

14. *"We support the affirmation of traditional Judeo-Christian family values and oppose the continued assault on those values."* The Constitution guarantees the right to practice any religion or not. Judeo-Christian values lead with feeding the poor, housing the homeless and clothing the destitute. See #13 above about Texas' standings on these issues. And these guys are afraid of Sharia Law... And who is assaulting these wholesome values? Not progressives. By the way, the founders, in many documents, established this nation as one free from religious dogma. You can look it up.

15. *"We affirm that the practice of homosexuality tears at the fabric of society and contributes to the breakdown of the family unit. Homosexual behavior is contrary to the fundamental, unchanging truths that have been ordained by God, recognized by our country's founders, and shared by the majority of Texans."* It must be a drag that natural men and women keep producing gay boys and girls. Too bad the founders didn't say anything about homosexuals. It must really chap the bottoms of Texas Republicans that the Supreme Courts around the nation and in Washington are declaring marriage equality to be a Constitutional right. What's really tearing at the fabric of society is poverty, failing education and few good jobs. Did God sign off on the Constitution?

16. *"We support objective teaching and equal treatment of all sides of scientific theories. We believe theories such as life origins and environmental change should be taught as challengeable scientific theories subject to change as new data is produced."* Evolution is not a theory, but a proven fact. The methods for change over time will be theoretical, but are supported by all research. Virtually all credible academics abide by the processes of evolution. Challenging theories is the very nature of science. So what do these folks want, really? Global climate change is being measured with mountains of new data every year. Over 97% of scientists are certain the climates around the world are definitely warming and changing due to human activity.

Meanwhile, I strongly advise all of you Republican readers to check your calendars and make sure you haven't had a *Twilight Zone* experience. Be assured; you have not. This is the real, albeit curious work of your party chieftains in Texas who think they can float out a new nation for you and me. The 2014 version of this document is only slightly less radical, but retains the same backward-thinking tenets.

Maybe this stuff comes from the dark depths of Rick Perry's laboratory of secession as he makes preparations to withdraw Texas from the United States and turn it into his own personal fiefdom. His anointed successor, Greg Abbott has pledged to follow Perry's "legacy" to the letter.

How much goofier can it get in Texas? Well, 67% of all eligible voters stayed home in 2014 and allowed a whopping 17% of the voters to elect Republicans across the board. Then, that was the national average too, so voter disgust remains at record levels. This is the prime example as to why the American citizen must take the country back from the corporate-sponsored politicians that we've been talking about.

Voter cynicism is understandable, but the only vehicle citizens have for change is the vote. Otherwise, it will take some sort of rebellion or revolution to regain our moral senses.

Chapter 15:   Grover's Groove

Fewer people amaze me. As I grow more "experienced" with every passing day. Then I heard parts of Grover Norquist's recent speech to the RNC and had a jaw-dropping experience. No pussyfooting around. No obfuscating language. No coded phrases. He just came right out and said that conservative leadership will come from the House of Representatives and the Senate. "All we need...", he said, "is someone in the White House to sign the bill." The bill he was talking about, of course, was one of Paul Ryan budget plans that dismantles the New Deal, the War on Poverty and the Great Society all at once.

Grover's groove is about making the President a figurehead for his idea about how this country should operate. This creature of the night thinks that poor people, unemployed people and ambitious, middle class people should chase the jobs to Asia and not burden his utopia with silly things like Medicare, Social Security, unemployment compensation, Medicaid, public education or just about anything having to do with "...the welfare of the people..." like that quaint document, our Constitution, requires our government to do.

The *Lord of Loopiness*, has given new meaning to the words hubris and arrogance. Then again, why shouldn't he. He's badgered almost all the Republicans in Congress into signing his pledge never ever to raise taxes, but to only cut them along with social services that several generations were promised and needed over the last 80 years, or so. It reminded me of a photo I saw of young men dressed in full battle dress clutching red flags emblazoned with twisted crosses and their right hands raised pledging absolute fidelity to their leader. I wonder how many German citizens thought that Adolf Hitler, the ultimate right wing extremist, was just a passing fancy and that no harm would come from his calculated arrogance.

The *Champion of Cheap* has reached a new low of depravity in this country with his career made from the droppings left from the late Milton Friedman's aborted take on neoliberal economics: *Supply Side Economics*. The ONLY people yelling for this are the 1% who are already incredibly rich and those who think they can become that way. This economic theory has never worked for any nation as a whole and has caused such a dramatic evacuation of capital from the infrastructure, the middle, or consuming class and the general welfare of the majority of the people anywhere it's been tried that the countries are barely able to function and end up with despotic dictatorships.

It should be mentioned again that Naomi Klein's award-winning best seller, *Shock Doctrine*, provides the historical and documented details for the failure of Friedman's disaster formula.

Grover the Great says, "Not to worry." As long as we have our mighty military and police to suppress the outcries of those lazy, indolent, good-for-nothing creatures known as citizens, everything is under control. Norquist would be better off if he actually did research with real facts, instead of talking to Friedman's ghost. Grover Norquist will soon find out that his agenda is deeply flawed and rational people will not abide by its guarantees for failure. Meanwhile, he makes fools of those who wrote the Constitution, adjudicated it and died defending and respecting it as the law of the land.

Who is this guy?

Chapter 16:   Unraveling Democracy

The *Citizens United vs. Federal Election Commission* Supreme Court decision tells us in certain terms: If you are not a major player in this upper echelon game now being developed in the ivory towers of corporate America, your rights, freedoms and understanding of the American way are also at risk to the whims of candidates now about to be attached to the strings of the corporate puppeteers. Make no mistake. The candidates who will emerge from this decision will NOT be part of any populist movement like the one that President Obama conducted. Those quaint little political actions by real people will be overwhelmed by corporate sponsored initiatives funded by virtually unlimited resources – like the Koch brothers' $900 million financial commitment to the Republican cause for 2016.

E.J. Dionne a major political writer for the Washington Post wrote a column on February 5th, 2012 titled "The Citizens United Catastrophe": "We have seen the world created by the Supreme Court's *Citizens United* decision, and it doesn't work. Oh, yes, it works nicely for the wealthiest and most powerful people in the country, especially if they want to shroud their efforts to influence politics behind shell corporations. It just doesn't happen to work if you think we are a democracy and not a plutocracy. The *Citizens United* justices were not required to think through the practical consequences of sweeping aside decades of work by legislators, going back to the passage of the landmark Tillman Act in 1907, who sought to prevent untoward influence-peddling and indirect bribery. "

Dionne adds: "Justice Anthony Kennedy's words in his majority opinion: 'The appearance of influence or access, furthermore, will not cause the electorate to lose faith in our democracy." How did he know that? Did he consult the electorate? Did he think this would be true just because he said it? The election of 2014 proved him wrong when 66% of the voters stayed home.

Justice John Paul Stevens' observation in his dissent reads far better than Kennedy's in light of subsequent events. 'A democracy cannot function effectively,' he wrote, 'when its constituent members believe laws are being bought and sold." He should also have added candidates for elected office.

Clearly, this product of judicial activism is currently reaping the whirlwind of corporations as people and money as speech. Mr. Dionne and I both agree that this was their intent all along. Remember, Justice Scalia helped found the *Federalist Society* and recruited Justices Alito and Roberts. This is an extremely conservative, agenda driven group that thinks the few should govern the masses. When the Constitution was drafted and finalized, the Federalists, led by Alexander Hamilton, lost the debate to the

Jeffersonians and from that emerged the Bill of Rights. Why else would the Texas State School Board eliminate the story of our third President? It's about *noblesse oblige* and slanting the history education for our children.

Add to this the Lewis Powell memo from 1971 where he demanded of the U.S. Chamber of Commerce that corporate/banking America join forces to do whatever it takes to influence Congress and the courts in overturning all of the New Deal laws as well as set up a ruling plutocracy that gave the moguls the legal right to do whatever they wanted to do. This is real history, not an opinion. The results of this "organization" gave us "K" St. people like Jack Abramoff who made influence peddling an art form. It gave us the revolving door for politicians becoming lobbyists (over 40,000 in Washington, D.C. alone). We saw the naked graft at work when Eric Cantor got primary-ed by a Tea Party incursion. It only took a few months before he announced his new banking job with a salary in the seven-figure range. This is just one example of the overt corporate influence on who will represent *We the people...*, and what will happen to them when they're done with doing that.

These events have combined to greatly damage the fabric of our nation. Combined, they are unraveling our Democracy as our citizens sit idly by and watch it happen. The ridicule heaped on the *Occupy* movements by the right wingers indicates they are afraid something will change their goal to have plutocracy instead of democracy. They want to stop it before it's too late and the people actually rise up and take back their country from those who would steal it from them and sell it to the highest bidder.

Chapter 17:   Is Anyone Thinking Correctly?

My friend and colleague, Mr. Steve Love, provided the basis for this piece. I have paraphrased for brevity. It is in keeping with the topics in this section to point out several things in the failed model of so-called "conservative" policies and politics. In reality, these policies are retrograde backwardness – a delicious redundancy.

Conservatives used to label liberals as pointy-headed idealists totally out of touch with reality. Conservatives claimed they dealt with how things really are (adults) while liberals were the adolescents lost in idealism. Conservatives claimed pragmatism while labeling liberals as ideologues trying to force a square world into their round-hole realities.

Now, it is the conservatives, the radical no-compromise political faction that takes its orders from free-market economists in their academic/think-tank ivory towers. They promote some ideal world that only exists in their imaginations or in historical revisionism. They are Adam Smith economists from the 18th century.

They talk about being faithful to the Founding Fathers' ideals, but are oblivious to the exclusion of women's suffrage and the horror of slavery. They overlook the fact that the Founders excluded provisions in the Constitution only to have to amend it with the Bill of Rights and several others.

People wonder why this Congress is at loggerheads with the President. Conservatives want to construct their particular ideal society with limited reproductive rights for women, no taxes, no immigrants, little government, limited voting, a meritocracy, total individual freedom and laissez-fair capitalism - a libertarian nirvana. Liberals will settle for a strong and vibrant middle class in a society that includes sufficient regulation that prevents abuse of rights, the economy and the environment.

The political arena is deadlocked because one side refuses to compromise *because of* their philosophy. Conservative, ideologically-based thinking results in people with a self-identity based on centralized dogma not on existential reality. Conservatives ask us to believe what they tell us not what we can learn on our own.

They listen to what Libertarians, talk show entertainers and think-tank talking heads say about what the world must become and is while closing their minds to the lessons of history. They argue that cutting taxes and government spending is how jobs get created while ignoring history from the 30s and 40s; the time when we came closest to full employment. It was the result of high taxes and massive government spending on the New Deal agencies and the war effort. These experts claim that we recovered from the Great Depression, not because of FDR's New Deal policies, but because of WWII, as though the high taxes and massive government spending of the war economy was different from that of the years preceding and following it. Actually, the War just put the New Deal into overdrive. The Keynesian methodology actually saved capitalism from itself and its wrong-headed notions about free market enterprise solving all issues.

The person who said that politics is the art of the possible was a liberal not a conservative. The obstructionist, filibustering conservatives in Congress are now the Luddite ideologues, whose refusal to learn from the past and take a pragmatic view of what is possible in a democratic society is the reason that Congress cannot address or solve the real problems of the country.

The best solution is the ballot box. If we are to make progress, the people cannot keep electing backward thinking ideologues who are owned by selfish, profit-motivated big money interests. The mid-term elections of 2014 was projected be a watershed event toward the direction our nation is headed. Most activists hoped that either the same old failed behavior would appear or people would actually turn out to vote and start letting their voices be heard through candidates who, hopefully, were not bought or paid for by corporate/banking America.

Sadly, the people voiced their disapproval of the entire process of democracy by staying home in 2014. Only 1/3rd of eligible Americans chose to vote. I see this as a most ominous occurrence that the people are willing to eschew their right to vote because they didn't like the process or the candidates. My message to those who didn't vote because of those reasons is: It's your fault! You allowed the process and the slate of candidates that appeared on the ballot without being active in that process.

What gives me some hope is the curious result of progressive agenda items in conservative states passing overwhelmingly while the "conservative" candidates were elected by a "whopping" 17% of the eligible electorate. I can hardly wait for 2016 when the nation will be ending two more years of Congressional gridlock and partisan vitriol.

Chapter 18:   Mandatory Laws

There is still a lot of buzz about the mandatory health care clause in the Affordable Care Act. This is not news. With a little research a person can discover that we've done this before. Our founding fathers (a much overused phrase) did this same thing in 1790 during our first Congress.

The mandate they passed then, required ship owners to buy medical insurance for their seamen. It was signed by 20 framers of the Constitution and George Washington himself.

In 1792, Congress, along with 17 Constitution framers passed another statute that required all able-bodied men to buy firearms. Congress decided it was a federal duty to buy and possess firearms. Even though 4 framers voted against this bill, Washington signed it into law. I'm sure the NRA and others clutching their guns today feel even more justified knowing that ancient fears of invasion or a tyrannical government still persist and must be defended against.

Congress in 1792 once again addressed the problem of mandatory health care for seamen. The original mandate didn't cover hospital stay, so Congress passed a law requiring the seamen to buy hospital insurance for themselves. This first-of-its-kind individual mandate requiring the purchase of health insurance was signed into law by President John Adams, one of the original founding fathers and framers of the Constitution.

In 2012 and we saw the battle joined once again between those who want everyone to be insured versus those who think that this mandate violates the Constitution. In view of recent case hearings, I wonder if Justice Scalia knows the above history being the constructionist pure soul that he is. I wonder if Chief Justice Roberts is aware of these precedents being the strict precedent adhering jurist that he is.

Doesn't it make sense to have a healthier population that is able to work when jobs need filling? A healthy workforce is a productive workforce. Why do we need middle men, aka the health insurance industry, raking 30%-60% off the top for their fees to push paper and figure out new ways to deny people coverage they are paying for?

What's the big deal about mandatory health care? We have mandatory retirement payments into Social Security. Some companies require their employees to contribute to the company retirement program. We require, in most states, that a driver have automobile insurance of some sort before he/she can obtain a driver's license or buy a car. So, what's more important, a car or your health?

The rest of the industrialized world employs some form of single-payer, government sponsored, universal health care. Their citizens live longer and are healthier than our citizens and it costs less per person than it does here. So, why are we wasting time and more money debating what is logical and right? After all, we have history on our side. We've done this before...and it works.

Chapter 19:   Why the Republican Model Fails
Every Test

Republicans ritualistically denounce President Obama as hostile to capitalism, disdainful of individual enterprise and lacking in ideas for reviving the economy. All they offered over the last six years were economic ideas that not only are inadequate for the purpose of reviving the economy, but were instrumental in creating the nation's current economic problems in the first place.

Republicans had little to do with creating the middle class, so they fail to address the pain of the middle class when their policies fail and the people suffer. The Republicans repeated familiar charges that Mr. Obama advocates a redistribution of wealth. In view of the growing gap between the rich and everybody else, plus the added benefit of having more people with more money spending it, this sounds like a pretty good idea.   Governor Rick Perry of Texas outright called the President a socialist – as if he knew what it meant. Mitt Romney, the last Republican Presidential candidate participated in the frenzied world of leveraged buyouts. Companies like his Bain Capital helped close 50,000 factories and shops while killing the jobs in them by sending them to foreign countries.

Leveraged buyouts were only one factor in the growth of the income gap. Also to blame were a host of benighted economic policies advocated by Republicans for the last thirty years. One of their favorite memes (lies or myths) was government spending being the sole cause of the federal budget deficit and cutting it the sole solution. In reality, it was tax cuts for the wealthy, an assault on social programs, tax loopholes and a deregulatory zeal that allowed a recklessness that led to near economic collapse. These factors, the Medicare Part D fiasco and fighting two illegal wars on credit cost the American taxpayer over $1 trillion dollars in debt. These are the gifts of George W. Bush and his advisors that just keep on giving. It was all exactly backward. Americans are angry about income redistribution — from the money going from the middle class up to the tiny sliver at the top, not from the top down. The poor have always been there and nobody seems to pay them much attention, mostly because they seldom vote.

The workable and proven solutions are policies that promote real job growth and help the middle class, not the Republican proposals of austerity and tax cuts as the solution to all problems. That's been tried repeatedly and has failed every time. Mr. Obama said it well a couple years ago: "We can't go back to this brand of 'you're-on-your-own economics.'" The Republicans continue to talk about a merit-based economy and call for lowering taxes and cutting spending. The so-called *sequester,* for example, not only cut spending, it cost us jobs and buying power to say nothing of taxes lost. This alone is proof that austerity only does nothing but make economic issues for the consumer classes worse. Most European economies are still struggling with austerity only and not making much headway toward recovery.

An op-ed by the *New York Times'* Thomas Edsall, entitled *What the Right Gets Right* polled a few conservative think-tanks and got what he called *ideological pap.* He decided to ask some liberals what the right gets right without going to the Roosevelt Institute or People for the American Way. He asks a few individuals who have evidently unconsciously bought into the GOP framing of issues and so reflect, not what the right gets right, but what the right would con us into believing that it gets right.

Sadly, Andy Stern, former president of the S.E.I.U and now a senior fellow at Columbia University's Richman Center, made five points in his response that couldn't be more pro-right if Grover Norquist and Newt Gingrich had written them. Here are his observations and Mr. Edsall's response:

"They appreciate more instinctively the need for fiscal balance." So this is why Romney's leadership role in Bain Capital is receiving such *high praise* from all but the Ayn Rand crowd? Where is that "balance" embodied in the tax policies of the last 30 years? I cannot imagine a more tone-deaf statement than to suggest the tax policies of the last 30 years have been *fiscally balanced.* The rich getting richer as the poor get poorer…where is the "balance" in that?

"They understand people's more innate belief in hard work and individual responsibility and see government as too often lacking that understanding." The *hard work* of hedge fund managers and top-500 corporate CEOs? Really? If "government" – dominated by conservative memes since Reagan – lacks an appreciation of "hard work and individual responsibility" why have so many in the middle class found *their* "hard work and individual responsibility" rewarded with stagnant wages at best, pink slips, lost health care and foreclosures at worst?

"They are more suspicious from a philosophical point of view of big government as an answer to many issues and are suspicious of Wall Street institutionally and not just their high salaries, and bad practices." Big government has been the target of right-wing hit squads beginning with the John Birch Society in the 1950s and has become an approved meme in polite society with Reagan's first inaugural address. When has anyone talked about the center of our financial industry as "big finance" and to fear *it?* Yet our public and private debt of $10.5 trillion in 1987 went to $43 trillion in 2006 -

a 410% increase - creating an international financial bubble that upon its bursting in 2008 destroyed $11 trillion of domestic wealth and $50 trillion of wealth worldwide! We haven't been cautioned about big finance because big finance has been the patron of the right and they have told us that we must fear "big government" but "big finance" - think 19% credit cards and adjustable rate mortgages - is "looking out for us." Right!

"They respect the need for private sector economic growth (although their prescription is lacking)." Hey, Andy, what is their "respect" worth if their policies show us that when in control they are committed to seeing Wall Street prosper and Main Street decline? They're like the guy who says, "Don't believe what you see with your eyes; believe what I'm telling you!"

"They are more pro-small business." On what planet have you been for the last 30 years? Drive through small town America and see what has happened to Mom and Pop stores there because of Wall Mart – the epitome of *big* – squeezing them out of business by the hundreds of thousands. The Waltons cannot be your hero and be pro-small business. That does not compute, Andy. The conservatives would love to have us believe they are for small businesses but small businesses have ever been the prey of big business and the big boys have the political clout and the right would never offend the big boys. Don't think you can make this sow's ear into a silk purse, my friend. Furthermore, the banking fiascos have made the banks turn off the spigot to venture capital and small business loans.

Chapter 20 The GOP Money Game

A little something from one of my all-time favorite Americans:

> "Republicans approve of the American farmer, but they are willing to help him go broke. They stand four-square for the American home-but not for housing. They are strong for labor-but they are stronger for restricting labor's rights. They favor minimum wage-the smaller the minimum wage the better. They endorse educational opportunity for all-but they won't spend money for teachers or for schools. They think modern medical care and hospitals are fine-for people who can afford them. They consider electrical power a great blessing-but only when the private power companies get their rake-off. They think American standard of living is a fine thing-so long as it doesn't spread to all the people. And they admire of Government of the United States so much that they would like to buy it."
> ~Harry S. Truman

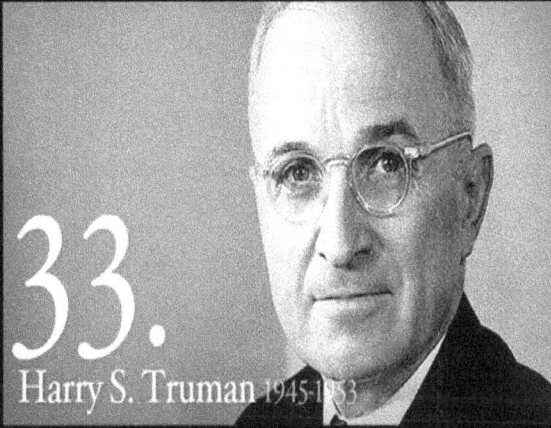

33.
Harry S. Truman 1945-1953

Money and power. Power and money. That's the name of the game in Republican politics. Not principle. Not vision. Not governing. Who are the core players in that money and power game? I have combed several lists of 'key' Republican players from the major forces on the Radical Right, the Libertarians and the Neo Cons. My top ten list represents the people who, through political clout, money, or both, are seminal driving forces that corrupt Republican politics and push it to the extremist regions that it inhabits today.

In a seemingly endless sea of Right-wing malefactors who have created part of the 35 year industry of political extremism that has driven millions of voters out of the GOP (and millions more away from the ballot box) and made it a rich, but minority party, it would seem like a daunting task to pick a ten most wanted.

My top ten, though, merit special attention because of the breadth of their influence, which is usually masked behind the web of phony grass roots movements, think tanks, and other big money sponsored professional media pundits of various merit. It is good to know who is pulling the strings of power.

This list is fluid as some of the usual crowd, like right-wing, radio-reactionary Rush Limbaugh, took a major tumble, opening space in the Ten Most Wanted.

They are:

No 10: **Roger Ailes** – Fox News' CEO ranks No. 10. Ailes may be America's leading propagandist, but his network, which has dominated the narrative lines of most conservative political stories for decades, has been losing its iron-clad grip.

Fox News owner Rupert Murdoch is an opportunist. Ailes is pure old-school Neo-Con, a true-believer in the Wall Street to Military Industrial Complex side of the party.

Ailes was able to build his "news" network into a powerful propagandist tool that has given lift to the Tea Party, marginalized the Occupy Wall Street movement, and put the far right's spin on political news out there as the story to debate for the other networks.

No. 9: **Frank Luntz** – Luntz is the propaganda lyricist to Grover Norquist's political orchestrations, a Sullivan to the master manipulator's Gilbert. Luntz, with degrees from University of Pennsylvania and Oxford, is the CEO of Luntz Research Companies, which offers "Strategic Consulting and Message Development," messaging, focus groups, surveys and other research for political and corporate campaigns.

Effectively he is a professional *mendast*, who finds alternative phrasings that allow his Far Right clients to twist political sentiment through their own misunderstanding and emotional responses to his clever wordings.

- It's not "global warming." It's "climate change" which sounds oh-so un-man-made. He advised the Bush administration to play up the "lack of scientific certainty" in the global warming debate, even though scientists were quite certain.

- To promote school vouchers that privatize the public school systems, he told his clients to call them "opportunity scholarships" rather than vouchers, which poll as unpopular with most average independent voters.

- He told oil company clients that offshore oil drilling is better expressed as "deep-sea energy exploration."

- Luntz was awarded the 2010 PolitiFact "Lie of the Year" award for his promotion of the phrase 'government takeover' to refer to healthcare reform, starting in the spring of 2009.

- He coined the term "death tax" to light a fire under average Americans about the reinstatement of an estate tax that really only affects the wealthiest 1%.

- Fighting reform of the abuses of Wall Street, Luntz urged opponents of financial legislative reform to say the legislation is filled with bank bailouts, lobbyist loopholes, and additional layers of complicated government bureaucracy.

You get the idea.

No. 8: **Sheldon Adelson**, one of the new Super PAC men, moves up into the A list of the Right Wing's most wanted by being the primary money man behind the Newt Gingrich campaign of 2012, but as the sixth richest man in the world, his deep pockets afford the NeoCon wing of the Republican Party lots of ad buys, robo-calling, and more.

Free to put millions from his international casino business into the 2012 GOP primary contest, he kept pal Gingrich's White House ambitions on artificial life support and almost sparked a real run for the Oval Office until Nasty Newt's odious personality and high-negatives with independent voters sparked enough cat-calling from the GOP hierarchy, Fox News and the other Right-wing punditocracy to take him out at the knees.

Adelson is still a huge giver to the GOP, and their senatorial campaign, with an eye towards anyone on the hard Right that remains pro-Israel.

He owns the newspaper equivalent of Fox News in Israel, Yisrael Hayom. It's a daily paper that is closely tied to the ultra-nationalist wing of the Likud party. He also is a big funder of Benjamin Netanyahu. I'm guessing he is thrilled with Boehner's boner of inviting Bibi to speak to Congress behind the President's back.

No. 7: **Foster Friess** – A long-time Bush supporter, Friess, who made his millions in the successful Brandywine Fund, is an odd combo: A Christian conservative *and* a Libertarian. On social issues, he leans towards the government getting into your business, and on business issues he leans toward the government getting out of *his* business.

He emerged politically when he set up the Super PAC Red White & Blue Fund to back Rick Santorum. Friess donated $689,000 to Republican organizations and the Bush presidential campaigns over the last decade. He has contributed millions to far-Right political causes and candidates.

Friess is a member of the secretive conservative Council for National Policy that coordinates objectives amongst the network of phony grass roots groups, think tanks, Super PACs and their wealthy funders.

He was acknowledged at the privately held Koch brothers' seminar in June 2011 in Vail, Colorado for donating at least $1 million to Koch-related causes.

Friess gives to Private Sector Solutions, a network of leaders developing private sector solutions to augment, preempt or replace government services. This is part of the neo-liberal economic plan of Milton Friedman, the destroyer of nations.

He has donated to LibForAll and other groups building a global counter-extremism network

He opposes national health reform through donations to the phony activist group Free Market Cure and other groups.

Friess backstops the DeVos family's bid to dismantle public education through Alliance for School Choice, All Children Matter and others. This is another brick in the neo-liberal, Supply-side economics wall.

He also backstops the FairTax project, legislation to replace the current federal system of a tax on retail sales, a tax that hits the working man hard and lets Friess keep even more of his "hard earned" money.

He is a rich ideologue who holds the most extreme right-wing social, religious and economic views, and has the millions to try and influence others by way of the web of faux special interest groups that he funds.

No. 6: **The Coors Family** – The Coors family, heirs of Adolph Coors, are fronted by great grandson Pete, and grandsons Joseph and William Coors.

They are anchor funders of far-right, phony grass-roots think tanks, and other organizations with a decided Libertarian bent, including the democracy-killing American Legislative Exchange Council (ALEC), the American Enterprise Institute, the Cato Institute, the secretive Council for National Policy, the Free Congress Foundation, the Heritage Foundation, the ultra-conservative Mackinac Center for Public Policy, the anti-union National Right to Work Legal Defense Foundation, and The Strategy To Privatize The Public Domain to name a few of the more than 40 organizations that use their millions to espouse the Far Right agenda.

No. 5: **The DeVos Family** – Not as well known as their pyramidic family business, **Amway**, the company's co-founder Richard DeVos Sr., his children and grandchildren are all big funders of the Far Right.

The senior DeVos also served as Republican National Committee finance chair.

The DeVos family contributes to anti-government anchors like the American Enterprise Institute, judicial manipulation via the right-wing Federalist Society for Law and Public Policy Studies, manipulation of the masses through the Heritage Foundation, the Michigan-centric far Right Mackinac Center for Public Policy, and some highly questionable interpretations of the Constitution via the National Constitution Center.

Extremely religious, Betsy DeVos is influential in school voucher funding that allows for school "choice" that brings religion in through the back door. They also work with smaller fry like James Dobson to promote organizations like the Family Research Council, and Focus on the Family.

Members of the family fund D. James Kennedy's Coral Ridge Ministries in Fort Lauderdale, FL. that produced an Ann Coulter documentary linking Darwinism with Hitler and the Holocaust which the Anti Defamation League of B'nai B'rith called "an outrageous and shoddy attempt by D. James Kennedy to trivialize the horrors of the Holocaust." Can it get much loopier than this?

No. 4: **Richard Mellon-Scaife** – A scion of the early capitalist Robber Barons, Richard Mellon-Scaife is a $1.2B trust-funder with a publishing business that makes him the Charles Foster Kane of his day. He is far more dangerous to the truth than Rupert Murdoch, because, unlike the Australian opportunist, Mellon-Scaife is a true believer.

Like Ailes, Mellon-Scaife tries to corrupt the fourth estate with a hard-right spin in his publications like the *American Spectator*, *NewsMax.com*, and the *Pittsburgh Tribune-Review*.

Mellon-Scaife is a DBC Charter Member with his money in numerous hard-right foundations that support more than thirty hard-right special interest groups and think tanks, including the American Enterprise Institute, the Cato Institute, the judicial-bending Federalist Society, L. Brent Bozell's Media Research Center, Grover Norquist's National Taxpayers Union Foundation, and more.

He guides four foundations with more than $385M in assets with the sole purpose of remodeling the United States Government in his self-centered Libertarian world view. The Sarah Scaife Foundation had $244 million in fair market value in 2009. The Carthage Foundation had $24 million, the Alleghany Foundation held $47 million, and the Scaife Family Foundation put $70 million to work for far Right causes and ideologies.

***No. 3:* The Koch brothers** – The Kochs are the most visible face of the Dead Billionaires Club. The owners of the largest privately held company in North America, Koch Enterprises, they move oil, own Georgia Pacific Lumber, and sell you Brawny paper towels.

Yes, the Kochs are big funders of the far-right Libertarian overthrow of the Republican Party. They are core funders of the American Legislative Exchange Council (ALEC), as closed to a "shadow government" as we've ever had. They are also major funders of the nation-wide *public policy foundation* network found in just about every state with various titles. Their father, Fred Koch, was co-founder of the John Birch society.

Yes, they host ultra-secret meetings to recruit and gather other billionaires and high-million millionaires to their cause of ripping down the federal government from the inside brick-by-brick.

They have Supreme Court Justices Scalia and Thomas in their back pocket, and can call them out to secret meetings without consequence.

The Kochs are big union busters as well, and the biggest backers of Scott Walker's union busting efforts in Wisconsin. Americans for Prosperity (AFP) is their biggest phony grass roots group, and should rightly be named Americans for the Koch Brothers' Prosperity. Their agenda largely serves the wealthiest of the wealthy, not the poor schmucks that they've convinced are aligned with their government-dismantling.

No. 2: Karl Rove – The man George W. Bush nicknamed "Turdblossom" lives up to that moniker as one of the top right wing supporters and election manipulators. Rove is the de-facto leader of the Neo-Conservative wing of the Republican Party. Politicians come and go, but Rove is a principal architect and crypt keeper of more than a generation of linkage between the money and power of Wall Street, big oil, the military industrial complex, big agribusiness, and the pharmaceutical industries to the NeoCon politicians, Astroturf groups, and think tanks that hold a handful of the reins of power. He began his "illustrious" career by being hired by George H.W. Bush as a political policy maker. Those Bushes.... The gifts that just keep on giving...

He has grown the NeoCon tumor on the American body politic, part of the same carcinogen that spawned a hard-right judicially activist Supreme Court that delivered the malignancy that was the George W. Bush administration, a pair of illegal wars, radical reshaping of civil rights, the festering boil of Wall Street greed that exploded in 2008, and more.

George H.W. Bush, George W. Bush, Phil Gramm, Ronald Reagan, Rick Perry and Kay Bailey Hutchinson have all been clients. Rove also generated the program at the state level for placing their Supreme Court justices that would then be tried at the federal level: Put partisan "activist" judges in place and then accuse the other side of doing it while you were doing it.

Rove's dirty tricks started with his early "prank" of using a false identity to gain access to the campaign office of Democrat Alan J. Dixon, running for Treasurer of Illinois. Rove stole 1000 sheets of campaign letterhead, then printed fake rally fliers promising "free beer, free food, girls and a good time for nothing." It didn't work, but his practice of underhanded dealing began.

He dropped out of college to run, ironically, for the head of the College Republicans in the Midwest in 1973. He held a bloodless coup by producing another version of their bylaws from the one that Robert Edgeworth, the other candidate, was running under. Things became so heated that they held two seaparate elections, and both were named to helm the same organization, at the same time. While lawsuits proceeded, Edgeworth leaked a recording to the *Washington Post* where Rove admitted that he had been rooting through people's garbage cans to get dirt on his opposition, in a mini-me mirror of the Watergate investigation that was going on in the same year.

Then RNC Chairman George H.W. Bush put Rove under the microscope, including having an FBI agent question him. Former Nixon White House Counsel John Dean, and alleged Watergate co-conspirator, who became the star witness for the prosecution, said: "[B]ased on my review of the files, it appears the Watergate prosecutors were interested in Rove's activities in 1972, but because they had bigger fish to fry, they did not aggressively investigate him."

Rove also had his hand in politicizing the Department of Justice with the political firings of seven U.S. Attorneys for failing to engage in political prosecutions that he had wanted carried out, but, under the cover of Executive Privilege from his years in the White House, he dodged another political bullet.

What has moved Rove up the list to No. 2, though, is his development of American Crossroads in 2010, another shadowy 527 Super PAC, to take advantage of the Citizens United decision. He amassed a very large war chest to try to stop President Obama's re-election (he failed and blew over $300 million in donor assets), and was the sugar daddy of the muddled and middling Mitt Romney campaign in 2012.

No. 1: **Grover Norquist** – He surpasses the more public Karl Rove in so many ways because he has elevated the power game on behalf of his elite Libertarian DBC clientele to Wagnerian heights. Norquist has shanghaied the Republican Party out from under its NeoCon masters by spending more than 35 patient, long years building his government wrecking crew from the ground up.

He is best known by the public for his infamous tax pledge, requiring all Republican incumbents who don't want someone competing in their primary to sign on or be targeted as a RINO (Republican in Name Only).

Norquist, working with low-lifes like convicted felon Jack Abramamoff and boyish "alternate reality" man, Ralph Reed has hand-trained legions of extremist, highly dogmatic Libertarian political warriors. The Tea Party, and the extreme hard right policies that career Republicans have taken in recent years to avoid extinction are all his handiwork.

The manipulation of the debt run up by the NeoCon side of the GOP into the phony "crisis" last summer, are all part of Mr. Norquist's handiwork.

Norquist has been adept at co-opting the Religious Right out from under the NeoCons by letting them put their extremist agenda into legislation, rather than giving it lip service. Why? It's another happy monkey wrench thrown into the system to destroy government from within. Rather than tackle climate legislation, the government is left paralyzed by hot-button issues like abortion and women's rights that distract intrest from Norquist's real putsch toward deregulation of his business backers and Paul Ryanesque changes to the social safety net and the tax system.

He was a driving force in the creation of the American Legislative Exchange Council (ALEC) a one stop shop for major corporations to come and have legislation written up, handed to a Republican congressman, and put through the pretense of the American political process to dismantle regulations or delay complying with environmental or societal responsibilities.

If you ever wonder why Republicans seem to turn against polling data showing them out of step with the will of the people, it is because the only will they answer to is that of Norquist and his wealthy masters.

The above commentary is part and parcel to the ongoing Republican meme that serves only corporate self-interests since the time of William Howard Taft. Theodore Roosevelt tried to introduce real American citizen agenda everywhere he served in government and became one of the most popular Presidents in our history. But the Republican Party, continuously being fed money by the corporate/banking elite, continues to try to destroy the life and well-being of the middle classes while totally ignoring the chronic poor. I am continually amazed at this in view of the fact that most consumers are middle class and they are the class that has made the rich richer. Furthermore, if the poor would be educated, trained and put to work, *they* would add to the consumer base. There is something very, very wrong with the philosophy that thinks the golden goose will live forever even if it is starved to death. Whatever happened to the old axiom: When we all do well, we all do well?

Chapter 21:   No Longer the Land of Opportunity

In January, 2012 Harold Meyerson published an article in the *Washington Post* that speaks eloquently to the Republican brand and how its model for governing fails every time. I paraphrase the pieces of the article in italics. My comments are in normal typeface.

From Mitt Romney *: "... Barack Obama has been replacing our merit-based society with an Entitlement Society. The coming election", Romney told Wall Street Journal editors last month, "will be a very simple choice" between Obama's "European social democratic" vision and "a merit-based opportunity society — an American-style society — where people earn their rewards based on their education, their work, their willingness to take risks and their dreams."* As we have seen all along, this was just part of the Republican fantasy promoted by those who don't understand that a totally merit-based society is not only unrealistic, but is bound to fail – as they have so often.

Romney continues to assert that his and the GOP's critique of Obama includes liberal thinking in America. He fails, however, to explain how and why the American economy declined during the past decade – in part because he would betray his lack of understanding of Europe's social democracies. They are much more "merit-based" than we are.

The best way to measure a nation's merit-based status is to look at its economic mobility between generations: Do children move up and down the economic ladder based on their own abilities, or does their economic standing simply replicate their parents'? As the American middle class has shrunk over recent decades, (Since the Reagan "revolution") *the idea of America as the land of opportunity has become a farce. A paper by Julia Isaacs of the Brookings Institution shows sons' earnings approximate those of their fathers about three times more frequently in the United States than they do in Denmark, Norway and Finland, and about 1¹ / ₂ times more frequently than they do in Germany. The European social democracies — where taxes, entitlements and the rate of unionization greatly exceed those of the United States — are clearly more merit-based than the United States.*

More measurements by which Europe's social democracies demonstrate more dynamism than our increasingly sclerotic plutocracy include: Unemployment rates in Northern European nations — as of October (2010), *Germany's unemployment rate was 6.5 percent; the Netherlands, 4.8 percent; Sweden 7.4 percent — are substantially lower than ours* (9 percent at the time of the article. We have since dropped to below 6 percent). *Denmark, Sweden, Finland and Germany in particular have sizable trade surpluses, while the United States runs the largest trade deficits in human history.*

There are multiple reasons why the nations of Northern Europe are outperforming us. But if entitlements and social democracy were anywhere near the impediments to enterprise that Romney claims, Germany would hardly be the most successful economy in the advanced industrial world, with those of Scandinavia close behind. Romney and the GOP are still hitched to Friedman's Supply-side economic theory. It is a shame to mention that Reagan so influenced Thatcher with Reaganomics that the United Kingdom used the stress of the Falklands war to implement this "austerity only" economic strategy from which they are still trying to recover.

*The reasons for **social democracy's** (emphasis mine) successes are clear. The Scandinavian governments commit to worker retraining and job relocation such that there is no major political pressure to keep failing firms in business; it's a policy that favors innovative start-ups. In Germany, management and unions **cooperate** to upgrade their products and their processes — partly because corporate boards consist of equal numbers of management and worker representatives.* We might recall that part of Lee Iococca's strategy to save Chrysler from bankruptcy in the 1980s included bringing the UAW to the boardroom table. *Germany's surge in exports may be somewhat attributable to its union workers agreeing to hold their wages flat (at levels still well above those of their U.S. counterparts). But their workers' willingness to sacrifice in order to stay competitive is surely increased by the fact that their CEOs on average make just 11 times as much as their workers. In the United States, chief executives make roughly 200 to 300 times (choose your survey) as much as their average employees' salary.* This is yet another factor in the inequality arguments that Republicans choose to ignore. Speaking of choosing surveys, look at those that show how much the CEOs are contributing to political campaigns and right wing propaganda mills.

Romney's characterization of our country as a merit-based society and his failure to notice the huge changes in economic rewards over the past three decades show how short-sighted and biased his and the GOP's view of economics is. During the 30 years after World War II, the average American family's income doubled, while chief executives' income was restrained, increasing by less than 1 percent annually, according to a 2010 paper by economists Carola Frydman and Raven Saks. Beginning around 1980, however, as unions were smashed, industry moved jobs offshore to finish off the unions at home. Executive pay skyrocketed while the incomes of most Americans began to flatten or decline. Meanwhile, financiers and corporate leaders were able to claim more and more of the nation's income for themselves. These facts and the obvious observations from the business pages illustrate how transparent the GOP/corporate/banking plan for hegemony over labor really is.

Corporate and bank leaders have been rewarded with huge payouts even when their corporation's performance has been disappointing. Conversely, while millions of Americans have maintained or upgraded their skills, but saw their jobs shipped abroad or downgraded. Is this a description of a merit-based society? How does it compare with that of mid-century America, when the rewards for work were distributed more broadly? Knowing these facts makes me think that somebody is lying about how our economy works for the people.

Romney and his Bain Capital buddies may view their wealth as the just rewards endemic to successful people in a merit-based society. But why are so few Americans sharing in those rewards today while so many shared in them 40 years ago? Are most Americans no longer meritorious? Or has our country ceased to reward any but the rich and powerful? I can't help but be cynical in that the perpetration of this great lie by those who profited greatly by destroying companies for his own, and their company's profit is still trying to promote the fraud. That said, the fact that so many working people still vote Republican tells us how naïve they remain, or how ideologically resistant they are to anything sounding liberal, even if those parts of the ideology are against their own best interests.

In the final view, the Republican Party has a severe identity crisis. They can't decide whether they embrace the Tea Party loonies (Cruz, et.al.), are isolationists (Paul), Moralists (Huckabee) or cultural warriors (Santorum). In any case, their bench of viable candidates for party and national leadership is terribly short and none of the "players" represent the heart and soul of the American people.

Chapter 22:   I'm Your Friend – Really!

Even though this book is dedicated to mostly progressive points and opinions, I can't in good conscience ignore my Republican friends. I have them, you know. They are terrific people, some of the most sincere and reliable people I've ever known. I hold great affection for them and it is breaking my heart to watch their dreams and expectations being shattered and hosed down the gutter like so much broken crockery. They don't deserve to be treated so badly by the Republican National Committee and its "leadership". The candidates they trot out for President and other offices are like so many one-trick ponies and truly embarrassing to you. Then again, that's what corporate/banking America is paying for these days, so I guess you're stuck with this lot.

Let me take this time to extend my sympathies and my heartfelt condolences to all Republicans who are true-hearted, honest, industrious, caring, generous, intelligent, aware, learned and curious. You are my friends. You are the kind of citizens this country depends on to do all the things necessary to maintain the highest standard of living mankind has ever known. All your lives you've been diligent and attentive and family-oriented. You've sacrificed to raise wonderful children and developed great careers at the same time. It's not fair that you good and true Republicans should be treated so badly and tarred by the brush of incompetent political organizations.

Today's Republican Party is no longer interested in compromise while you, my friends, have had to compromise daily throughout your lives. Today's Republican Party is still fighting against the New Deal, while 3 generations of Americans have been treated to comfortable retirements and sane, fair and judicious labor laws to say nothing of intelligent and necessary banking regulations that kept our savings and personal retirement funds safe from vulture capitalists causing them to disappear altogether. The Republican Party has won a few of those fights and almost destroyed our banking, savings and retirement infrastructure in the process. Why, they're even suggesting that your Social Security funds be turned over to those very banks that blew trillions of depositor monies on hare-brained investments with our tax dollars and bad loans while insuring themselves against the losses. How could they treat you so badly? You deserve better than that. Why didn't you take them to task and demand better representation?

Well, while you had your head down and were working so hard to support and grow your families, the Tea Party came in and hijacked the remaining reason and sanity from the RNC. What a slap in the face that must have been. It's bad enough that certain factions of the RNC hijacked Christianity and turned it into another instrument of hypocritical propaganda. Now this! Jesus, the Lord and Savior, was committed to the poor and the unfortunate, but now we have self-ordained right wing pundits telling us that the poor and the weak are merely lazy and don't deserve our help. I don't think you need to be included in that hypocritical conversation, do you? It wasn't that long ago that Congressional Republicans actually wanted to expand food stamps and other social services.

You, like me, were brought up to respect our teachers and to work hard in school so we could have a good life, know the difference between right and wrong and have abilities and skills developed in school such that we could tackle problems and tasks when we were grown. Today's Republicans want to cut schools, or privatize them so that only the rich get to send their kids there. They want to blame teachers (especially unionized teachers) for everything wrong with schools, learning, curriculum and your kids. They think that every parent is perfect and that every teacher is a drag on society even though they get paid like servants rather than the developers of young minds. None of us deserves that kind of representation in government at any level.

So, my dear Republican friends, what are we going to do about this? Are you going to persist with your choice of political affiliation even though it is working very hard against your best interests, or are you going to consider an alternative path? You don't have to vote a straight party ticket, you know. With a little diligence you can determine which candidates and which issues are in your best interests.

Not all Republican or Democratic candidates are our best representatives. We have to learn about them, my friends, then make the correct choices and not for political reasons, but for our families and our nation.

Chapter 23:   The Time for Lying is Now

A recent blog piece by Mark Sumner succinctly summarized the state of the Republican Party and its crumbling legitimacy for representing the American people. My analysis follows:

Ideological fights in Congress are nothing new to American government, but these are uniquely dangerous ones now, because the basic Republican operating philosophy is fear mongering. When people are afraid they do irrational things and that's what the RNC is counting on to get votes for their candidates because people are afraid, not because candidates make sense.

The time is long past when ideas contested for history's approval. It's not even that what's now coming from the political right consists of 100% emotional, fear-based dogma without factual basis. The Republicans' staked out position is one requiring constant lies. There is a kind of impudence among Republicans that doesn't even try to merely distort or shade the facts rather they shove the lies right into our faces. Rand Paul's recent bogus description of the contagiousness of the *Ebola* virus is a perfect example.

Another perfect example is the lie about President Obama being the "food stamp president" even though more people joined that program under Bush. This truth avoidance is part of the Republican Bush-distancing plan. Blatant lies extend through every aspect of the Republican platform, such as it is, for the simple reason that Republicans are devoid of ideas that haven't been repeated failures for anyone but the richest citizens.

With the recent publication of the Senate's investigations into U.S. torture during the Bush years, the pushback from the Bushites is shriller than ever. The GOP is so very desperate to save the legacy of Bush and tarnish that of Obama that they will keep denying the facts and truths to the end.

The economy crashes under Republican policies...repeatedly. EVERY time the Republicans are in charge of the nation's economy, it falters, crashes and creates great hardship for the people at large. It crashed due to tax cuts, deregulated markets, restricted unions, massive environmental regulations cuts, lowered trade barriers and enormous Pentagon spending. This is the failed dogma of Republicans since Lincoln's death.

The Republicans got what they wanted when Bush was appointed/elected, and said it would make us all wealthy and create jobs. They got unlimited wealth for CEOs, unlimited banking "creativity" with other peoples' money, trade agreements that guaranteed manufacturing could move to the cheapest, most desperate labor sources available, massive cuts in capital gains taxes and large boosts in wealth from estate tax freedom. They got record oil and gas drilling freedom, record giveaways of public land and the middle classes shouldering more of the burden so those job creators (the rich) would be free to work their magic. They even gave the already profitable pharmaceutical giants a trillion dollar gift with Medicare Part D. In case you missed it, none of these things worked for anybody BUT the richest Americans. There was NO trickle down, the money trickled UP. The Wall St. gamblers nearly destroyed the world's economy with "creative" investments, loans and self-saving insurance against loss using our taxes as the back-up insurance. They invested privately, but the debts were paid by the public. That's the Republican idea of economics, ethics and respect for working people everywhere.

Recently, a very successful German business owner was interviewed by an American journalist with taxes being the main theme of the conversation. When the German CEO told the reporter that he was taxed at about 55% with no loopholes, the reporter almost feinted. The reporter kept poking at the tolerance of the CEO for accepting such high taxes. The CEO said that he was doing very well and didn't mind paying his taxes. The reporter, still aghast, kept at the "absurdity" of those high taxes. "Look!", the German said. "I don't see any sense in being a rich person living in a poor country."

I don't hear ANY Americans saying things like that.

Today, the Republicans cannot justify their claims that the Democrats or President Obama are responsible for the fragile economy or the civil unrest beginning to sweep the nation. The truth is that the economy crashed because taxes were cut, preemptive wars were fought on credit, banking and investment regulations were removed and unions were made scapegoats – as they always are when Republican policies fail. They can't blame any of the failures from the Bush years on President Obama, but, of course, they do.

The lies continue with attacks on the science of climate change and evolution. They pontificate how gay marriage is a threat to "traditional" marriage and the family unit, disregarding the people who are trying to employ such values. They shake their heads at the perceived threat of illegal immigrants stealing American jobs and living off our taxes, but ignore the fact that the farmers and hoteliers would lose profits if the immigrants they hire were paid minimum wage. Most American citizens simply won't do that kind of stoop labor for minimum wage. The complaints about state of the national debt and the effects of the President's health care plan continue to go on to the point of becoming clichés. The Republicans simply can't admit the truth about the economy, because they are responsible for its collapse in

2008 and have done nothing to help a recovery. They can't and won't admit that their policies directly caused the worst economic failure in American history since the last time these same policies were tried in the 1920s. They can't admit those truths, of course, because they would bring down their house of cards.

The truth is the Republicans have nothing to offer, least of all a plan for governing. Conservatism is no longer about politics. It is a cult that requires certain phrases be repeated, certain hatreds be fed and that purity of message be maintained regardless of truth or facts. This schism with reality is increasingly large and obvious; obfuscation replacing reason and fact.

Real history scares and confuses today's Republicans because truths and facts undo their ritualized beliefs. This defines a *true believer.* The Republican publicity machine now tries to rewrite its own history as well as history that actually worked. They rewrote Reagan who raised taxes and increased debt, rewrote FDR who created policies that actually worked and saved capitalism, rewrote that the founding fathers never owned slaves, never supported government regulation of the economy and never wavered in their love for a religiosity that didn't yet exist.

The real danger isn't that someone might listen to the Republicans. The danger is that we might forget that they're lying. Too often Democrats, including this President, have felt that the best way to handle Republican lies is to compromise. You can't compromise with those committed to altered reality as *true believers.*

91

Part III

Public Education

A successful man is one who can lay a firm foundation with the bricks others have thrown at him.

-David Brinkley

It's become almost un-American to admit that for a sizable number of our young people, college is a waste of time.

-Mike Rustigan

Chapter 24: The Evolution of Learning and Teaching

Serious research into primate behavior really didn't start until Jane Goodall amazed the world with her patient and superb summary of observations of chimpanzees in the Gombi forest of East Africa. The things she discovered linked certain behavioral similarities to the human end of the order *Primates.* Most interesting of all was the apparent teaching and learning going on between adults and younger members of the troops.

There are, in addition, certain inherent reflexes seen in both major groups of apes, our closest current relatives, and humans. The clutching instinct of infant humans is a copy of what baby primates do almost across the board. Why? Well, the infants are required to hang on to mother while mother goes about searching for food and shelter. The infant can cling to the fur and even nurse while being transported. Humans lost their fur to keep cool as they became long-distance runners, but the infantile instinct to clutch a finger is still there.

When the mechanisms of evolution caused the original ape ancestor to undergo division into modern apes and species leading to the genus *Homo,* certain aspects of success were retained by both. Learning and teaching were two of those. Without learning and teaching, subsequent generations would not possess the traits or behaviors that led to their success. The brain in the *Homo* line developed differently and with more capacity to reason and, perhaps, imagine than the ape lineage. This ability to imagine and reason had to provide successes as well as failures. Depending on the biological/survival stress placed on the individual, success HAD to exceed failure in experimentation and implementation of new ideas and "technology". A stone tool, for example, is infinitely more technological than a twig or a stick. A stone that was purposely shaped to perform one or more tasks was an enormous leap forward in technology for the emerging species of our lineage.

There are stone implements found in proximity to various species of our ancestry over more than 3 million years. That means that technology is very ancient and became an integral part of ALL the species in our branch of evolution. So, who was the first to invent the shaped stone implement, and how did that idea get passed along to subsequent generations over millions of years? Moreover, as time wore on, the sophistication of the stone implements increased until they became part of multi-part weapons and tools. Obviously, these implements were the success stories, because here we are today; our ancestors were not only *required* to be successful with their technology, but they had to be able to pass it along to subsequent generations effectively enough such that the growing imagination in the enlarging brains of our ancestors (by now, certainly members of the genus *Homo*) produced improvements along the way. A secondary factor for this learning was that it added more individuals to hunt and gather and produce viable offspring to ensure the tribe's success.

Great volumes of paleontological and archaeological research show, in detail, the evolution of human technology from the most ancient of times to modern times. The question we pose here is: How did we get from there to here?

It may sound like a rhetorical question until one examines the intricacies of the technological advances themselves. The wonderful series by James Burke, *Connections* demonstrates how technology advances from a series of "ah hah!" moments coupled with lengthy refinements of an invention or improvement. Some of the refinements have led to epiphanies that changed the course of the human condition and history. The point is that refinements are impossible without the passing of knowledge and experience from one generation to the next. We humans, after all, only live to an average age today of around 65 years, planet-wide.

In that span of years each human, in his or her immediate environment, must learn the skills and behaviors that allow them to live successfully enough to be able to reproduce and thrive to some degree. When Hilary Clinton wrote her book, *It Takes a Village* she implied that each village is its own schoolhouse and each of the members are teachers. We humans are unique in this respect because of the volume of learning that must be imposed on village members from the beginning of their lives.

Primates are, generally speaking, *altricial*. That means that they are born virtually helpless and remain dependent on parents for food and protection for long periods of their lives. The opposite of this is seen in mammals that are producing in greater numbers, are herd types and are subject to predators as a main food source. These animals, like the plains animals of East Africa, give birth to *precocial* young that are able to walk and even run in a few hours after birth. They still need mother for milk and defense, but they are able to move with the herd and are thus somewhat protected from predation.

The human brain is not fully developed at birth much as the body remains virtually helpless for months. Learning, however, begins early, even pre-natal in the human brain. The natural sense of rhythm and sound patterns is formed by the first sound the fetus hears, its mother's heartbeat. The capacity of the brain to learn, how it learns and how quickly it learns varies widely across the population. There are, however, certain aspects – in a normal, healthy brain – that seem to be "hard-wired". Language and visual behavior cues are not all unique to humans, but require significant exposure at certain ages to optimize the development of those two main aspects. These two things are essential to the passing of information. Without these two significant evolutionary factors, we probably wouldn't be reading this material, never mind writing it.

As our inventions became more sophisticated and our successes as a species became connected to them, it was imperative that this information be passed along to tribal members at first, then whole societies. From a time when tribal members learned the skills of survival, knapping flint spear points and arrowheads, for example, to modern times where virtually the entire technological suite of information is available on the internet. Today's information totality is so sophisticated and specialized that additional learning is necessary in order to use it.

So, from the first primitive lessons of tool making, camp making, food processing, protective clothing, territory or resource defending, etc., of primitive humans, to today's massive educational systems around the world, we have centered our existence on learning and teaching what we have learned. This means that our current and future successes as residents on Earth are irretrievably tied to education. Without it we will fail absolutely, or revert to simpler, less sophisticated lifestyles where fashion is replaced by bare survival; flights to distant planets replaced by fierce competition for drinking water and arable land. Looking around the world of humans today, all these levels exist in some form or other. Nevertheless, the central, most important aspect of each of those societies is education. Clearly, we are "hard-wired" to teach and learn to perpetuate our species' survival.

Any society that insists on cheapening or altering pure learning from pure information, untainted by political or social distractions runs the risk of failure as a society. Our recorded human history shows us that in several famous examples. There must be many unrecorded instances at the tribal level where learning stopped and the tribe failed. We are the most adaptable species that ever lived on Earth. Our ability to adapt rapidly through our behavior and inventions separates us from the "natural" rules of evolution. The most significant of these is our ability to learn and reason from what we've learned. We all stand on the shoulders of those who came before. Each of us contributes our little bit to the knowledge base for future generations.

Chapter 25:   Education in America: The Beginning of Greatness

During the formation of our country in the late 18ᵗʰ century, our founders struggled to find a model upon which to build this new nation. Some, led by Alexander Hamilton favored a more "traditional" approach by declaring that a ruling class should administer the law while everyone else went about their business of making that ruling class rich. These were the Federalists. Nowhere in their musings known as the *Federalist Papers* did they consider anything like educating the mass of the people.

Fortunately, a more egalitarian point of view prevailed, mostly at the behest of Thomas Jefferson. His ideas formed the basis for establishing a national public education system in the 19ᵗʰ century. By 1791, 14 states had their own constitutions and 7 of those had specific provisions for education. Jefferson believed that education should be under the control of government, free from religious biases and available to all people irrespective of their social status. Other proponents of educating the public during this tumultuous period in our nation's history included Benjamin Rush, Noah Webster, Robert Coram and George Washington. These provisions did not preclude private or parochial schools, but they allowed the states to fund schools for those who couldn't afford private ones. They came to be known as *public schools.*

Even with the support of influential people and state funding, the education system remained localized and available only to wealthier people in the 1840s. Education reformers of that day wanted to expand the concept of public education to a much wider application; indeed made available for all who wished to attend. Horace Mann began publishing the *Common School Journal* which took education issues to the public. He and Henry Barnard argued that "common schooling" would create good citizens, unite the society and prevent crime and poverty. Their work resulted in elementary level education becoming available to all citizens by the end of the 19th century.

Massachusetts passed the first compulsory school attendance laws in 1852, with New York doing the same in 1853. By 1918 all states had passed laws requiring children to attend at least elementary school. The Catholic Church, of course, opposed common schooling and created its own parochial schools. This action was supported by the U.S. Supreme Court in 1925 in the *Pierce v. Society of Sisters* case. This decision allowed children to attend private schools if they so chose.

The first publicly supported secondary school in the U.S. was the *Boston Latin School*, founded in 1635. The curriculum in secondary schools at this time was difficult and specialized, so attendance was minimal. By the middle of the 18th century, however, Benjamin Franklin recognized the need for more skilled workers, so he helped develop a new kind of secondary school. The *American Academy* was established in Philadelphia in 1751. Schools like this eventually replaced the Latin grammar schools adding to the rise in those attending higher schools. From 1900 to 1996, for example, the percentage of teens who graduated high school rose from 6% to about 85%. During the 20th century, most states added compulsory education laws requiring children to attend school through age 16. These actions plus the other major events of the 20th century (two world wars, the Great Depression, the technological explosion) all contributed to the need for more education. The 1920-40 years were dubbed the era of "progressive education". This allowed the focus of education to shift to intellectual discipline as well as more industrially oriented, vocational curricula at the same time.

These shifts resulted in the 20th century seeing a steep rise in post-secondary education. At the beginning of the century, only 2% of Americans aged 18-24 were enrolled in college. By the end of the century, over 60% were enrolled, approaching 14 million students attending about 3,500 4-year and 2-year colleges and universities. The Morrill Acts of 1862 and 1890 provided *federal* support to state universities and many land-grant and state universities were established through gifts of federal land.

The years following World War II saw millions of war veterans take advantage of the new G.I. Bill and attend college instead of just trying to re-enter a declining job market. This is no small consideration when we realize that these were the people that not only created the largest and most productive non-military economy in the history of mankind, but also expanded our technological capability to actually fly men to the moon and bring them back safely.

Administration and Control

Generally, the states have taken on the responsibility of managing and controlling public schools with the local communities having the largest role in the direct management of them. The federal and state governments provide funding, thus most teachers and administrators are technically state employees. The state school boards tend to be responsible for teacher certification, overall curriculum supervision and a variety of other school and school district events like athletics. Property taxes for schools are generally levied by the communities through elections. Local school boards administer personnel issues as well as the "bricks and mortar" of district maintenance.

By mid-20th century, most states took an active regulatory role by consolidating school districts into larger units that shared common procedures. In 1940 the United States had over 117,000 school districts, but by 1990 that had decreased to just over 15,000. In 1940, local property taxes financed 68% of public school expenses while states only contributed about 30%. In 1990, local districts and states *each* contributed 47% to their schools. The federal government added the supplement.

Other government actions improved and expanded public education infrastructure, curriculum and opportunities. The *Smith-Hughes Act of 1917* provided funding for vocational programs in schools, for example. In 1958, Congress passed the *National Defense Education Act* then the *Elementary and Secondary Education Act* of 1965. These two landmark statutes for the first time addressed education inequalities for poor children as well as upgrading education in heretofore neglected subjects like science, mathematics and foreign languages.

Additional legislation directed at our educational systems in this period included the *Vocational Education Act* of 1963, the *Manpower Development and Training Act* of 1963 and the *International Education Act* of 1966.

Equal Education for All

Racial and gender equality has been a constant factor throughout the history of public education in the United States. People of color and of different nationalities have reaped both rewards and hardships by being introduced to our public schools. For a very long time it was thought to be "un-ladylike" for a female to be educated in anything other than the arts and skills pertaining to child rearing and domestic tranquility. Those difficulties and notions underwent significant change over the period of our existence as a nation. World War II, for example, forced women to enter the manufacturing labor force *en masse*. With a larger population of single women during and after the war, the female education paradigm changed forever.

The first black slaves arrived in the American colonies in 1619. By mid-19th century, the black population was estimated to be 4.5 million. The earliest education provided for these people came from Christian missionaries who also were trying to convert them to that faith. The Southern states, of course, opposed educating blacks to ensure their hold on the slaves' behavior. The education of black people remained very low until Lincoln's *Emancipation Proclamation* in 1863. Black literacy rates in the 1860s were about 5%, but rose to 40% by 1890 and 70% by 1910. Sadly, not much improvement has been made since. Black children in the United States consistently score lower than white children in literacy. There are many contributing factors for this disappointment, but chief among them is poverty.

In 1954, the U.S. Supreme Court *unanimously* ruled that racial segregation in public schools was unconstitutional with the landmark *Brown v. Board of Education of Topeka* case. Despite vigorous resistance from most southern states, the federal courts had largely succeeded in eliminating systematized segregation in southern public schools. Today, there is much less racial tension in public schools, but inner city schools across the nation tend to be populated by mostly black or Hispanic children. The segregation now has a fluid real estate component.

Women were also discriminated against in American public schools. Girls and women were often shunted into separate curricula that school boards thought appropriate, thus creating quality of education discrimination. With the emergence of the women's rights movement during the 1960s, huge inroads were made to force schools to provide equal quality education for females as well as males. In 1972, Title IX of federal education amendments prohibited discrimination on the basis of gender for educational institutions receiving federal money. Even so, women still do not receive equal pay for equal work as men throughout most professions.

Equally disappointing is the conservative push for school vouchers as an "option" for parents to send their children to schools of their choice (read: private schools) without having to pay for it. In my book, *A Worm in the Apple*, the details of this wrong-headed idea are shown and discussed. Basically, though, the tax money needed for vouchers gets taken from the districts that are mostly already poor and suffering from difficult local environments. Furthermore, once the "good" schools are full, the poor kids wanting to go to schools in "better" neighborhoods simply are denied that choice. Add to all that the stigma placed upon the kids in the "poorer" schools that they are even less worthy than before and you have a nation and a system eagerly trying to tear itself apart.

Chapter 26:   The Real Value of Teachers

The January 15th edition of the Austin American-Statesman published Nicholas Kristoff's (who writes for the *New York Times)* imposing piece about the value of good teachers. He opens the article with the poignant question: "Suppose your child is about to enter the fourth grade and has been assigned to an excellent teacher. Then the teacher decides to quit. What should you do?" His point is that a strong teacher has much more of a lifetime impact on a child than a weak one. He points out that a good 4th grade teacher makes students 1.25% more likely to attend college and 1.25% LESS likely to become a pregnant teen.

A great 4th grade teacher, research shows, produces adults that earn, on average, $25,000 more over a lifetime than those students emerging from a poor 4th grade teacher's classes. An average class size will mean that its overall lifetime gains will be around $700,000. It may not seem like all that much, but when considering the impact on the nation as a whole, it is a huge amount of wealth and value added to the society. That's just from the 4th grade. Extend that premise throughout a child's education and the earnings numbers more than double per person. Furthermore, a 2014 report states that a 2-year community college degree is worth a lifetime earnings increase of about $250,000 over a high school graduate.

The research was done by economists at Harvard and Columbia universities and underscores the cumulative value of an excellent teacher. Conversely, a very poor teacher has the same effect as a pupil missing 40 percent of the school year. We wouldn't tolerate that absence rate and would consider it an unacceptable truancy. So why would we tolerate a poor teacher? The study glibly suggests that parents collect money to force the poor teacher to retire because it holds the children back so much.

In my book about public education, *A Worm in the Apple: The Inside Story of Public Education* about how to find, train and retain very good teachers. By letting a poor teacher into the classroom in the first place we create an inherent inefficiency, so starting at the beginning is the way to avoid or minimize this situation.

It isn't hard to see that prolonging the stumbling education system is a most serious threat to our national economy and the well-being of our country. All our politicians are wailing about this or that foreign threat, but are failing to address our most important one: failing our children.

None of the current administration's plans or ideas, and none from the current population of Republicans address this issue with much energy at all. Until we the people stand up for our children and their education what we'll get is more of the same at best, and most certainly a continued deterioration as the likely outcome of inaction.

Why, for example, do politicians cut libraries and school funding FIRST before cutting anything else when budgets get tight? It's like eating the seed corn. If we don't educate our children to increasingly high levels of excellence we guarantee that our nation will soon become a second class nation – or worse. It already shows in comparative international test scores where the gap between foreign students and ours is growing at an increasing rate. Diane Ravitch's book, *The Death and Life of Public Education* addresses that issue and many others.

One dramatic example of the conservative attack on education is highlighted by an MSNBC blurb that decries the labeling of the G.I. Bill as "welfare". It was the G.I. bill that let our returning veterans go to college and quadrupled our college graduates in just one generation to say nothing of the huge economic expansion it engendered. That's not socialism or welfare. That's progress and growth for all classes of worker. By the way, those returning GIs ended up fostering the space program that put Americans on the moon. How's that for teacher and education accountability?

We must change the role of the teachers' unions to ensure excellent teachers enter each classroom. But we have to pay these people wages similar to their equally educated peers in the private sector. Most other civilized nations do this with their teachers, why not us?

Why aren't we willing to do that and all the other things? We already have laws that fund vocational education in schools. Why aren't schools funded accordingly? It's all for the future success of the country after all.

Chapter 27:   The Death of Learning

I dreamed that I was in Heaven and allowed to watch the history of the world at my leisure. I saw a garden full of children learning their lessons. Adults were attentive and helpful. They spent time teaching each student the parts they didn't understand during the primary lesson, which was taught before the whole class. The teachers had teachers' aides, the ratio six to one, which empowered the classroom environment. As a team, they had the time, energy and manner to precipitate a positive educational experience, and that alone incited the students to love learning and embrace their own unique talents. The instructors, provided with plentiful resources to teach their students how to perceive learning as a joyful adventure, thrived; and the children learned to reach for the best within themselves and desired to do more than merely survive.

Then I saw the time when my country had just sent a rocket soaring to the moon with astronauts. We were number one in almost every category under the sun -- our dreams continually climbing.

I glanced at an angel, who fluttered one of her wings in a small circle, indicating that I should change the view of history. Unsure if I even wanted to see the other side of this scene, I politely tried to decline. But she insisted, fluttering her wings again, more insistent this time.

Obediently, I turned myself upside down and looked into Earth's history.

Ronald Reagan stood at the presidential podium, making a vow to American parents. They were a small group, but their school-aged children certainly mattered to them. He asked if he could reduce our students' Federal Education Funding, claiming we were in fine shape educationally; our country was headed in the right direction and we knew where we were going. So he said. However, the economy was in the tank, and the president wanted a sacrifice. This was in 1982.

He asked our families to donate three years' worth of Federal Education Funding -- not all of it, mind you, just over a third -- to prop up our sagging economy, keep corporations in business and usher in new technology and the Computer Age. By doing this, our government could help businesses to create jobs that would turn the economy around. He promised that our kids wouldn't lose much ground, and whatever was lost scholastically would be rapidly restored when -- after the third year -- Federal Funding would be fully reinstated, and generous corporate grants would be donated as rewards for what we had done.

"How will it be better then? It is good right now. Why change what is working for our American children?" a spectator asked from the crowd.

Our President's voice was a distant echo, but I'm sure I heard him say, "This plan will secure jobs for years to come, because of the trickle-down theory. You see, men run corporations and these men realize what you've given, the true sacrifice you've made. They will want to give back generously to those who gave to them, and after their companies have recovered, they will happily offer enormous grants to our schools to help catch our kids back up. These men are as concerned as you. You see, they are Americans, and they have children too."

Doing a double take, I realized I was a bystander in that crowd. I stood in the back of the audience, interested, but immobilized. I didn't understand how this "plan" would benefit our country's children.

"I remember that," I told the angel.

The blanket of clouds was now so large it surrounded her, and she looked like she was wearing a dress with petticoats.

"Whatever happened to that promise?" I asked. I fast-forwarded quickly, tilting my hand to the right. After awhile I looked inside again, watching the last of the three long years without teachers' aides and other resources. Every parent saw the difference. Yet, our day had finally come, our citizens sacrifice was made, and today we would have our nation's education funding fully reinstated. I stared at the man we trusted to be President.

"Our economy was all messed up and we're still not doing well enough," Reagan was saying. "Besides, I think each State should take care of its own Public Education. It's their responsibility, after all. Why is it the federal government's burden to take care of your State's children? Teachers want more control over what they teach in the classroom anyway. I say we give them this privilege along with the enormous debt. Besides, in some States the lottery will make up for the missing support, and of course I'll create the 'Block Grant,' but I won't give you any more money."

I looked for an indication of the generous corporate donations, but I couldn't see them anywhere, and the States, unprepared for the broken promise, couldn't afford the imposed costs. With sadness, administrators reduced school funding even further by increasing class-size and terminating thousands of teachers. The rules were changed at the end of the game, and our American children were the losers.

"We never got that money back, did we?" I sighed, deeply disappointed in all of us for our silent consent. I my view to the right again. "What are these, anyway -- our modern day sins?" I asked in dismay, pointing toward the scattered spheres that lay all around me. The angel was leaning comfortably against the jumbled mass of fluffy blanket, busily knitting. Casting my eyes down, I stopped my hand and focused on the scene below.

George H. W. Bush was in office; average American families were becoming homeless. In an effort to save his neck, he cut school funding to the bone. Schools couldn't afford even the most basic supplies, like chalk, books and paper. Through his action, Bush sent a message loud and clear for all corporate entities to hear -- we don't take care of our own. The whispering quickly started, "Shh... taxpayers don't think supplying paper to Public Schools is important; pass it on."

104

I fast-forwarded the scenes just a tad, so I could see the response of the citizens. Looking down, I was surprised to see my own dad purchasing boxes and boxes of bond paper at an office store. "I'll be damned if I'm going to let my kids and my relative's kids go to schools that can't afford paper," he muttered under his breath as he stacked another box of paper inside his hatchback, fighting the war alone.

"I didn't know about that. All I knew, at the time, was that the problem at our neighborhood schools was somehow magically solved," I explained to the knitting angel. I noticed that the cloud fabric had grown so large, it wrapped around her shoulders like a shawl. "Who would have thought, my own dad was Santa Claus." I couldn't help but smile.

Fast-forwarding again, I watched the images pass and remembered what I had carelessly forgotten. Students, overpowering the limited teaching staff, took over classrooms and whole school systems. Metal detectors were installed in the worst offending districts. School buildings filled with mold, started crumbling; trailer homes, used as a temporary classroom shortage solution, became permanent fixtures. Art, music and extracurricular programs were eliminated, considered unimportant. Classrooms became overcrowded, the pupil-to-teacher ratio, forty to one; and instructors, having no time to teach, were transformed into glorified babysitters and behavior wardens. The students, consistently shoved into the cracks, felt forced to abandon their dreams. Our children began to believe, because of their limited base of knowledge, that they had only two choices: whether to be a victim or a bully.

"Surely this got better when Clinton came into office." I couldn't remember why, but it sure didn't improve much. After watching events scroll by for the longest time, I finally saw the flawed reasoning for our nation's continued under-education of our children. We were supposed to work our way out of the deficit and pay off our debt first. Then, we would not only revitalize our educational standards, but our entire social infrastructure; putting our public purpose programs first, getting them back in order by modernizing our antiquated systems to better serve our citizens' needs.

And work we did, until our debts were paid. When everyone in the middle class was having a fabulous day, some money returned to our schools in the form of the 'Block Grants' that we were previously told about. These newfound riches disappeared into the pockets of countless administrators, who thought a hefty pay raise and extravagant benefits for themselves were long overdue. But after the folks who worked off school grounds got their fair share, there were only a few pennies to spare, and teachers still had to buy classroom supplies for the students they taught. The increase in education funding had no results accountability attached.

Moving events forward again, I knew what was coming, but kept watching -- I didn't know why -- Columbine, metal detectors across the nation, elimination of school lockers and the introduction of thirty-five-pound backpacks on sixty-pound children. History is unimportant because it isn't on the test. I sat there, immobilized. By skimming fast-forward, I saw, across the span of time, the steady dumbing-down of our nation. As the dreams of countless students died, their grief transformed into anger and hopelessness. American children, having no voice, acted out, and on the nightly news adults could hear their primal screams.

To make up for this indiscretion and ignoring compounded inflation, Bush Jr. matched Kennedy's education funding dollar-for-dollar; and then we gave the money we saved to people who didn't even need any. Bush Jr. required states to adhere to the *punishment only* scheme of *No Child Left Behind* if they wanted any Federal money for education. All schools were required to have a 95% test success rate by 2014, or they would be closed. As I look at the end of 2014, I see that only 25% of the schools have "succeeded" with the test scores, but few are closing. One asks why a multi-billion dollar "program" is being wasted and ignored. The answer is because it didn't work and created more problems than it solved. Way to go, Jr.

And to top it all off -- as if this wasn't enough -- parents recognizing the suffering of their own children, faced limited choices and in desperation started an all-out housing war in an attempt to outbid each other in the "good" School Districts. Working more hours to pay the enormous living costs and keep foreclosure at bay, took concerned parents right out of their new homes; and the kids, left alone to fend for themselves, had no guidance. The poorest kids from the poorest neighborhoods received NO help because they couldn't pass their tests. Their hopes and dreams of escaping abject poverty remained unachievable...just as they've always been.

Watching this compressed history lesson about how the United States fails to educate its children from above, I had to wonder why we even bothered. Our political learning is arrested and remains in the 19th century while the rest of the world aspires to greater things. There are now 7.6 billion of us on Earth, yet the "richest" country on Earth insists on destroying the education system that worked so well when we held it in a higher national priority than we did war making. Now, war making exceeds all other priorities.

How interesting. I wonder what today's children will learn from that?

Chapter 28: Where We Went Wrong and How to Fix It

Some will herald the start of a new school year by celebrating the extra-curricular ceremonies surrounding athletics, band and cheerleaders. I love all those things too, but there are more important things to discuss. In order to achieve or regain the ideals of Jefferson regarding educating our citizenry, we first have to discover how we lost our way and how we allowed our children to flounder in the squalor of materialism and self-indulgence. Someone said to me that the current preoccupation with communication devices has created a society of hyper-connected isolation. This comment doesn't even approach describing the generations of 147 character idiots we're producing. Our kids will all have arthritic thumb joints by the time they're thirty...along with diabetes.

The task at hand is nothing short of rebuilding our moral compass as a society and a community. Daily activities, known affectionately as *the rat race* have the rats winning. Our parents are running around trying to keep their personal finances and families afloat in an ever increasing maelstrom of family dysfunction and career and economic degradation. These pressures affect us all whether or not we have children or are directly associated with their education. Teachers all know that they are increasingly absorbing child rearing as part of their jobs. We also see teachers being increasingly targeted as reasons for our children's failures in school and in the workplace. In some cases that is a valid concern. In most cases it is a canard from those who choose not to take responsibility for raising their children or want to pay for their worl-class education.

Politicians have been exploiting the structural weaknesses of the parents' lack of attention and the teacher's organizations to further this avoidance of responsibilities by their voters. The natural tendency for teachers is to put their heads down and go to work doing what they do best: caring for and about the children in their classrooms. The teachers have, therefore, given de facto approval for the destruction of public education by political entities that see it as merely another source of revenue. *No Child Left Behind* is the culmination of this attack on public education. Its unholy stepchild, *Race to the Top,* followed to exacerbate the statements associated with the perception of "just throwing money at the problem". I will illustrate for you why that is and what we can do about it to achieve the lofty, yet practical goals necessary to return our nation's vigor to the top tier.

Thomas Jefferson did point out the need for educating our citizens: *Every government degenerates when trusted to the rulers of the people alone.*

The people themselves therefore are its only safe depositories. And to rend even them safe, their minds must be improved to a certain extent.

Horace Mann took it one step further:

Never will wisdom preside in the halls of legislation, and its profound utterances be recorded on the pages of the stature book, until Common Schools *...shall create a more far-seeing intelligence and a purer morality than has ever existed among communities of men.*

By the end of the 19th century the rural schools built half-century earlier were deteriorating and the flood of immigrants from Europe overwhelmed the urban schools. The industrialists proceeded to bash the public schools, such as they were, for emphasizing intellectual development instead of preparing these kids for vocational jobs in their factories. Sound familiar? Indeed, in those days, one didn't need to have a teaching license to teach children. So, politicians placed their cronies in classrooms to prepare the kids for the industrialists.

It wasn't until the agricultural "revolution" took place in the early 20th century with the advent of artificial fertilizer and improved agricultural mechanical devices that more children entered school from rural areas than ever before as their chores became less time consuming. This, coupled with the explosion of the industrial sector created more needs from business and industry for people who knew how to read and write. These series of events came in handy when World War II happened and we had to innovate like never before.

I graduated from high school in 1960. I would like to see our modern high school students receive the same, excellent education I did before I die. It won't be as difficult to do as one might think. The model and methods already exist. The necessary data, enriched information and tools for access are so much greater today, that the only thing keeping this leap forward from happening is society's will to do so.

It is saddening, in a way, that someone has to write essays like these, but it *is* necessary if we expect to remain a viable nation.

Every Child Left Behind

It is clear to all professional educators that this law, *No Child Left Behind,* is by far the worst thing to happen to public education in our country's history. All of the school bashing, teacher bashing and phony testing regimes just nibbled around the edges of the intent of certain political entities to either destroy public education completely, or dilute it to the point where it is irrelevant in the world economy. It is hard to conclude anything else when you see the sustained and increasingly strident attacks on our schools and teachers by conservatives with a clear political agenda. What, exactly, are conservatives conserving?

When one considers those responsible for introducing this misbegotten law to the American people for the sake of accountability of teachers and other educators, we begin to understand why it is such a flawed idea and plan. The real intent, therefore, is something else entirely. My generation was educated in public schools. We were responsible for initiating the computer age and engineering those machines and disciplines that landed men on the moon. The next generation was educated in public schools and did the things that produced the greatest economic, technical and social expansion in the history of mankind in spite of wars, debt and scandal. How's that for accountability? Did the teachers of those generations do their jobs? We know the answer to that.

There are at least seven things that should disqualify the NCLB law from our education environment.

1. The law states scientific research to support its thesis. But the research cited does not support the school reform actions, indeed, the data argues against it.

2. NCLB relies solely on *punishment* for schools that don't have all 37 subgroups of test data meeting minimum requirements. If one criterion fails, the whole school fails. This is especially damning for schools with high diversity in race, socio-economic and performance categories.

3. The law requires that all students (100%) be proficient in reading and mathematics by 2014 even though the tests keep changing and the student diversity continues. I wonder how our special needs kids and ESL kids and those in socio-economic groups that start school 2 years behind in verbal skills will make ever make it to these arbitrary goals.

4. As a result of #3 above, California and many other states, including Texas, will have 99% failing schools by 2014. In those states that are currently leading the nation in test scores, only 95% of them will be classified as failing in 2014. This almost sounds like a conspiracy to close all public schools since private schools aren't measured by NCLB. As it happens, private school students do about as well on national tests as public school students. Fortunately, the Obama gave states waivers against this egregious provision.

5. Schools that fail to make the minimum achievement for 2 years running must offer all its students options to attend other schools.

Schools can also be classified as failing if fewer than 95% of the students show up on test day. Recall the recent case of Pearce Middle School in Austin, TX. Eighty percent of its students do not speak, read or write English at grade level. A significant percent of those kids are illiterate in *Spanish.* NCLB drove the superintendent to announce the closure of Pearce with the reassignment of those kids to another nearby middle school that had failed for the last three years! Fortunately, sanity prevailed and the rolling wave of failure was averted. Pearce remained open and education proceeded forthwith.

6. NCLB relies solely on state mandated testing. The breadth and strongest part of our public education idea, diversity of topical subjects, is disregarded. We talk about providing opportunity for character development and sound, healthy children, but none of those things are part of NCLB. Diane Ravitch, one of the early proponents of NCLB, and a Bush insider has come out against this law, saying that it is a huge mistake.

7. NCLB begins testing in 3rd grade. It ignores the first years of development through age 7, those years that are most important in either the development or stifling of a child's potential. There is no provision for attending the needs of those in the lower socio-economic classes yet those children are expected to succeed to arbitrary standards by third grade. Children in poorer families are exposed to a fraction of the vocabulary of those children in less poor homes.

Michael Birnbaum, a staff writer for the Washington Post wrote an article on 23 November 2010 detailing pertinent examples of why NCLB is so wrong.

Students transferring from failing schools in Prince George's County, Virginia are overwhelming the few successful schools in their areas, an unintended byproduct of the *No Child Left Behind* law.

The issue arose recently, when the parents of nearly 3,000 middle-school kids learned just days before school started that they could switch their children to the only two non-specialized middle schools in the county that met the law's performance goals. About 200 families accepted the offer. The flurry of transfers (more than 700 in Prince George's this year across all 12 grades) packed classrooms while underscoring an unintended consequence of NCLB. It demands steadily rising achievement (all students are supposed to pass benchmark tests by 2014) and, as a result, more schools fail every year.

Student-hopping to more successful schools leads to dwindling populations and funding for the weakest schools, and over-crowding for the better ones.

School leaders are concerned that these moves could jeopardize any fragile progress at the failing schools. And parents of children at the successful schools worry that the wave of new students will overwhelm teachers and drag down the only programs that are meeting the new standards. Both of these concerns were validated by the end of the first school year.

"This is a worthy impulse that turned out to be an un-keepable promise all over the country," said Chester E. Finn Jr. of the Thomas B. Fordham Institute, a prominent advocate of more rigorous standards. "The number of schools being deemed in need of improvement is becoming vastly more than anybody in their right minds can expect to actually be improved."

The transfer requirement, in which school systems must allow students to transfer from high-poverty schools that repeatedly fail, has created similar problems in the past for struggling school systems around the country, including New York City and suburban Atlanta. They and other systems have responded by limiting the number of students who are allowed to transfer.

"We are taking a much more flexible approach with regard to choice," said Carmel Martin, assistant secretary in the Office of Planning, Evaluation and Policy Development at the Education Department. "Having this federal mandate, which is a one-size-fits-all requirement, doesn't make sense to us," she said. Around the country, only 1 percent of students who are eligible to transfer take advantage of it, she said.

But a proponent of *No Child Left Behind* argued that the transfer requirement has done some good, even as he acknowledged that it wasn't perfect. You'll notice that the reporter was not able to get quantified reasons regarding that "good".

"We kind of got put into a corner" during negotiations, said Sandy Kress, one of the authors of the law. "We wanted there to be greater choices: to private schools as well as across school districts." Kress said the compromise, which limited choices only to public schools, "was less desirable" and led in part to the problems school districts now face. But the performance standards are attainable", Kress said, and the law was designed to put pressure on school systems to improve. I can't help but feel the drumbeat of elitism from these statements.

Our children are not lab rats, least of all variables in political experiments. What might start out as a politically expedient idea, will almost certainly end with results adversely affecting the children. The first chapter in this section described the importance of learning for the success of the community's long-term plans. Perhaps we should just let the teachers do what they do best, support them fully, pay them well and let the test scores take care of themselves.

A Summary of Solutions

There are several successful models around the world upon which we could build a better, more interesting and fairer system for educating our children. Consistent with the theme of this chapter, it starts with the teacher.

Most countries in industrialized Europe and Asia recruit teachers from the top tiers of their colleges and universities. We do not. Other countries pay for their recruits' specialty education, preparing them for the classrooms. We do not. Our potential teachers either take out loans or work extra jobs to pay for their teaching credential requirements. Other countries pay their teachers salaries nearly equal to those of their equally educated peers in business and industry after an "apprentice" program with a master teacher as mentor. Our teachers' salaries begin at about two-thirds of their peers' salaries in business and see the gap widen every year thereafter.

Most industrialized nations in Europe and Asia have a national curriculum that is flexible enough to accommodate certain socio-economic areas and their citizens plus add subject diversity for the arts and vocational needs. Our curriculum may or may not be managed by the states, and is sometimes managed by the districts. Those other countries used to have very narrow curricula, but expanded them by modeling what ours used to be from decades past.

We emphasize extra-curricular activities, but the other nations limit those to what they can afford. Children in every industrialized country in the world attend school for over 200 days. Our children average 180 days. The school day in most other countries is 8 hours long. Our children are in class from between 4 and 6 hours per day.

I've discussed the testing issues, but it should be noted that most other countries have exams for grade level advancement and perhaps a nation-wide test. Teachers are delegated the job of administering "normal" evaluations of students in their classes.

Our children score poorly on international tests on similar subjects at every grade level. We do not rank first in any. Clearly THIS indicator tells us that increased rigor in our curricula, longer school years and longer school days is necessary to keep up with the information explosion as well as prepare our children for the world marketplace. The competition is not going away, and if we have any pride left in ourselves, we will step up and prove our greatness as a people by making our children the best educated in the world – once again.

Chapter 29:   The "Super" Who Gets It

John Kuhn is a public school superintendent. Most amazingly, his school board actually has his back. He is superintendent of the Perrin-Whitt Consolidated Independent School District in North Texas. He is assuming the status of Patrick Henry on the abomination known as "school accountability."

He's become a firebrand on behalf of an increasing number of Texas school districts — over 100 — that have signed a resolution saying standardized testing is "strangling" their schools.

"The government has allowed state testing to become a perversion, growing like Johnson grass through the garden of learning and choking to death all knowledge that isn't on the test," writes Kuhn. I'm guessing he means both the Federal as well as the state governments since it was George Bush's hare-brained idea to hold teachers accountable in the first place.

He said at a "Save Our Schools" rally in Austin, Texas, recently, that this fixation on testing "is killing ancient wisdom like debate, logic and ethics — deep human learning that once provided this state a renewable crop of leaders who knew courage instead of expedience, truth instead of spin, and personal risk for the public good instead of personal enrichment and re-election at all cost." If one reads some of the Texas Republican Party platform presented in an earlier chapter, one will see that it is the stated *intention* of this political party to kill those skills.

It takes a little time to see the causal link between "school accountability" and the venal state of today's politics, but after observing and studying this linkage in Texas, the bosom of the "accountability" cult, it is clear that this linkage is real.

As Kuhn notes, Texas, which cut $5 billion from public schools in 2011, spent $500 million on a new generation of tests (STAAR) to further strangle them. Thankfully, in 2013 the legislature cut many of those tests and added back about $1 billion in school spending. Since 1999, the spending on Texas public schools has *declined* on a per student basis, still it costs Texas taxpayers $100 million per year – paid to a British testing consultant and management firm – for creation and administration of these tests; all at the expense of classroom days meant for learning.

Kuhn isn't the only one using "perversion" to describe the testing overemphasis bleeding public education of its vitality. Former Texas Education Commissioner Robert Scott (A Perry appointee, no less) concurred, calling the extensive testing a "perversion of its original intent," one that led states to increasingly control every wink and nod of every educator in every state.

"What we've done over the past decade," said Scott, "is we've doubled down on the test every couple of years and used it for more and more things to make it the be-all, end-all" of K-12 education. "You've reached a point now where you've got this one thing that the entire system is dependent upon. It is the heart of the vampire, so to speak."

In today's political stewpot, what Scott and Kuhn said takes guts, but if one pays any attention at all to public education as it is now practiced, one could not possibly come to any other conclusion. Our students are being cheated out of their basic education, thus making them *less* competitive in the world marketplace for good jobs and decent careers.

One problem is that unlike educational leaders who follow Kuhn's outcry, too many districts want robots who speak in numbers, rubrics and algorithms. They seek data-driven humanoids bearing the latest scripted methods for teaching, often costing an arm and an elementary school. They guarantee higher test scores. They occasionally deliver those numbers, but at what cost? Several districts have been found to cook the numbers and hold out students who are chronic failures or somehow not "qualified" to take the tests. They will then promote them forward two or more grades to allow them to miss the tests. This fiddling of children's lives ended when legislative initiatives required students pass the tests to earn a diploma.

Kuhn said of the testing system: (it) "has sought to make our children quantifiable shells of people, their guiding light of curiosity snuffed out by an idiot's opinion of what constitutes a human education." I agree. Only an idiot would shift our education system in this direction. Remember: *NO CHILD LEFT BEHIND.*

Worst of all, this testing regimen and idea was invented and implemented by those who are more inclined to eliminate public education and replace it with vouchers for "private" schools and other agenda-driven entities. The "accountability" idea ends up punishing and shaming students and schools for things that are not necessarily in their control. What I mean is that history shows that poorer demographic schools have ALWAYS done less well on standardized tests nationally. By threatening to close down failing schools – which NCLB does – the burden of failure lands on the poor....again. For-profit schools have been shown to be not necessarily more successful than their public counterparts and some are an outright scandal, taking money without enrolling students. Kuhn calls this the "engine of shame."

115

Kuhn: "No matter what, the only crime of the public school teacher in 2013 is his or her willingness to embrace and teach broken children. If that's a crime, then find us guilty. If caring for the least of them makes us unacceptable, then bring on your label gun. We're not afraid."

I wish he hadn't used the word "gun".

There are pundits and authors who see a more sinister angle to this debauchery of education by "conservative" politicians, or politicians who are beholden to the interests of their benefactors. It's been long noted in the world of propaganda that an ignorant population that has few learning or thinking skills is more easily led and convinced to follow leaders and agendas that are actually working against their own best interests. a major implementer of a political agenda-lead education.

Chapter 30:   How Long Can We Do It This Way?

One of the sure things in life is the extinction of a species if it insists on eating its young. If this happens often enough, there are insufficient breeding opportunities and the species loses genetic vigor and thus its ability to adapt to changing environments. The same can be said for how our human consumer-oriented economy works and the impacts it has on our children.

The fact is we don't really have a consumer economy; we have a consumer *growth* economy. Our national wealth is predicated on how our businesses *grow*. If all businesses grew to their potential, they would consume resources, energy and human capital at ever-increasing rates. That seems to be the whole idea these days. This thinking assumes we have unlimited resources, energy and human capital. Our resources are limited by the size and make-up of our planet and what lies within our reach. We have virtually unlimited solar energy for the next 4-5 billion years, but we refuse to make that availability a number one priority for fueling our lives and lifestyles because it doesn't show short-term profit and growth of financial capital. That brings us to human capital.

Education in the United States has deteriorated for any number of reasons and our children are the victims of this creeping incompetence. I say "incompetence" because everything that drives the consumer growth economy is impacting public education. The notion that private schools will provide needed competition for public schools is ludicrous due to the many factors that make them different. Besides, studies continue to show that public schools are about as effective as private ones in educating children even as our public schools deteriorate at the hands of politicians. Why would we want to have schools competing for quality education with one another anyway? Wouldn't it be better if ALL schools provided excellent education?

The politicization of schools reached its low point with *No Child Left Behind* and its barely better *Race to the Top,* such that testing becomes more important than learning. The cheating and expense involved in these programs for political gain negates any benefits to the kids and only benefits those politicians who have convinced enough voters that the testing racket is good for their children. Texas, for example, spends $100 million per year on state-wide tests written and distributed by a British consultant firm. Texas' students continue to rank near the bottom in achievement by any measure.

Meanwhile, we have social issues of working people scrambling to make the American Dream come true while other political and financial pressures keep their salaries stagnant and their buying power lowered. The destruction of labor unions is the chief culprit for stagnant/declining wages. The children who need nurturing are ignored by working parents, single working parents and too often, no parents at all. Their anxiety levels, exacerbated by testing regimes forced upon them causes their learning abilities to be altered or disabled. On my first day of teacher education I learned that a hostile or anxiety-ridden classroom stifles learning, yet everything we do with public education seems to add to that dysfunction.

I keep reading about how the current generations of children are going to have it worse than their parents. No kidding. How else could it be when the engines of economy, consumers, are asked to work more for less, our teachers are overworked, underpaid, given too many students, denied their abilities to teach due to the testing racket and attacked mercilessly by so-called conservatives as the reason our children aren't competitive with the rest of the world. What else would we expect? The "system" insists on proceeding counter to its intent and philosophy.

The consumer economy is cutting the ability of the consumer to consume. Good paying jobs continue to be scarce and only low-paying jobs are abundant, yet the business community howls about a minimum wage that pays a whopping $13,000 per year. By the way, we spend $40,000 per year per imprisoned inmate, 75% of whom are functionally illiterate. Skilled worker jobs go begging because we've cut vocational education in our schools. The resources the economy requires grow scarcer while the environment in which we live is put at increasing risk to acquire new ones. Our children are being ignored, dumbed-down and, ironically, sheltered more from learning the survival skills in our world economy. Instead, they are being inundated with violent video games that promote shooting and killing as their themes, the more realistic the better.

I may be old-fashioned, but all this sounds like we're not only eating our children, we're showing them how to eat *their* children too. Maybe we have it all wrong. Maybe we should be moving toward a *sustaining* economy that actually conserves those things important to our survival as a species, never mind a society. We're running out of time to decide what we're going to do if we want to carry on this experiment in democracy. How much longer will the working people go before they finally rebel? How many times can the *Corporatocracy* break the hearts of the people who are making it ever richer?

118

Chapter 31:   The Kids are All Right

Much to my shock and amazement, as I researched the topic of public education, I discovered that our country didn't emphasize everyone fulfilling Jefferson's ideal of an educated populace until the 20th century, coincident with the industrial revolution and a couple of really horrible wars. It finally dawned on the leaders of our society that education was good for the masses instead of just for the elite.

What I also found out was that public education has been used as a political football for just about as long. THAT discovery was most revealing in that it explains much about how shallow and idea-free so many of our politicians are. Teachers and the public school system have had political bull's eyes painted on them for decades to slake the thirst of the political machines at every level.

I admit I drank the Kool-aid about tests and test scores as an indicator of the success or failure of our public schools. I recently read a book entitled *Education Hell: Rhetoric vs. Reality*, by Gerald Bracey. In that book, Dr. Bracey illustrated the facts and fiction of testing and test results. As a former industrial engineer I have some grip on statistics and the test results that get published by the media are "scrubbed" just about every way one can imagine. That scrubbing is done to promote political agenda.

During the Reagan administration we heard the idea of vouchers replacing public schools by allowing public tax money to go to private schools. This tenet was coupled with the notion that the Department of Education should be eliminated; indeed, Gingrich's *Contract with America* called for that also. The idea here was to save the government billions of short-term dollars so they could build another aircraft carrier, or something. As an aside, the Reagan administration did give the Navy its 600 ship fleet, but ran up a $6 trillion debt (1985 dollars) in doing so. That's the kind of fiscal restraint we've come to know and expect from both Republicans and Democrats since.

Arne Duncan was plucked from the canyons of Chicago to put more testing on our kids while getting them to spend more time in front of a computer. Great. We then have a former Bushite, Diane Ravitch, who initially supported *No Child Left Behind,* but now says it was the wrong approach. She also adds that 90% of charter schools have results equal to, or worse results than public schools, yet Duncan and Obama want to expand charter school funding. One has to wonder why we are so eager to make public education a profit center instead of the noble institution Jefferson, et. al., intended it to be. So, after billions of dollars spent on high stakes testing with the sword of Damocles hanging on every question, one of the original experts says it's wrong. In my newly found awareness, I see all this testing as yet another ill-conceived idea to fix what isn't and hasn't been broken.

Our schools are NOT broken. They are just underfunded where it matters most. We have and are spending billions of dollars on stuff that is wrong and doesn't matter anyway – high stakes testing. I once saw a travel show filmed in a West African country. The scene that stays with me was one of a classroom full of small children learning the English alphabet. The classroom had no chairs or desks, only a ceiling and a small lectern. The teacher and students conducted the lesson with hand-held slates and a piece of chalk. That was it! The teacher employed the Socratic Method for engaging children in pronunciation and application of each letter. She was wonderful. Tears filled my eyes. *This* is where the money needs to spent: on teachers!

The point here is that the vast majority of our teachers know how to teach. I've suggested before that most of us are hard-wired to teach. Teachers that also coach need to decide which they'd rather do. Many coaches teach academic courses, but with our emphasis on athletics and the revenue they generate, the academics suffer. We have decided that that is what we want. O.K., but let's make sure our coaches can teach the academics with rigor and thoroughness. Then the kids might not feel they are being neglected academically.

The kids know how to learn if they're given just the least bit of encouragement. In Colin Powell's report on education around the country, it stated that the number one cause for high school dropouts is *lack of interest*. When the curriculum has been dumbed-down to accommodate unnecessary tests and teachers are directed to "prepare students for the test", what else would we expect?

The kids are all right. Put the money where it matters, then watch them soar. Reward them and their teachers for that instead of threatening them with punishment based on bad data. Most countries whose students surpass ours on international evaluations pay their teachers equivalent salaries to other professions with equivalent education. Teachers in those countries are respected as valuable members of the community – just as we used to do – instead of some impediment to a child's "freedoms".

Chapter 32:   Fixing and Changing the Education Paradigm

So, what is the complete job description for being a modern classroom teacher in today's America? One little summary captures it well:

- Walk into the classroom everyday populated with 25-35 students and fill their every waking moment with the love of learning.

- Instill a sense of pride in each student's ethnicity, modify their disruptive behavior, observe any signs of abuse and censor their T-shirt messages and dress code violations.

- Continue to wage war on illegal drugs, warn them about sexually transmitted diseases, check their backpacks for weapons and, at the same time, help raise their self-esteem.

- Teach patriotism, good citizenship, sportsmanship, fairness, how to register to vote, how to balance a checkbook and how to apply for a job.

- Check for lice and other parasites, maintain a safe environment, look for anti-social behavior and make sure every student passes the mandatory state exams even though some rarely come to school or complete their assignments.

- Make sure all learning disabled students get an equal education regardless of the severity of their condition.

- Communicate regularly with parents by letter, phone or e-mail.

- Stay current on new materials and methods in the subject area.

- Write and submit copies of lesson plans each week.

- Attend faculty meetings, chaperone school activities, sponsor a club or activity if not a coach, and attend fifty hours per year of required professional development workshops.

- Write a professional development portfolio project every year.

Teachers and teaching must be moved to the top or near the top of the respected professional positions. Why? Because parents are working too hard and putting in too many hours into their jobs to supplement the learning that happens at school and simply don't have or make sufficient time for leisurely discourse with their children, thus transferring that responsibility to teachers. The same respect and sense of community necessity, therefore, must be given to teachers as the community gives those factors to doctors, dentists, police and firemen. This is our 21ˢᵗ century American "village".

Of all professions, teachers increasingly serve more as the pivotal point than any other in our children's lives from which they emerge as success stories ...or not. Changing the paradigm for public education will not be *easy* or *cheap*, two words that are currently part of the current paradigm. We as a nation must, for the first time, invest in our public education on a scale of such magnitude that the price tag is not mentioned. The necessary actions to return our public education's excellence level to the world's best must be performed irrespective of cost. Since we have never done that before and there isn't any known precedent of this magnitude, the exact cost is unknown. The payback and returns on that investment are obvious; we've seen this with our successes of the 20ᵗʰ century. If we don't do it, our fate as a nation is ordained and certain. Our Secretary of Education must be a driving force, not a Presidential toady. That cabinet office must break its paradigm of cronyism and being beholden to big business and take an overall plan for excellence all the way down to the district level in every state. I realize this is a massive undertaking, but so was going to the moon. We just have to be motivated enough.

Here are several actions that will get us on the road to an improved public education paradigm:

1. Increase the number and quality of teacher education programs in our colleges and universities. School districts should also establish scholarships for high school students going to college if they come back and teach for five or more years in that district.

2. Abolish or streamline the way teachers gain and lose their jobs. Train the principals better in personnel matters and give them more authority in the hiring and firing process so that competent and excellent teachers will be hired and retained. KIPP charter schools do this with outstanding results. If you are worried about unions, pay the teachers a salary competitive with other professions and watch the unions disappear.

3. School boards or state education agencies need to hire superintendents with cost-conscious and value-added skills instead of Ed.D. (Doctor of Education) types who perpetuate bureaucracies as usual. Many of these people are well intended, but are so hung up on their own dissertation topic that they try to implement their program

without proper oversight, time or resources. Some ideas and programs are good, but it may take several cohorts of kids to go through them in order to realize results, good or bad. Many ideas get truncated and replaced with something else when the first year or two doesn't yield the intended results. The superintendent gets fired and the merry-go-round starts all over again.

4. No pass-no play rules must be employed where they don't exist and enforced where they do. Teachers and principals who have never been out of a classroom since kindergarten should take paid periodic sabbaticals to work in the real world with real workers to get a feel for what the expectations are for their students when they graduate. They will then teach their academics from the point of view of how those skills are applied in the working world.

Over the last twenty years, I watched our country struggle to provide world-class quality education for our children and continue to fall further behind the rest of the world. I am sick and tired of cartoonists, late night talk show hosts and conservative media pundits publicly bashing our schools, our students and our teachers without willing to offer non-politically motivated solutions to the problems they perceive.

The following are some ideas developed with the help of my spouse, my friends who have or have had children in schools and my colleagues at every level of experience.

1. Repeal the *No Child Left Behind* Act and return to responsible student assessment methods that measure the *child's* progress, not the schools' based on inconsistent and arbitrary standards set by politicians.

2. Each state, based on Federal Department of Education guidelines for curriculum in all subject areas (required as well as electives), should develop detailed curriculum requirements for each subject by grade from kindergarten through high school graduation. Teachers, both new to the job and experienced, must be required to know those curriculum requirements in their subject areas. The validity of their teaching certificate will depend on that knowledge as well as the overall *pedagogy* of their subject.

3. Teachers will submit to their principals a yearly outline of their lessons that satisfies the checklist of topics required by the state's requirements. Teachers will then submit lesson plan summaries weekly to their principals so that the administrators can check off each requirement and detail item as it is taught by each teacher. Principals will periodically submit these checklists to their superintendents for review to ensure that each teacher is staying

current to his or her outline. The superintendent will submit the final checklists to the various curriculum directors at the state level and establish feedback loops between teachers and principals to ensure proper communication and curriculum rigor. Teachers who consistently fail to meet the curriculum requirements should be dismissed or re-educated.

4. Class sizes should be maximized at twenty-five for non-laboratory courses. For laboratory classes in science, domestic engineering (home economics), art and vocational courses like machine or auto shop, the maximum should be twenty students. These numbers are based on research that indicates optimum maximums for a variety of teaching techniques like expert groups, student interaction activities as well as for safety considerations. Traditionally large group classes like physical education and band should be sized at the discretion of the principal.

5. A district in Colorado Springs, Colorado made an executive decision that their elementary school population maximum would be six-hundred, their middle schools 1,000 and their high schools 1,800. As the limits were approached, they would ask the district to build them another school. The community completely bought into this plan, and as a result student performance on national level tests for all grades is still some of the best in the nation.

6. Let football stadiums be funded by revenue generated from admission and concession monies generated by all the athletic programs, not from bond issues attached to building new or refurbishing older academic buildings. If teams want to have bigger stadia, raise ticket prices until they get the money. As I see it, the fans will pay as much as required in order to attend their local high school's games. Fund raisers for band uniforms, cheerleader uniforms, drill team equipment and other necessities supporting extra-curricular activities have been going on for years. School districts should promote more opportunities for these money-makers instead of bleeding off more tax dollars from academics.

7. Each community should hire an independent auditor to periodically examine the value added by central office staff and examine staffing levels. This should also be done at the state level to keep these bureaucracies from growing into unmanageable, expensive and wasteful behemoths filled with cronies. As a former industrial engineer who has performed similar audits on businesses, I assure you that the fees of the auditor will be made up many times over from the money saved and costs avoided by running a streamlined operation.

8. Combine common functionary duties in educational regions such that individual districts will not have to establish redundant staffs for things like personnel, purchasing and maintenance management. The central organization of these things will streamline the districts so that they can better serve the students.

9. In view of the current public discussions on child and adult obesity, I recommend mandatory physical education classes for all non-physically challenged children. I also recommend that these classes include significant cardio-vascular exercise. As corny as it sounds all research points to healthy bodies supporting healthy brains. Besides, other research shows that physically fit children tend to get into less trouble in and out of school. Our physical education instructors are very good at providing this environment. School districts should also promote fitness programs for their teachers and staff so that those personnel can also be at their best every day. Teachers modeling good eating habits will help the students do the same.

10. Eliminate sugar from the school drink and food vending machines. Sugar and caffeine are an unhealthy combination in a learning environment for developing children. We have known about this for many years, but often, due to lack of funds, school districts are forced to become billboards for corporations at the expense of the child's health and educational environment. An added benefit is that the teachers, by not having this stuff to eat and drink, will be healthier too.

11. Provide only healthful, cafeteria-prepared foods for the lunch lines. Balance the proportions of protein, fat and carbohydrates in each meal to meet the requirements of the age group being fed. University book shelves are groaning under the weight of the research defining those parameters. Will it cost more? Probably. Why? Because the district will have to purchase more perishable food and hire more food preparation personnel that actually know how to prepare healthy dishes. In concert with this idea, districts should send recommended diet suggestions to parents with cost/savings analyses for various foods and their nutritional value as it relates to the optimum development of their children. If we're going to teach our children how to eat healthfully, and their parents don't know how to do that, we should educate the parents too.

12. Recruit teachers from the top tiers of college graduates and from pools of under-employed professional people who have lost their jobs to outsourcing. Pay for their year of teacher education and student teaching.

13. Raise teacher and administrator salaries to a level equivalent with their equally educated counterparts in business, industry and government. Teacher salaries, after a probationary period must be increased at least fifty percent from current levels in order to parallel their equally educated fellow Americans in other careers. Not only will that engender respect for teachers from the more cynically secular among us, but it will provide incentive and competitiveness for those teaching jobs. I feel secure in suggesting that a newer, higher salary structure will attract more capable people to the teaching profession and hold them there. In the foreign countries that treat their teachers this way, their students are outperforming ours by double-digits on any test you want to name.

14. Teacher incentive pay is a current topic of some interest. In view of the fact that our inner-city schools exhibit very high teacher turnover rates, added financial incentives may reduce that situation. There are also acute shortages of mathematics, science and special education teachers everywhere. Paying these disciplines higher salaries may also help reduce those shortages. Teachers who *do* stay on the job in an inner-city school for extended periods should also receive some sort of incentive. I suggest paying decade bonuses to teachers and administrators who stay with their districts for ten, twenty, etc., years. There are those who linked these kinds of incentives to the peculiar notion of merit pay for teachers based on student performance measured by standardized test scores. I've already been through that and I can't find a way that is fair and makes this idea valid. You can find more detail on this topic in my previous book, *A Worm in the Apple: The Inside Story of Public Education.*

15. Eliminate the volumes of unnecessary paperwork that contributes nothing to the learning of our children. This applies to administrators, non-teaching professional staff and teachers. Special education personnel at all levels in each state must find ways to streamline their documentation requirements while still complying with the appropriate state and Federal laws. When each new report or required form is created it takes that much more time away from what that faculty or staff is supposed to be doing to educate children.

16. Funding schools in any state should be *zero-based.* That means that the base cost of operating buildings including support and maintenance staff is determined for all the schools in the district each year. The best estimate of student population for the entire district for each year will determine the teacher count and their salaries based on teacher/student ratios mentioned in item #4. Add in the consumables for the whole operation, administrative and academic, and each district will identify the funding necessary to function for that year. The state and Federal funding pool will be established based on all the above data with contingency additions derived from previous budget history of overages. Any other extra projects or unexpected expense must require financial or practical justification and approval by the school board, if locally funded, or the state, if the needs are on a larger scale. Large scale capital projects would require a bond issue vote by the entire community served by that project. This method will greatly reduce the influence the Federal government exerts on states' education systems, but will more exactly justify how the money is spent and how much is needed from one year to the next. Accounting history will also help districts make sound fiscal decisions.

17. Lengthen the school year to at least two-hundred days of class. We are the only industrialized nation that does not send its children to school for two-hundred days or more. The rest of the industrialized world has found a way to do that without destroying anyone's profitability. These added days can come from the overly long winter break, the summer break, Spring break and so-called *in-service* days. The extra twenty days are the minimum needed to adequately cover all the material in many classes. The rate at which science is expanding and the fact that history keeps marching on alone justifies this increase. The success of the KIPP (*Knowledge Is Power Program*) schools and others of its type is an example of obtaining excellent results from applying more rigorous curriculum in a longer school day with top-tier, well-paid teachers in limited size classrooms over a longer school year. These academies take inner-city, low achieving students and bring their skills up to grade level quickly. Teachers are well paid and the principals have absolute control over hiring and firing teachers. Bad teachers don't last long there. Results are paramount for the faculty to retain their jobs.

18. Improve the ratio between teachers and administrators so that the principals and assistant principals have more time to supervise, assist and otherwise help teachers do a better job. The recommended closer working relationship between professionals cannot help but make teachers, especially the newer ones, more confident, innovative and efficient.

19. With the growing number of foreign immigrants bringing children into our schools, I suggest that each district have an English language academy. I understand that we cannot do bilingual education for all the different languages we import, but research shows that total immersion in English in a non-intimidating environment will yield desired results more quickly than current inclusion programs. We

absolutely must get these children to obtain language skills equivalent with their grade level as soon as possible so they can learn and enjoy the regular curriculum. This idea is especially productive for the youngest children as their language learning optimum age range is 3-7 years. What makes this item even more urgent is that many of the immigrant children are functionally illiterate in their native language having no skills or knowledge of grammar and spelling to begin with.

20. Re-establish strong vocational curricula in our secondary schools to provide for those children who won't or can't go to college. 75% of the freshmen entering college do not graduate in four years and half of them don't get a degree at all. Some vocational programs are capital intensive in that expensive machines and equipment must be purchased and maintained. Insurance liability also increases as does the specter of lawsuits. These factors act as disincentives for vocational programs where district or school funding is restricted. Nonetheless, I strongly believe that if our country is going to regain the manufacturing and industrial vigor and prominence it lost or gave away to Asia, vocational programs are necessary. When I read about un-skilled young men and women just hanging around on the corner because they are not employable, I am convinced that these skill-related curricula would give these kids a better chance to stay out of trouble, away from drugs and gangsters and allow them to *earn* their way to a better life.

21. Review everything related to special education. This area will require perhaps the most reorganization and financial expansion of any topic previously mentioned. Review the *least restrictive environment* decision-making process so that regular classes aren't reduced to the lowest common denominator of learning due to the quantity of learning disabled children present in any class. Many of our special children can manage in some classes, but not others; it isn't fair to the "regular" children to have their lessons diluted or restricted because of the few special needs kids. In order to balance this out so that the special needs kids get *their* excellent education is hire many more special educators and add new and better methods and materials to the special education curriculum. Of course, improved salary schedules for this specialty is necessary.

22. Perhaps the most difficult to implement of all my suggestion is to re-prioritize, as an entire society, the emphasis on athletics, band and cheerleaders. These "ABCs" of education must be replaced with a different series in the alphabet: knowledge, learning and motivation to learn, my "KLM" plan. Extra-curricular activities are fine, but the excessive time, money and attention spent on them is clearly reducing

the quality of education our children are receiving. Newspapers should publish reports of earned grades in our schools and compare them to other schools just the way they report scores of athletic events. Parents must, of course, be the driving force behind this idea. If they lack the will to change how we educate our future citizens, we have little or no hope of competing in the future world economy and will have wasted the vision of our founding fathers and a few others who built our nation into the greatest society the world has ever known.

Part IV

Race in America: Consequences of Institutionalized Hate

One of the penalties for refusing to participate in politics is that you end up being governed by your inferiors.

- Plato

Give me your tired, your poor, your huddled masses, yearning to breathe free, the wretched refuse of your teeming shore. Send these, the homeless, tempest tossed to me. I lift my lamp beside the golden door.

- Inscription on the Statue of Liberty

Chapter 33:   Lincoln's Second Inaugural

Fellow-Countrymen:

At this second appearing to take the oath of the Presidential office there is less occasion for an extended address than there was at the first. Then a statement somewhat in detail of a course to be pursued seemed fitting and proper. Now, at the expiration of four years, during which public declarations have been constantly called forth on every point and phase of the great contest which still absorbs the attention and engrosses the energies of the nation, little that is new could be presented. The progress of our arms, upon which all else chiefly depends, is as well known to the public as to myself, and it is, I trust, reasonably satisfactory and encouraging to all. With high hope for the future, no prediction in regard to it is ventured.

On the occasion corresponding to this four years ago all thoughts were anxiously directed to an impending civil war. All dreaded it, all sought to avert it. While the inaugural address was being delivered from this place, devoted altogether to saving the Union without war, insurgent agents were in the city seeking to destroy it without war—seeking to dissolve the Union and divide effects by negotiation. Both parties deprecated war, but one of them would make war rather than let the nation survive, and the other would accept war rather than let it perish, and the war came.

One-eighth of the whole population were colored slaves, not distributed generally over the Union, but localized in the southern part of it. These slaves constituted a peculiar and powerful interest. All knew that this interest was somehow the cause of the war. To strengthen, perpetuate, and extend this interest was the object for which the insurgents would rend the Union even by war, while the Government claimed no right to do more than to restrict the territorial enlargement of it. Neither party expected for the war the magnitude or the duration which it has already attained. Neither anticipated that the cause of the conflict might cease with or even before the conflict itself should cease. Each looked for an easier triumph, and a result less fundamental and astounding. Both read the same Bible and pray to the same God, and each invokes His aid against the other. It may seem strange that any men should dare to ask a just God's assistance in wringing their bread from the sweat of other men's faces, but let us judge not, that we be not judged. The prayers of both could not be answered. That of neither has been answered fully. The Almighty has His own purposes. "Woe unto the world because of offenses; for it must needs be that offenses come, but woe to that man by whom the offense cometh." If we shall suppose that American slavery is one of those offenses which, in the providence of God, must needs come, but which, having continued through His appointed time, He now wills to remove, and that He gives to both North and South this terrible war as the woe due to those by whom the offense came, shall we discern therein any departure from those divine attributes which the believers in a living God always ascribe to Him? Fondly do we hope, fervently do we pray, that this mighty scourge of war may speedily pass away. Yet, if God wills that it continue until all the wealth piled by the bondsman's two hundred and fifty years of unrequited toil shall be sunk, and until every drop of blood drawn with the lash shall be paid by another drawn with the sword, as was said three thousand years ago, so still it must be said "the judgments of the Lord are true and righteous altogether."

With malice toward none, with charity for all, with firmness in the right as God gives us to see the right, let us strive on to

*finish the work we are in, to bind up the nation's wounds, to
care for him who shall have borne the battle and for his
widow and his orphan, to do all which may achieve and
cherish a just and lasting peace among ourselves and with all
nations.*

Here we are today with our first black President who is only half black
and that half is of direct African descent. He is the son of a Kenyan father
and a white Euro-American mother. Specifically, Barack Obama is not of
slave ancestry, but is reflecting on that American blackness because he is not
all white. At least that's how many on both sides of the color line see it.

The fact that this President has created an environment for a whole
new repertoire of dog whistle racism shows how deep and wide the racist
nature of our culture truly still is. In many places in this book, race plays an
important, if not essential role in the topic at hand. I wish – I truly wish
with all my heart – that we Americans had moved past the scourge of
intellectual waste; the waste of hate and prejudice for the simplest of reasons.
The tribal imperative – "you're not like me" – still hangs us up from clear
thinking and true community and national brotherhood, the key to our
ultimate salvation as a society.

I suspect Lincoln understood how difficult things would soon be, but I
don't think he expected it would take 150 years to overcome the hate. It will
take longer. Then, he didn't live through the second horror of the 19th
century, *Reconstruction.* That dreadful squabbling by the post-war political
extremists fomented the egregious exploitation of the ashes of the South and
the degradation of what was left of its populace by carpetbaggers and a host
of other charlatans. White southerners have a right to harbor loathing for
"Yankees", but does it have to be this long in overcoming those sins of the
past? And why harbor resentment for black people as well? Hasn't 300 years
of slavery and social pariahship (new word) been enough of a punishment for
just having black skin? When DO we bind up our wounds completely? When
will the southern Christians walk the walk of their "savior" and accept all
men as partners on this, our only planet?

The whole world wonders....

Chapter 34:   Has It All Been for Nothing?

A friend recently asked me if all the civil rights work we did in the 60s and 70s was worth it. He, like me, was in the "dumps" over the recent Supreme Court ruling that section 5 of the Voting Rights Act was obsolete and even prejudicial. The question that kept nagging us was: Why didn't the law just get expanded to cover the other states that were excluded from this provision? Instead we heard something quite different.

Robert Parry recently wrote a book titled *Secrecy and Privilege: Rise of the Bush Dynasty from Watergate to Iraq.* He said, "Neo-Confederate members of the Supreme Court are gearing up to restore white rule over America by tearing up the Voting Rights Act." He wrote this before the court announced its decision, and the right-wing majority of the Supreme Court validated that prediction. It means that jurisdictions with a history of racial discrimination in voting will be free to impose new obstacles to voting by constituencies that tend to vote for Democrats. Already in Texas and several other states Republicans are jumping for joy that they can once again help ensure their voting dominance and keep white-dominated rule in government. As the election of 2014 pointed out, voter suppression schemes worked. Over 600,000 people of color, the elderly and even students were prevented from voting because they didn't have the correct or enough "legal" identification" or were temporarily living out of state. This was just in Texas.

The Republicans' aggressive gerrymandering of congressional districts has ensured a continued GOP majority in the U.S. House of Representatives although Democrats outpolled Republicans nationwide in *Election 2012*. This green light to renew Jim Crow laws also comes at a time when Republican legislatures and governors across the country are devising new strategies to dilute or stop the votes from minorities and urban dwellers to protect GOP power - especially within the federal government. Some GOP-controlled states, that tend to vote Democratic in presidential elections, are now considering apportioning presidential electors according to these gerrymandered districts to give Republican presidential candidates most of the electoral votes even if they lose the state's popular vote.

The five partisan Republican Justices showed us all how much they wanted to do their part in devaluing the votes of blacks, Hispanics, Asian-Americans, and young urban whites. The GOP justices indicated during oral arguments that they sought excuses to strike down the heart of the Voting Rights Act. Extremist Justice Antonin Scalia shocked the courtroom when he dismissed the Voting Rights Act as a "perpetuation of racial entitlement," suggesting that the right of blacks to vote was some kind of government handout. Equally troubling was the remark from Justice Anthony Kennedy who insisted that the Voting Rights Act, which was first enacted by Congress in 1965 and was renewed unanimously by Congress in 2006, was an intrusion on Alabama as an "independent sovereign," a phrase from the states' rights language reminiscent of the Old Confederacy. The five Republican justices, including Roberts, Thomas and Alito, seem to have absorbed a Neo-Confederate interpretation of the Constitution that conflicts dramatically with what the Framers intended.

The language about "independent" and "sovereign" states was part of the *Articles of Confederation*, which governed the United States from 1777 to 1787. They proved to be so disastrous that George Washington and James Madison insisted that the Articles be tossed out entirely during the writing of the Constitution in 1787.

General Washington, in particular, hated the concept of "independent" and "sovereign" states because he saw how badly that worked when trying to supply his troops during the Revolutionary War. The states often reneged on their promises to provide support, and the central government had little power to override them. They acted as little fiefdoms as their "leaders" saw fit. Washington correctly saw that forming a nation from these factions was hopeless. Indeed, even during the Civil War, Jefferson Davis had huge problems getting states to supply the Confederate armies in the field due to "sovereign" issues.

With the *Articles of Confederation* failing as a governing structure, the Constitutional Convention in Philadelphia was instructed to propose amendments. Washington and Madison eliminated the Articles in favor of the new Constitution. It is this Constitution which made federal law supreme and transferred national sovereignty from the 13 states to "We the People." All language about state "sovereignty" and "independence" was expunged, though the Framers left the states substantial control over local matters. The tensions between the federal government and the states continued, however, especially over the South's insistence that slavery be made permanent. Among the compromises in Philadelphia, was a particularly offensive clause that counted black slaves as "three-fifths of a person" for the purpose of electoral representation. Slave states also wanted their "peculiar institution" extended to incoming states to prevent non-slave states outvoting the slave states in Congress. Ultimately, this dispute led to Southern states seceding from the Union after Abraham Lincoln's election in 1860.

The North's "victory" in the Civil War seemed to establish the supremacy of federal law as expressed in the Constitution. The Thirteenth Amendment was enacted in the waning days of the conflict, abolishing slavery once and for all. The Fourteenth and Fifteenth Amendments then established the principles of equal protection under the law, including the right to vote. Still, the former slave states didn't stop trying to limit voting for the blacks. With whites reasserting their racial supremacy and their political dominance through electoral trickery and terrorist violence, the states of the Old Confederacy created a Jim Crow system of racial segregation that included devious means to rob African-Americans of the voting franchise. Today, conservative groups supported by the Koch brothers still maintain active research on how the 10th Amendment can be used to foster Libertarian agendas. Even Rick Perry, the outgoing governor of Texas has mentioned the 10th Amendment as a possible doorway to secession. I guess some people have to re-learn history every day.

The civil rights struggle of the 1950s and 60s, pushed the federal government to address these racist laws and actions. This intervention produced an angry white backlash in the South which resulted in an overwhelming shift to Republican dominance there.

Over the past half century, wealthy right-wing Republicans, have invested millions of dollars in "think tanks" such as the Heritage Foundation, Cato Institute and The Federalist Society. All of these organizations are dedicated to cherry-picking the nation's early history to transform America's founding narrative into its own, opposite one. Through these attempts to rewrite history, they turned Washington and Madison, devoted Federalists, into states' rights lovers and federal government haters. They did this by forgetting the facts and replacing them with *states' rights* language from the *Articles of Confederation.* This rewrite of history makes states "sovereign" and "independent" from the U.S. Constitution, the document intended for "we the people." (See Robert Parry's *America's Stolen Narrative* for more on the way right-wing historians attempt to rewrite historical documents and events).

Unfortunately, it's not just the right-wing historians that emphasize the 10th Amendment over the large number of rulings that define Federal supremacy over state laws. The five right-wing justices on the Supreme Court are the product of right-wing fueled misinterpretations of U.S. history and Neo-Confederate revisionism. These men absorbed this ersatz history as they rose through the ranks of right-wing ideology and institutions, and are now in position to impose their false constitutional thinking on the United States, particularly as those theories relate to the present Republican ideological crisis with the country's changing demographics.

As the white population shrinks to below 50 percent, the only way to sustain white control is by devaluing minority votes.

Chapter 35:   Pink Palms

Due to a lack of pigment cells, melanocytes, human palms are either pink or some shade of "flesh tone". It is curious that when we buy paints, "flesh tone" is almost always white-ish. Today's economics in the United States is so shifted to the upper echelon of the wealthy, that what's left for the rest of us makes us more alike than different. The 1% is 99% white, while the black and brown people in the top 1% are mostly star athletes and entertainers. The notable exceptions include some loony entrepreneurs like Herman Cain – he of the 9-9-9 economic plan that would have destroyed the world's economy.

It's time to resurrect and focus on the 99% movements in order to save democracy from the oligarchs pursuing the prophecies of Karl Marx with all speed. In *Das Kapital* Marx predicted that unregulated capitalism will destroy itself from within. Between 2001 and 2006, fifty-three percent of every dollar earned in the United States went to the top 1%. The bubbles burst and the economy tanked a year later, but those who bet against themselves with derivatives and other instruments of screwing-everyone-else ended up collecting billions while millions of people lost their jobs (700,000 per month), their health care (60+% of bankruptcies were attributable to health care costs irrespective of insurance) and their abilities to contribute to society. It should be noted that the Labor Department has produced all sorts of data showing how much LESS American middle class workers earn than they did before the Bush debacles. So much for THIS iteration of supply-side economics.

Meanwhile, the banking industry managed to wangle a few trillion dollars out of the Federal Reserve to save themselves from themselves and followed the letter of their executive contracts paying said executives their required billion dollar bonuses for doing such a fine job. This must be the new reward-for-excellence program that I slept through in American Government class.

Today we see "intellectual" combat between the naysayers and scientists who actually follow the rules of the scientific method. Most of these naysayers also call themselves "conservatives". Backwards seems a better word. As Carl Sagan once said, "We live in a society exquisitely dependent on science and technology in which hardly anyone knows anything about science and technology." And Fox News wasn't even around when Sagan said that.

While I'm quoting famous Americans, Abraham Lincoln dropped a dime on my favorite villains when he said, "I see in the near future a crisis approaching that unnerves me and causes me to tremble for the safety of my country....corporations have been enthroned and an era of corruption in high places will follow, and the money power of the country will endeavor to prolong its reign by working upon the prejudices of the people until all wealth is aggregated in a few hands and the Republic is destroyed." How did he know? Did he see 2014 through a glass darkly? He said these damning words in 1864, six months before the end of the Civil War. He had to see what the MILITARY INDUSTRIAL COMPLEX looked like even then.

Americans have this thing about applying sainthood to certain leaders. Ronald Reagan has been sainted over and over with aircraft carriers, countless roads and buildings and an airport in Washington, D.C. named after him. Yet, his administration set league records for criminal indictments and convictions, an $8 billion loss in the S & L scandals and over 130 investigations regarding defense contractor corruption…to name just a few things. Did I mention the Iran-Contra debacle? Clearly if his record is examined with a clear eye, the Reagan years are among our most grievous. Then, of course, the Republicans, their Supreme Court Justices and misguided voters picked George W. Bush to set new lows in every category for national progress.

Notice that our recent ills are attributable to Republicans almost exclusively. From the 20th century until today, Republican Presidents have created monstrous economic problems for the 99%. Even the attempted rollback of women's rights in society is on the table for Republicans which makes me say that a woman voting for a Republican is like a chicken voting for Colonel Sanders. Indeed, why would anyone in the 99% vote against their best interests? The rich do NOT create jobs. They DO promote illegal war. They DO cut taxes for the rich and corporations while raising the tax burden on the working classes – who can't find good paying jobs anymore. This all sounds like a formula for Lincoln's disaster.

Those of us down here in the nether regions of American society no longer can look at one another and discern our place by skin color, gender preference, or any other phony divider. All we have to do is look at our palms and see that we are all in this together and that we'd better start asserting ourselves, or Lincoln's and Marx's prophecies will certainly come true.

Chapter 36:   Slavery and the Modern Capitalist

In April of 2012, Joshua Freeman and Steve Fraser wrote a lengthy piece (from which I quote – italics - and paraphrase extensively) describing a new kind of slavery conducted by corporate America and the capitalist spirit. They begin with:

"All told, nearly a million prisoners are now making office furniture, working in call centers, fabricating body armor, taking hotel reservations, working in slaughterhouses, or manufacturing textiles, shoes, and clothing, while getting paid somewhere between 93 cents and $4.73 per day."

The writers call this "sweatshop labor", but a little digging shows that it is something more sinister than that *birth-of-the-industrial-revolution* horror show. *Penitentiaries have become a niche market for such work. The privatization of prisons in recent years has meant the creation of a small army of workers too coerced and right-less to complain.*

Prisoners have not found a legitimate place in today's American economy. Their ranks are increasing to the point where the United States leads the world in actual and per capita incarceration. This population provides a huge labor base for those who desire to pay very low to no wages. As the prison system becomes more commercialized with companies like *The Corrections Corporation of America* or *G4S (formerly Wackenhut)* who sell inmate labor at sub-minimum wages to Fortune 500 companies like Chevron, B of A, AT & T and IBM.

These companies can, in most states, lease factories inside prisons or hire out prisoners to work on the outside. All told, nearly a million prisoners are now making office furniture, working in call centers, fabricating body armor, taking hotel reservations, working in slaughterhouses, or manufacturing textiles, shoes, and clothing, while getting paid somewhere between 93 cents and $4.73 per day.

It's hard to imagine a more compliant labor force where the worker has no rights of any sort, can be disciplined on the whim of the "supervisor" and is excluded from all other labor laws of the land. This is really a Dickensian 19th century model where convict labor was "normal" for confinement at "hard labor". This situation emulates a time when, similar to today's economy, capitalists thought that capital accumulation was a top priority crisis.

Some historians call the span between 1870s – 1890s "the long Depression" caused, in part by frequent investment panics and slumps, mass bankruptcies, deflation and self-destructive competition among businesses that were especially designed to depress labor costs. Sound familiar? The political pressure to commit austerity instead of capital investment is specifically designed today to shrink the society's wages for the working classes. There is no capital problem today, except that it isn't working capital. It is sitting in a variety of banks to avoid taxation. This is the new capitalism of the 21st century.

Convict labor is once again an appealing way for business to address their overwhelming desire to cut wages and benefits. The taxpayer, ultimately, pays the wages of the prisoner-based labor force. Penal servitude may now seem like a barbaric throwback to some long-lost time that preceded the industrial revolution, but that is incorrect. From its first appearance in this country, it has been associated with modern capitalist industry and large-scale agriculture.

That is only the first of many misconceptions about this peculiar institution. Infamous for the brutality with which prison laborers were once treated, indelibly linked in popular memory (and popular culture) with images of the black chain gang in the American South, it is usually assumed to be a Southern invention. So apparently atavistic, it seems to fit naturally with the retrograde nature of Southern life and labor, its economic and cultural underdevelopment, its racial caste system, and its desperate attachment to the "lost cause."

As it happens, penal servitude -- the leasing out of prisoners to private enterprise, either within prison walls or in outside workshops, factories, and fields -- was originally known as a Yankee invention.

First used at Auburn prison in New York State in the 1820s, the system spread widely and quickly throughout the North, the Midwest, and later the West. It developed alongside state-run prison workshops that produced goods for the public sector and sometimes the open market.

A few Southern states also joined in. Prisoners there, however, were mainly white men, since slave masters, with a free hand to deal with the

140

"infractions" of their chattel, had little need for prison. The Thirteenth Amendment abolishing slavery would make an exception for penal servitude precisely because it had become the dominant form of punishment throughout the non-slave states.

Those men AND women sentenced to "confinement at hard labor" were not restricted to digging ditches or other unskilled work. Prisoners were employed in a broad range of tasks from rope- and wagon-making to carpet, hat, and clothing manufacturing (where women prisoners were sometimes put to work), as well as coal mining, carpentry, barrel-making, shoe production, house-building, and even the manufacture of rifles. The range of small and larger workshops where the felons served made up the heart of the new American economy.

While observing free-labor textile and convict-labor mills, during a visit to the United States, novelist Charles Dickens couldn't tell the difference between them.

State governments used the rental revenue garnered from their prisoners to meet budget needs, while entrepreneurs made outsized profits either by working the prisoners themselves or subleasing them to other businessmen.

After the Civil War, the convict-lease system metamorphosed. In the South, one of several grim methods, including the black codes, debt peonage, the crop-lien system, lifetime labor contracts, and vigilante terror, were used to control and fix in place the newly emancipated slave. Those "freedmen" were eager to pursue their new liberty either by setting up as small farmers or by exercising the right to move out of the region at will or from job to job as "free wage labor", but were thwarted in this by imposed constraints on their movements.

It is inaccurate to assume that the convict-lease system was exclusively the brainchild of the apartheid, all-white "Redeemer" governments that overthrew the Radical Republican regimes (which first ran the defeated Confederacy during Reconstruction) and who used their power to introduce Jim Crow to Dixie. In Georgia, for example, the Radical Republican state government took up the convict-lease initiative soon after the war ended. They did this because the convict-lease system was tied to the modernizing sectors of the post-war economy throughout Dixie.

Convicts were leased to coal-mining, iron-forging, steel-making, and railroad companies, including Tennessee Coal and Iron (TC&I, a major producer across the South), especially in the booming region around Birmingham, Alabama. More than a quarter of the coal coming out of Birmingham's pits was mined by prisoners. By the turn of the century, TC&I

had been folded into J.P. Morgan's United States Steel complex, which also relied heavily on prison laborers.

All the main extractive industries of the South were, in fact, wedded to this system. Turpentine and lumber camps deep in the fetid swamps and vast forests of Georgia, Florida, and Louisiana commonly worked their convicts until they dropped dead from overwork or disease. The region's plantation monocultures in cotton and sugar made regular use of imprisoned former slaves, including women. Among the leading families of Atlanta, Birmingham, and other "New South" metropolises were businessmen whose fortunes originated from the dank coal pits, malarial marshes and isolated forests in which their *unfree* peons worked, lived, and died.

The Southern system also stood out for the intimate collusion among industrial, commercial, and agricultural enterprises and every level of Southern law enforcement as well as the judicial system. Sheriffs, local justices of the peace, state police, judges, and state governments conspired to keep the convict-lease business humming. Indeed, local law officers depended on the leasing system for a substantial part of their income. They pocketed the fines and fees associated with the "convictions," a repayable sum that would be added on to the amount of time at "hard labor" demanded of the prisoner.

The arrest cycle was synchronized with the business cycle, timed to the rise and fall of the demand for fresh labor. County and state treasuries similarly counted on such revenues, since the post-war South was so capital-starved that only renting out convicts assured that prisons could be built and maintained. It was a kind of self-fulfilling business enterprise; capitalism with almost zero labor expense.

There was, then, every incentive to concoct charges or send people to jail for the most trivial offenses: vagrancy, gambling, drinking, partying, and hopping a freight car, tarrying too long in town. A "pig law" in Mississippi assured you of five years as a prison laborer if you stole a farm animal worth more than $10. Theft of a fence rail could result in the same.

In the North, where 80% of all U.S. prison labor was employed after the Civil War, and which accounted for over $35 billion in output (in current dollars), the system was reconfigured to meet the needs of modern industry and the pressures of "the long Depression." Convict labor was increasingly leased out only to a handful of major manufacturers in each state. These textile mills, oven makers, mining operations, hat and shoe factories -- one in Wisconsin leased that state's entire population of convicted felons -- were then installing the kind of mass production methods becoming standard in much of American industry. As organized markets for prison labor grew increasingly oligopolistic (like the rest of the economy), the Depression of

142

1873 and subsequent depressions in the following decades wiped out many smaller businesses that had once depended on convict labor.

Companies leasing convicts enjoyed authority to dispose of their rented labor power as they saw fit. Workers were compelled to labor in total silence. Even hand gestures and eye contact were prohibited for the purpose of creating "silent and insulated working machines."

Supervision of prison labor was often shared by employers and the prison authorities alike. Many businesses continued to conduct their operations within prison walls where they supplied the materials, power, and machinery, while the state provided guards, workshops, food, clothing, and what passed for medical care. As one observer put it, "Felons are mere machines held to labor by the dark cell and the scourge."

Free market industrial capitalism, then and now, invariably draws on the aid of the state. This might be shocking to the Hayek/Friedman school of economists, but in that convict labor system's formative phases, the state regularly used its coercive powers of taxation, expropriation, and incarceration to free up natural and human resources lying outside the orbit of capitalism proper.

In both the North and the South, the contracting out of convict labor was one way in which that state-assisted mechanism of capital accumulation arose. Contracts with the government assured employers that their labor force would be replenished anytime a worker got sick, was disabled, died, or simply became too worn out to continue.

Penal institutions all over the country became auxiliary arms of capitalist industry and commerce. Two-thirds of all prisoners worked for private enterprise.

Even today, government is once again providing subsidies and tax incentives as well as facilities, utilities, and free space for corporations making use of this same category of convict labor. A principal objective in using prison labor is to undermine efforts to unionize.

Opposition to convict labor arose from workingmen's associations, labor-oriented political parties, journeymen unions, and other groups, which considered the system an insult to the moral codes of egalitarian republicanism nurtured by the American Revolution. The specter of proletarian dependency haunted the lives of the country's self-reliant handicraftsmen who watched apprehensively as shops employing slave-wage labor began popping up across the country. Much of the early agitation by unions was aimed at the use of prisoners to replace skilled workers while unskilled prison labor was initially largely ignored.

It was bad enough for craftsmen to see their livelihoods and standards of living put in jeopardy by "free" wage labor, but is was worse still watching unfree labor do the same thing. At the time, employers were turning to that captive prison population to combat attempts by aggrieved workers to organize and defend themselves. On the eve of the Civil War, for example, an iron-molding contractor in Spuyten Duyvil, north of Manhattan in the Bronx, locked out his unionized workers and then moved his operation to Sing Sing penitentiary, where a laborer cost 40 cents per day, $2.60 less than the going day rate. It worked, and Local 11 of the Union of Iron Workers quickly died away.

The workingman's movement of the Jacksonian era was deeply alarmed by the prospect of "wage slavery," a condition conflicting with their sense of self as citizens of a republic of independent producers. Prison labor was a sub-species of that dreaded "slavery"; a caricature of it.

Throughout the Gilded Age of the 1890s, convict labor served as a magnet for capitalists trying to get the cheapest labor possible. But prisoner rebellions became ever more common, particularly in the North where many prisoners turned out to be Civil War veterans and dispossessed working people who already knew something about fighting for freedom and against oppression. Major penitentiaries like Sing Sing became sites of repeated strikes and riots; a strike in 1877 even took on the transplanted Spuyten Duyvil iron-molding company.

Above and below the Mason Dixon line, political platforms, protest rallies, petition campaigns, legislative investigations, union strikes, and boycotts by farm organizations like the Farmers Alliance and Grange cried out for the abolition of the convict-lease system, or at least for its rigorous regulation. Over the 19th century's last two decades, more than 20 coal-mine strikes broke out because of the use of convict miners.

The Knights of Labor, that era's most audacious labor movement, was particularly involved. During the Coal Creek Wars in eastern Tennessee in the early 1890s, for instance, TC&I tried to use prisoners to break a miners' strike. The company's vice president noted that it was "an effective club to hold over the heads of free laborers."

Strikers and their allies affiliated with the Knights, the United Mine Workers, and the Farmers Alliance launched stealthy attacks on the prisoner stockade, sending the convicts they freed to Knoxville. When the governor insisted on shipping them back, the workers released them into the surrounding hills and countryside. Gun battles followed.

In the North, the prison labor abolition movement went viral, embracing not only workers' organizations, sympathetic rural insurgents,

144

and prisoners, but also widening circles of middle-class reformers. The newly created American Federation of Labor denounced the system as "contract slavery." It also demanded the banning of any imports from abroad made with convict labor and the exclusion from the open market of goods produced domestically by prisoners, whether in state-run or private workshops. In Chicago, the construction unions refused to work with materials made by prisoners.

By the latter part of the 19th century, state after state pushed penal servitude toward extinction. New York State, where the "industry" was born and largest, killed it by the late 1880s. The tariff of 1890 prohibited the sale of convict-made wares from abroad. Private leasing of convict labor continued in the North, but under increasingly restrictive conditions, including Federal legislation passed during the New Deal in the 1930s. By World War II, it was virtually extinct.

Convict labor even ended in Tennessee, Louisiana, Georgia, and Mississippi by the turn of the 20th century. Higher political calculations were at work in these states. Established elites were eager to break the inter-racial alliances that had formed over abolishing convict leasing by abolishing the hated system itself. Too often it ended in name only. It is a wonder to what extent white people will go to foster racism.

What replaced it was the state-run chain gang, although some Southern states like Alabama and Florida continued private leasing well into the 1920s. Inmates were set to work building roads and other infrastructure projects vital to the flourishing of a mature market economy and to the continuing process of capital accumulation. In the North, the system of "hard labor" was replaced by a system of "hard time," that numbing, brutalizing idleness where masses of people extruded from the mainstream economy are pooled into mass penal colonies. The historic link between labor, punishment, and economic development was severed, and remained so... until now.

"Now," means our second Gilded Age and its aftermath. In these years, the system of leasing out convicts to private enterprise was reborn. This was a perverse triumph for the law of supply and demand in an era infatuated with the charms of the free market. On the supply side, the U.S. currently holds captive 25% of all the prisoners on the planet: 2.3 million people. It has the highest incarceration rate in the world as well, a figure that began skyrocketing in 1980 with Ronald Reagan's election as president. Since the 1970s American industrial corporations have found it increasingly unprofitable to invest in domestic production. Instead, they have sought out the hundreds of millions of people abroad who are willing to, or can be pressed into, working for far less than American workers.

145

Consequently, American workers - disproportionately African-Americans - found themselves living in economic exile, scrabbling to get by. They began showing up in equally disproportionate counts in the country's rapidly expanding prison archipelago. It didn't take long for corporate America to come to view this as another potential foreign country, full of cheap, local and subservient labor.

What began in the 1970s as an end run around the laws prohibiting convict leasing by private interests now became an industrial sector in its own right: employing more workers than any Fortune 500 corporation and operating in 37 states. The ultimate irony is that our ancestors found convict labor obnoxious in part because it seemed to prefigure a new and more universal form of enslavement. Could its rebirth foreshadow a future ever more unnervingly like those past nightmares?

Today, we are being reassured by the president, the mainstream media, and economic experts that the Great Recession is over, that we are in "recovery" even though unemployment is still almost 6% and American businesses still refuse to invest in new technologies, clean energy projects and their subsequent job expansion. The new (2015) Texas legislature, owned and operated by big oil, is considering legislation to stop subsidizing alternate energy and abandoning state sponsored alternate energy projects altogether. Today, "recovery" means that the mega-banks are not dealing with imminent bankruptcy, the stock market has made up lost ground and keeps setting new records for growth, corporate profits have achieved record levels, and notoriously unreliable employment numbers have improved by several percent.

What accounts for this peculiarly narrow view of recovery, however, is that the general costs of doing business are falling off a cliff as the economy eats itself alive. The current celebrated recovery owes thanks to local, state, and Federal austerity budgets, the starving of the social welfare system and public services, rampant anti-union campaigns in the public and private sector, the spread of sweatshop labor, the coercion of desperate, unemployed or underemployed workers who accept lower wages, part-time work, and temporary work, as well as relinquishing healthcare benefits and a financially secure retirement. Again, the Texas legislature is also mulling cuts to teacher retirement benefits even though it maintains a $130 billion portfolio and hasn't raised retiree benefits since 1999. In sum, the contract between American labor and business is broken with the attendant loss of hope and incentive to work toward a future success.

This downward spiral of the working classes toward becoming an underclass begins to look much like the prison labor environment of decades gone by. The question really becomes: How long will the American worker

and free persons put up with this spiral before committing to outright
rebellion?

Chapter 37:   Unavoidable Conclusions

There comes a time when one has to draw conclusions that one would rather not draw. I just re-read one of my earlier books and was surprised at how many times I repeated the same theme, but with new same evidence and with the same passion. The re-read exposed several main points to be hashed over and over, most of them related to Barack Obama being our President and how our form of socialistic capitalism is being perverted and altered to undermine our democratic republic.

I've written many essays about Glass-Steagall and how it worked and why it was repealed. I stomp into dust the vagaries of *Citizens United v. Federal Election Commission* and its blank check for corporate America to have direct influence over our national governance. I took Milton Friedman and his puppets, Ronald Reagan and both Bushes to the woodshed for mindlessly following the tenets of *Supply-side Economics*, the operating system that has destroyed (and continues to do so) many economies, large and small, throughout the world. Frankly, I surprised myself at how many ways I could say the same things about the same topics.

The extreme, supersonic lurch to the right by so-called conservatives over the last 30 years, or so, has created a nation in which I did not reside until my 40th birthday. Since then (1982) we've been careening toward a precipice for failed nations at an increasing rate.

It began in earnest with the election of Ronald Reagan, our most overrated President. St. Ronald lied to us about taxes, Granada, the Soviet Union's ability to kill us, the Panama Canal, Lebanon, labor unions and the infamous arms-for-hostages deals with Iran. We can only imagine how loud the screeching for impeachment would be today if President Obama got caught in any of these shenanigans. Instead, schools, aircraft carriers, an airport and countless streets are named after "the Gipper". As it is, the gridlocked Congress, that has thwarted every imaginable benefit to the people, has threatened to go forward with impeachment (Republicans) if President Obama has the temerity to issue executive orders that actually do good things for the citizens of the United States. Is this the kind of cooperative spirit that our founders envisioned?

Bill Clinton, lied to us too, but meantime created a "pay-as-you-go" budget scheme and a *Workfare* program to put chronic welfare recipients to meaningful work. These things, among other ideas, created a $200 billion budget surplus. While doing these things he endured a first-of-its-kind negative media blitz sponsored by the political right wing, aka the Republican Party. They tried to impeach Bill Clinton, but somehow couldn't come up with sufficient "high crimes and misdemeanors" to do it, especially since his accusers were hustling their own mistresses into hiding.

It tasks me to list (again) the horrors of both Bush presidencies. It is easily found everywhere not spelled Heritage Foundation – and the like. During these most recent Republican administrations the damning of the Presidents, their administrations and anything they tried to do, were not overtly obstructed, there was no back-peddling on ideas by one party or the other and there was totally insufficient checking and balancing of the usurpation of the power to make war from the Congress by the Executive. Article 1, section 8 of the Constitution gives Congress the power to declare war, not the President. The War Powers Act is a heinous piece of legislation giving Presidents the power to send in military power whenever they see fit; it totally flies in the face of what the founders envisioned. Every President since Kennedy has used these powers to put our people in harm's way causing the deaths of millions of other people around the world. But Republicans and their donors love war, so this law will remain on our mistakes list.

Since we haven't learned from our mistakes and wrong turns since 1981, there can be but few conclusions: Money and corporate power is now our governing philosophy. Anything that causes any discomfort for businesses and their moguls is wrong and needs to be quelled or outlawed. Any political action that actually benefits anyone but the richest citizens must be attacked and ignored at all costs. Taxation is evil and we'll just have to make do with what we have...unless it's something for the military. Any new revenue streams are dangerous and must be avoided. Working classes will just have to "eat cake" since we choose not to support them in their hours of need irrespective of the circumstances – like sending their jobs to China.

Finally, the most poignant conclusion that may be drawn in today's news and political environment is that we have a brown man in the White House, and anything he does or tries to do is not going to happen. No subtleties here: Mitch McConnell and the rest of the GOP are openly defying this President's actions or ideas even when they are their own in origin. Every lie coming from right-wing talk radio, the Tea Party blabbermouths and John Boehner underscores how racially divided this country still is. We were NOT ready for Barack Obama or any other person of color to be our president even though it was the right thing to do.

Some will say I am playing the race card. Well, yes, I am, because it's the card that is on the top of the deck. It is the card that must be played. It is the obvious conclusion to political events surrounding this administration. Even good news is spun into anti-Obama hate rhetoric. It's disgusting. I'm ashamed of what is being trotted out as representing the nation. Shame on the media. Shame on the Republicans. Shame on all those who lead with the hate card instead of the "best-ideas-for-the-United-States (aka, "...*the general welfare of the people.")* card.

Chapter 38:   A Failure in the Republic

Maybe I read too much non-fiction. Maybe I care too much about how our country behaves and operates. Maybe I think it's too important to prepare for the future for the coming generations. I am filled with foreboding when I see mothers with children and pregnant women. Why? Well, I think it's because it looks like we've lost our way as a nation – a democratic republic – and our minds as a people. It seems that all the good work that was done in my lifetime is being undone – with prejudice – in a flash of time. What happened?

Barack Obama happened. Progressively thinking people hoping for the next leap forward in our society saw a charismatic leader, a dreamer, a thinker, a good man and someone who they felt wanted them to succeed. Around 5 million more people voted for Mr. Obama to be their President instead of his Republican opponents *twice.* But it seems that the moment his hand came off the Bible after he pledged to defend the Constitution against all enemies, foreign and domestic, *his* enemies dropped their façade of decorum and went for his and the national throat. No other statement told us what the intent of the "opposition" was more than Mitch McConnell's sanguine statement about making Barack Obama a one-term President. In a delicious twist, it was the first of countless mistakes made by the Republicans.

Sadly, though, the process by which our naïve, new President used to develop the Affordable Care Act, failed to accept the peoples' desire for universal health care: the public option. Polls showed that over 60% of our fellow citizens wanted this. They didn't get it because President Obama thought he could reconcile differences and compromise with the Republican minorities in both houses of Congress. He failed to recognize his enemy. There was going to be NO compromising by the Republicans with this President . Even though the ACA was basically a Republican/conservative idea and plan, one that worked for governor Mitt Romney in Massachusetts, these Republicans weren't having any of it. "Obamacare" became the word of derision, passionate dislike, aka, hatred, and still resonates today and was a major issue in 2014's mid-term primary election season as the reason for people to vote Republican. Can this hypocrisy by Republicans be anything else but dog-whistle racism?

Never mind that it was a GOP plan. Never mind that it IS WORKING for the benefit of the poor and the unemployed, the ACA is anathema to Republican politics. Why? The obvious answer is because a non-white Democrat President put it forth in the face of overwhelming health care insurance lobbying - $1.4 million per day. Republicans decided that they just wouldn't accept a victory for the people of our country because it was introduced by Barack Obama. At least that was the front story. The real story is probably about how the insurance and drug industries could potentially lose money. They haven't.

The fight continues for the implementation of the ACA with Republican governors refusing free Federal money for increased Medicaid benefits that support the ACA. These governors are willingly hurting their own constituents because of *Obamacare*. Thousands in those Republican-controlled states will die unnecessarily due to lack of Medicaid funds. Yet people still vote for Republicans.

But it really isn't about Obamacare, is it? No, it's wider and deeper than that. While we subsidize corporate farms and oil companies with our taxes, we pay for it by cutting SNAP and welfare benefits for our most needy citizens as we also keep increasing our military/security budgets. By the way, ironically, many of our military veterans depend on SNAP benefits to help raise their families. While Republicans keep telling us how they want government off our backs, they impose their ideological agenda on women's reproductive rights and restrictions on voting rights, our most sacred freedom. Republicans can't even find good news from a returning POW without dumping on the President for doing the right thing. The amazing hypocrisy of Republicans exhibited in the case of Sgt. Bowe Bergdahl is breathtaking in its craven openness; it's like they don't care if they look like idiots, just so they can get in another shot at embarrassing this President. A military tribunal eventually decided he deserted his post, but he was awarded the opportunity for a fair hearing on U.S. soil because of the President's dealing to get him back home.

Perhaps the country wasn't really ready for a man of color to be President. Perhaps the roots of slavery and its associated racial bigotry run too deep to be killed outright by a mere 150 years, countless battles between races, lynchings, segregation, Jim Crow and all the rest of the horrors since the Civil War. Since slavery and the associated racial separations predate our nation's founding, perhaps we are not yet ready to make the intellectual leap out from under the slimy rock of antebellum primitiveness and racism.

Living, as I do, in Texas, I see and hear first-hand the dog whistle racist verbiage, the slavish adherence to Fox News hate and propaganda and the insistence that anything "liberal" is evil. Texas Republican politicians exhibit almost no grace, civility or intelligence, thus justifying the laughing stock title bestowed on them by the rest of the country at large. The Tea Party in Texas keeps producing a constant validation of their intellectual dwarfism, outright hatred for anything not them and a remarkable ignorance of truth and fact, especially toward the Constitution which they hold most dear. These traits are symptomatic of our nation's current confusion about its direction socially and economically.

The economic ideas of Milton Friedman thrive in Texas even though they've been shown to produce social malaise and corruption beyond description everywhere they've been tried and implemented. In Kansas, the implementation of deep and broad tax cuts consistent with this kind of "supply-side" economics has produced a functional and financial disaster. So, naturally, in 2014 the people of Kansas who voted re-elected all their Republican representation that caused this mess. The preoccupation with Libertarianism associated with this philosophy is exploited by such unsavory characters as the Koch brothers of Kansas. These people support hundreds of right wing groups all of whom are trying to undo the New Deal and harm the social services for those not as fortunate as themselves. Billionaires must control the working people in order to become....billionaires. The Kochs recently pledged to spend nearly a billion dollars on the 2016 Presidential election...for a Republican, of course.

As with most of the nation, Thirty percent of eligible Texas voters are un-registered. In anything but full national elections, less than 50% of *registered* voters do their duty and vote. This means that the Republicans think they're right, because Republicans, for all their misguided ideologies, vote. It also demonstrates that negative campaigning and perverted elections cause a cynicism in the electorate that causes it to mostly stay home on election day. In other words, the GOP political strategies are working at the expense of the guaranteed freedoms in the Constitution.

If the majority of citizens don't vote, they deserve what they get in political representation. If we don't think, we remain a backward, racially driven people. If we remain selfish, self-centered, self-indulgent and self-righteous, we will never escape the shackles of our own historical shame. In the 2014 mid-term elections, over 60% of eligible voters stayed home and allowed the Republicans to have a "victory" across the board. The percent of people actually voting for a Republican anywhere was around 17% of those eligible; hardly the stuff of a working democracy.

Chapter 39:   Capitalists Unchained

It's hard to escape the racial dog whistles coming from various segments of our society. I spoke with an "enlightened" friend the other day who told me that in his life's adventures he has seen and heard all the things that came with the Jim Crow era in the South. There are those who will not enter a restroom if a person of color is in there, will not sit next to "one of those people" on public transportation and will not drink from the same water fountain, etc., etc.

I went back to Ohio for my father's funeral in 1977 and heard the same sort of racial slurring I heard a decade earlier from people my age and younger. I had just spent the last decade in California learning to accept people of all shades, religions and interests. Some things in some places just didn't change. More recently, I've had occasion to talk to old friends from my home state and the "stuff" about our President, and the dog whistle comments about everyone else who doesn't look like them was like fingernails on a blackboard to me. I guess some folks have tried to alter their views, but I think there is an ingrained bias that people learned from their earliest days in "Lilywhiteville", USA.

What does this have to do with capitalists and capitalism? We have to go back to the 15th century when Europeans discovered sugar and the traders and entrepreneurs of the time decided to make it a Western industry (See Chapter 1). Muslim caliphs had already taken sugar to the ceremonial levels in their cultures, but Europeans saw ways to make profits. How right they were.

The August, 2013 issue of *National Geographic* includes a brief history of the sugar industry, and the most significant part of it is that slavery was necessary to make the profits. Since the work of growing, harvesting and processing sugar cane is brutally difficult, only forced labor could do the job consistently and, coincidentally, for maximum profit, thus linking sugar and modern capitalism forever.

Columbus planted the New World's first sugar cane on Hispaniola and the Caribbean sugar industry was born. Feckless West African leaders of the time (15th-16th century and beyond) were eager to sell their miscreants, slaves and captive enemies to the European slave traders and the race was on toward the sugar boom. Of course, there were all sorts of slave rebellions in the New World and the Europeans had to quell them or perish.

Slavery, paradoxically, was not born of racism, but the economic necessity of no cost, minimum maintenance, forced labor turned those who were slaves into lesser beings in the minds of those who developed the sugar

– and finally the cotton industry in North America – empires for the rich. That said, it isn't a large leap to see why people of African origin in the Western hemisphere, or at least in predominantly white-controlled countries there, experience an inherent prejudice and racial bias against them: Even today black people are still considered less than fully human in some parts of the southeastern United States and elsewhere to where that ingrained bias was transferred. Racial resentment in the Northern U.S. is also understandable since even before the Civil War, blacks seeking freedom from slavery took jobs for much less pay than whites would or could work for. It looks like capitalistic economics is restrictive of overcoming such bias.

The prejudice toward black people took an odd turn for me when I was in college. I asked a classmate who was from Africa (Kenya, I think) if he felt comfortable around black Americans. He looked at me askance and said that he was from royalty and would never associate with the descendants of slaves. I was still growing up back then.

Even the great documents of the United States illustrate a double standard with the *all men are created equal* phraseology offset by the 3/5 of a person language still present in the Constitution. Why hasn't that been expunged from it? The 13th, 14th and 15th Amendments had plenty of room for that language.

Recently, a Russian historian sagely commented that Karl Marx didn't know much about communism, but knew a great deal about capitalism. In *Das Kapital* Marx described the scenario of capitalism that we see happening in Western civilization today. How did he know? Well, he understood that the root of capitalism is greed, cheap labor, or no labor cost whatsoever. Slavery and robotics are, therefore, the two most important aspects of capitalism even though it takes highly skilled labor to build the robots. That labor, unlike slavery, becomes just another part of the cost of doing business and robots last longer and don't demand benefits. By lowering or eliminating labor costs, profits increase. That is the basic mantra of capitalism.

In John Helyar's excellent book about Major League Baseball, *Lords of the Realm* the struggle of the capitalist owners of the teams to maximize profits at all costs dominates the narrative. At an owner's meeting, Ted Turner, then the owner of the Atlanta Braves commented on his colleagues' attempts to restrict court-ordered free agency that put salary caps on their payrolls by saying, "Gentlemen, we have the only legal monopoly in the country and we're (screwing) it up." Such is the mindset of the capitalist who has much and always wants more.

In Gene Klein's (late owner of the San Diego Chargers) book, *First and a Billion*, he describes an NFL owners meeting where the owner of the Atlanta Falcons (What is it about Atlanta?) proposed increasing revenues by lining the fields with criss-crossed field stripes. Why? Because he said that that would give him double the 50-yard line seats when the teams played one half going in one direction and the other half in the other direction. Since he charged premium prices for 50-yard line seats, he'd increase his revenue. You can't make this stuff up, or as Klein put it, "It proves that you don't have to be smart to be rich.

So, from the sublime (racism) to the ridiculous (professional sports ownership) we come to a crucial time in our preoccupation with money, government and human interaction. President Obama's presence and one-time popularity have opened the can of latent prejudice (Tea Party) while giving previously hopeless people hope and inspiration to achieve and grow individually and as a people. Will capitalism join this discussion, or will it continue to destroy public education, outsource jobs, expertise and the middle class in order to meet the quarterly report expectations of the stockholders?

Will capitalism remain chained to the limited philosophy of *profit at all costs*, or will it realize that the long-term existence and quality of life of a nation is more important than 3-month cost sheet segments? Will capitalism liberate itself from its own self-imposed slavery of mindless searches for profit at the expense of people and the Earth it so wantonly exploits? What happens when we run out of those things to exploit? Who will be the slave and who will be the master then?

Taken to its end game, those who advocate the strategies, i.e., Republicans, are signing their own terminations, because in doing so, the end game for capitalism is *plutocracy*. The very fact that a mere 400 American capitalists control more wealth than 60% of the rest of their countrymen shows how the end game will look in the near future: A plutocracy run by oligarch billionaires who want it ALL.

Chapter 40:   The Accurate Obama

This essay is in no way meant to define the Obama administration as anything close to perfect. Instead, it is intended to put accomplishments in perspective with facts instead of political hyperbole so often used by pundits, writers and people who generally don't have a clue about anything except their own biases and agendas.

Let's begin with the Bush "legacy" from 2001 to 2008. The components of these years have been mentioned previously, but the summary includes unfunded wars, unfunded spending explosions in national security and military hardware, torture, the unfunded mandates of the *No Child Left Behind* disaster, massive tax cuts for the most affluent Americans, massive taxpayer money giveaways to the drug, oil and agriculture industries and the deregulation of banking and Wall Street practices that generated the tsunami of greed that nearly collapsed the world's economy. Try as one might, there is little good to find that serves the peoples' welfare. I can find none.

So, in 2008, the voters of the United States elected a brown man to be President. Almost immediately, the complaints, invectives and lies started emanating from the Republicans left standing. They told us how the recession was made worse by Obama's policies even while the economic numbers did a sharp reversal from their downward trends after he took office. There are several key statistics that prove how craven the lies from the Republican Party are:

- The stock market as almost tripled from just over 7,000 (DJI) to over 17,000 at this writing in late 2014.

- The country has stopped hemorrhaging jobs overseas and as of November, 2014 showed 56 straight months of job growth. It should be noted here that during the Bush years, almost 6 MILLION jobs were allowed to flow to China, India and Latin America while corporate vultures like Bain Capital (Mitt Romney's organization) closed over 50,000 factories and sold off the hardware to foreign businesses. The buildings housing those business are being dismantled and sold to China as scrap.

- The national deficit has been cut in half. Remember when Dick Cheney said that deficits don't matter while he was helping to spend our nation into oblivion, but when it came to election season, suddenly deficits were a big deal.

- Unemployment has been halved, though the average wage has risen only slightly by the end of 2014, for the first time in 20 years. The new job quality and pay are significantly lower than before Bush.

- A stimulus package to bail out failing banks and the auto industry were begun under Bush – as the Republicans panicked again – but was insufficient to kick the recovery into high gear. The Obama administration failed to listen to real economists and only provided about half of the money needed to create a rapid recovery. In all fairness to the President, the banks sucked up a few trillion dollars to pay off their executives for doing such a fine job.

- The drop in economic growth in 2008 was 9%, the most since the Great Depression. Since 2009, economic growth has *improved* by several percent every year.

- The keepers of the flame of small government added over 1 million employees to the Federal payroll, while the Obama administration cut over 300,000 Federal jobs by 2012.

- The Bush administration spent over $5 TRILLION of borrowed money on the wars and the giveaways, while the Obama administrations will see its spending increases amount to a "mere" $1.4 trillion by 2016 – barring any emergencies...like another war.

- The Bush administration was too busy exploiting "political capital" in Iraq to look after the health of the American people. Instead, it created Medicare Part D which prevented the Medicare services from negotiating best prices of services and drugs....to say nothing of the infamous "doughnut hole" for the people least able to pay for thousands of dollars of drugs at inflated, non-regulated prices. The Obama administration embraced a Heritage Foundation idea and, with the "help" of the Congressional Democrats, created the Affordable Health Care Act, aka, *Obamacare.* It worked in Massachusetts for then governor Mitt Romney and was a Republican think-tank plan. Since the 2010 implementation of this law (The Republicans offered NO input for its creation, development and implementation even though it was their idea in the first place. Even the Heritage Foundation itself distanced itself from the ACA when the brown guy took it on.) Even with a very bad start, the ACA has allowed over 10 million previously uninsured people to get affordable health care. The constant fight from Republicans is mentioned in several other chapters, but the bottom line is that *Obamacare* worked and costs have come down, no matter how often some wild-eyed junior Senator (Cruz) tells us it is an illegal law.

The caveat here is that never has such strident opposition been applied to a President for everything and anything he tried to do to improve the situation in the nation. One would think that we'd have learned our lessons from the 1920s, but no... Our backward-thinking "conservatives" had to play their political game against the brown guy. Even during FDR's *New Deal* machinations, when he indeed played fast and loose with the government's operations and the Constitutional strictures of the executive branch, did the Republicans issue such mindless rage against a President. Why else would Republicans reject their own ideas? Why else would they openly commit to obstructionism? The answer is because it's about racism lying under the surface and professional politicians forgetting that governance is their job, not the promotion of negative agendas or being reelected at all costs – including the overall health and strength of the nation. The Republican abandonment of governance is craven, unholy and will create a schism among the people for decades to come no matter who gets elected in the future.

The anti-Obama hatred is especially virulent in the South. The right-wing extremists there almost never use the "N" word, but the code words are fantastic in their imaginative use as substitutes. I never imagined this sort of behavior in the last half of my life. My naiveté has been shattered and turned into deep cynicism toward my "fellow Americans", many of whom think that secession from that "liberal, Yankee" country is a good thing. It told me how deep the remaining scars are from the Civil War and the horrors of *Reconstruction* – that time when radical politicians once again failed democracy and allowed the lesser angels of human nature to stitch the country back together. That stitching is soaked in blood and stupidity, greed and ignominy and soils the dignity of the 700,000 Americans who died while under the misguided illusion that we should be one country working together for the betterment of mankind.

Maybe Lincoln was wrong. Maybe the South should have been let go in 1860. History tells us that the South felt as if they were being subjugated by a foreign country while they built an entire economy on subjugated human beings. Yes, from a moral standpoint, Lincoln did the right thing by "freeing" the slaves, but it required three Constitutional Amendments to do it, all of which were vigorously contested by the Congress. The resentment of having slavery abolished is still very much alive today in the South. Even Ted Cruz, the most disturbing creature to be elected to Congress since Michelle Bachmann, said in an interview that there are those that think that without the abolition of slavery, Barack Obama wouldn't be President and that he and others thought that was a good thing. Even more astounding was Justice Clarence Thomas's defense of slavery as part of the original Constitution. Thomas is just another gift from the Bush family that keeps on giving. What makes this commentary even more absurd is that Justice Thomas is black and his spouse is white and a leading activist in the Tea Party which is *profoundly* racist.

You can't make this stuff up.

Chapter 41:   Nothing to Offer

In 1955 Robert Ruark wrote his Pulitzer Prize winning novel, *Something of Value*. A movie by the same name starring Rock Hudson disturbed many, as did the book, because it addressed the Mau Mau uprisings in Kenya in the early 1950s. But on the first page Ruark included a Basuto proverb: *"If a man does away with his traditional way of living and throws away his good customs, he had better first make certain that he has something of value to replace them."* I have written previously about Mitt Romney's *corporate vulturism* and how the Bain Capitals of our country stripped away traditional ways of living and threw away good customs without replacing them with anything of value. Since 2001 and the great de-regulation, for example, over 50,000 U.S. factories have closed and their equipment sold and their jobs sent to other countries. THAT is what corporate vulturism does. It does NOT create jobs in the United States.

After the Democratic Convention in Charlotte in 2012 it became clearer than ever wherein the values of this country lie, at least among those who would presume to govern our great nation. It wasn't so much the passionate speeches by politicians, but more those by the regular citizens from whom values and customs have been stripped and who want something of value to replace them. More clear indication of this thesis came to mind when I read and heard so-called conservative pundits and the Republican candidates continue to attack Barack Obama about anything and everything that THEY were responsible for.

They handed a nation to him on the brink of collapse, complain about him not fixing their mistakes fast enough and now want to replace him with someone who advocates repeating the behaviors that caused our problems in the first place. That illogic boggles the mind until you realize who and what are promoting these lines. A leading conservative pundit, Charles Krauthammer, thinks President Obama is insincere when he says he loves his country and the people in it. How does he know? The Tea Party pokes fun at how the delegates looked at the Democratic convention. Did they ever see how stupid they look in their 3-corner hats with dangling tea bags?

The Republicans have no strategy except to attack Barack Obama. They have thwarted everything he suggests including their own ideas. They have no justification for their obstructionism except that they are not in power to continue the dismantling of not only the middle class, but anyone else's bones they can pick. Of course, the race thing hangs on their every word. Indeed, virtually all but a very few of Obama's most passionate critics are white. I am a critic of Obama's and I'm white, but I don't use race as a reason for my critiques. My criticism of this President is that he so foolishly kept thinking that the Republicans actually intended to be his partners in governance. They are not.

It is a disgrace to those who fought and died for our freedoms that veterans were never mentioned by the Republican candidate for President at their presidential convention. It is a disgrace to everyone in this country that their people stood there and lied through their teeth about almost everything and blamed the President for their own irresponsibility. It is a disgrace to the process of electing representation that these people have such little regard for those who made them rich and indeed spit at them by telling them that it's their fault they are poor.

These people have to attack women's rights by forcing government intervention upon them while saying they are against government interference in peoples' lives. One is forced to ask if the only Republican value is self-interest, or just hypocrisy by itself.

If the way to govern a nation is to ignore the needs of the majority of its citizens and fill the pockets of the wealthiest to overflowing while giving nothing of value back to that nation, then the oppressed of that nation will revolt just as the people of East Africa revolted to end the mindless and heedless exploitation by the European colonists.

The people of the United States deserve something of value from those who would govern them, not the denial of opportunity by those who won't.

Part V

Guns and the American Way

A Well regulated Militia, being necessary to the security of a free State, the right of the people to keep and bear Arms, shall not be infringed.

- The Second Amendment to the U.S. Constitution

The gun lobby's interpretation of the Second Amendment is one of the greatest pieces of fraud – I repeat the word fraud – on the American people by special interest groups that I have ever seen in my lifetime. The real purpose of the Second Amendment was to ensure that state armies – the militia – would be maintained for the defense of the state. The very language of the Second Amendment refutes any argument that it was intended to guarantee every citizen an unfettered right to any kind of weapon he or she desires.

- Warren Burger, Chief Justice of the U.S. Supreme Court

Chapter 42:   Is it Our Right to Be Slaughtered?

Senseless episodes of shooting and killing innocent people keep occurring. Sometimes it's a panicked policeman, but mostly it's a shooting by a citizen against another citizen. The deranged, lone wolf shooters are becoming increasingly adept and successful at achieving their goal of slaughtering as many people as possible. It seems that schools and children are the "best" targets because they are vulnerable and trapped in a classroom.

This may or may not be due in part to interactive training using sophisticated shoot 'em up video games. On the other hand, much credit certainly goes to the easy availability of high-powered handguns and rifles with oversized magazines and unlimited access to ammunition. Additionally, more than passing credit also goes to various State Legislatures for their determined work to loosen gun laws and generally try to circumvent any Federal control or oversight of gun sales. However, it is without question that the greatest contribution to the tragedies at Columbine / Virginia Tech /Aurora /Newtown, etc. is made by both chambers of Congress' complete intimidation by the NRA that results in not a whisper of possibility of even beginning discussions about *trying to maybe* take steps to address the problem of repetitive human shooting galleries. In the 2014 mid-term elections, though, several states voted for mandatory background checks even though the majority of voters were "conservative". Maybe they realized that the word *conservative* meant to preserve something – like peoples' lives.

The Founding Fathers gave us the Second Amendment that guarantees the right to own and bear arms. This was a grand idea at inception: Young America had no standing army to defend its borders or repel attacks. Every citizen was expected to be ready at a moment's notice to take up arms and go into battle to defend America. Nowadays there are local police and sheriffs as well as the National Guard for domestic troubles, with the Army, Navy, Air Force and Marines constantly available to handle foreign battles. They are our well regulated militias.

The need for the average American to own firearms to form a militia has rendered the Second Amendment "quaint" to quote a previous statement on personal rights. In the 18th century, most people owned a gun to hunt food and defend against predators like wolves. Gun technology in the 18th century was limited to the muzzle-loaded musket that took a minute to load and fire a single shot.It would be a rare exception when someone had more that the one gun – a rifle or shotgun. Today we are economically and legally able to buy a huge variety of weaponry including military grade assault weapons and high capacity magazines for most pistols and rifles. These things take seconds to load and reload and can fire dozens of rounds per minute. It is often the case where the most expensive piece of hardware in a person's home is their gun.

Since there is no outcry from the public that is heard by the Congress, there is no motivation for them to act, and so the slaughter will continue. The "make my day" and "stand my ground" laws brought to the legislatures around the country from right-wing groups like ALEC enable the politicians to accept the gun lobby as their partner instead of their constituents. Apparently it is our right, as guaranteed by the Constitution that anywhere in America and without warning someone will act on the notion to kill everyone in sight. It's a big country with lots of people so the odds *you* will be present for one of these episodes is very small. So instead of banning assault weapons and high capacity magazines or closing gun show loopholes we merely shake our heads, mourn the dead and then shrug, and celebrate that the Second Amendment gives us the right to be slaughtered. It's what the Founding Fathers intended... right?

Chapter 43: The Second Amendment: Beginnings and Present

Recent mass killings of our citizens by other citizens who enjoy the right to keep and bear arms kicked off many debates and calls for more laws, regulations and restrictions on the weapons used in some of these incidents. Advocates of Second Amendment rights divide themselves into the camps of fear of government tyranny and a more rational position of examining the legal and necessary aspects of firearms control. Note that the latter group does not advocate the confiscation of legally owned firearms. Controls like gun owner registration, magazine limits and automatic, military type weapons do not infringe on anybody's rights to bear arms. Anything else becomes either political agenda or fear-mongering. The fact that there are over 300 million guns legally owned in this country speaks volumes about our national confidence and trust in one another.

History documents interpretive evolution of the Second Amendment. A recent analysis in *Truthout* written by Thom Hartmann suggests that this idea of bearing arms is unique to the United States in that its original intent was to preserve slavery and to prevent slave rebellions. Since there was no standing army and the economic backbone of southern colonies (soon to become states) was slavery, pre-revolutionary "slave patrols" and militias were necessary to preserve the peace and economics of the times.

This was, of course, the root for the words that became the final version. *But (Patrick)Henry, (George)Mason and others wanted southern states to preserve their slave-patrol militias independent of the federal government. So Madison changed the word "country" to the word "state," and redrafted the Second Amendment into today's form:*

*"A well regulated Militia, being necessary to the security of a free **State** [emphasis mine], the right of the people to keep and bear Arms, shall not be infringed."*(Hartmann)

For southern colonies to accept the Constitution and become part of the United States of America, this bow to slavery's preservationists had to be incorporated as a compromise, from which we still suffer consequences. Some analysts, sociologists, and ideologues think 'modern' attitudes toward gun possession are rooted in this early fear of rebellious black men being armed. It is almost as if white people fear that an angry black mob will arise and slay them in retribution for prejudice, hate and slavery. Such fears had some justification in the 1960s and '70s, when militant black groups formed to resist suppression by white society. It seems that our militarized police departments are tickling the tail of this black dragon today with incidents of oppression of the black communities, especially when guns are involved. The so-called *Stand Your Ground* laws invented by the Koch brothers' funded ALEC organization have fueled more overt use of firearms by "normal" citizens in "defense" of their person.

Since the end of the Civil War, the interpretation of the Second Amendment has been addressed by the Supreme and lower courts regarding who has the continuing rights to carry what kind of weapon to wherever they want including marching in ad hoc military parades with arms. Note that our state militias (the "well-regulated militia"), now known as the National Guard, no longer search slave quarters for signs of rebellion and insurrection; the state guard units are at the command of the state governors for use in emergencies affecting the people of that state to supplement law enforcement and maintaining order. We have seen racial issues require Federal troops to enforce segregation laws because racist governors (Faubus of Arkansas and Wallace of Alabama) chose not to deploy guardsmen to allow black students to attend previously all-white schools. We are now seeing fearful governors of Texas and Arizona using National Guard troops to police the border with Mexico for reasons known only to their prejudices. Since most "illegal" entrants into our country are unarmed, it is curious to the author why we must present an armed, militant face to our neighbors.

Even older historical legal decisions and factors define America's existing relationships with guns. Spanish conquistadors used them to intimidate Native Americans while gaining footholds on this continent. Over the next 350 years, theirs and descendants of other Europeans used more guns of ever-higher technology, assuring conquest of the indigenous peoples and making North America an extension of Europe.

With economically driven exploitation of the New World, cheap labor became necessary, and nothing was cheaper than slavery. Immigrants from Great Britain, Holland, and France created massive slave trades in the Caribbean and the Americas by the involuntary displacement of Africans. These African countries also sold their own miscreants into indentured servitude to rid themselves of the expense of jailing them for petty crimes and misdemeanors. These human beings required oversight to keep them working and prevent them from rebelling against their bondage. Rebellions against their bondage occurred by the hundreds, of course, so the gun was used when the whip could not maintain control. Economic absolutism is a powerful motive for the use of powerful weapons. See Part VI for summations of this topic.

Westward-bound settlers before, during, and after the Civil War used the gun for gaining food and defense against resentful Native Americans. The concepts of stealing land and breaking treaties required the necessary enforcement of rebellion. The repeating gun became part of our national culture and was the single most important instrument in securing the continent for today's society. States such as Wyoming, Montana, and Alaska still promote a pioneer spirit. Coincidentally, they also lead the nation in gun ownership per citizen and the number of gun-related deaths per 100,000 residents. (*Mother Jones*)

History is a great teacher. It can trace events like pearls on a string. Demand from slave owners to maintain a militia to prevent slave rebellions morphed into ghastly social exercises having unintended consequences based on historical misconceptions. Today almost anybody can own guns, and unhinged individuals have the capability to create mayhem with previously unparalleled technological efficiency. The lengths to which people go to address their fears in this modern world of comfort and plenty act as a mirror into their souls and their situational awareness. It also illustrates how our primitive notions about competition and self-preservation are so close to the surface of our actual behavior.

Historical realities of the origin of the Second Amendment conflict with the spirit underlying legislative attempts to regulate today's gun culture. We no longer have slaves, per se. We now have a well-regulated militia along with social traditions and laws intended to prevent mayhem. When Barack Obama was elected in 2008, gun sales skyrocketed and racist militias increased many times. When he was re-elected in 2012, gun sales skyrocketed and racist militias multiplied. These data are the loudest dog whistles of all regarding the reasons for how racism influences our pathological attraction to guns.

Why, then, do we need so much individual firepower? Those who fear the tyranny of government surely understand that it is the voting public who elects that government. If the government is so corrupt such that it DOES become tyrannical and "We the People" do nothing about it, we have only ourselves to blame. Guns have nothing to do with this process. Maybe it's not the fear of tyrannical government, but the fear by white people of black and brown people trying to take over the country.....or something.

168

Chapter 44:   The Tyranny of Fear

For the several months since the dreadful tragedy in Newtown, CT I resisted writing any formal pieces discussing the issue of guns. Then, a deranged and unhinged former FBI agent e-mailed me an article written by the editor of something called *The Natural News*, Mike Adams. It was so shocking and disturbing that I had to say a few words for those sane people left in the world.

The great G.B. Trudeau published a flashback strip in the morning's paper this same day highlighting the title of this article. The radio talk show host is interviewing and being interviewed. The question asked of the host by the guest is, "What are you like as a people?" The host answers by saying that two sets of facts define our current state of mind. In 2001, 19 people with box cutters crashed airplanes into two office buildings and the Pentagon killing 3,000 people. Our response was invading two countries that killed hundreds of thousands of innocent bystanders, one of which had nothing to do with the attacks, and creating an entire bureaucracy (Homeland Security) at the cost of a few trillion dollars. During the next seven years, the commentary continues, over 270,000 Americans were killed by domestic gunfire for one reason or another. Our response to that was to weaken our gun laws. The kicker is that the interviewee is a "little green man" from another planet who says he can't comprehend the answer.

The answer to both these inputs is fear: mind-numbing, logic crushing, civilization destroying fear. Here's the opening sentence from Mr. Adams' bizarre piece of over 5, single-spaced pages of overbearing fear exposition:

> *By screaming about how they wish to destroy the Second Amendment and disarm the American people, collectivist* (I think this is code for "socialist) *media gun grabbers and "school shooting doomsday" fear mongers* (People being shot at should be afraid, shouldn't they?) *have managed to do exactly what they hoped NOT to do: They have pushed **millions of AR-15s and hundreds of millions of rounds of ammunition** into the private hands of Americans.*

So, if I understand this correctly, it's the people afraid of being shot, or having their children shot by AR-15s that are forcing "millions" of other Americans to go out and lay down $1,000 or so for an assault rifle. Does this mean that those "gun grabbers" want the highly armed public to defend themselves against random shootings by equally armed madmen? Who is afraid here?

Adams goes on to rail against the "gun grabbers" who are out to destroy the Second Amendment and thus antagonize the gun rights folks who will not give up their guns for any reason. This guy continues to describe a scenario where the country will erupt into a shooting war if Obama and Biden "overplay their hands" and try to confiscate assault rifles. The term "gun grabber" is used about a dozen times in 2,000 words, so Adams' fear is evident: He cannot imagine standing before his fellow neighbor unarmed. How do people like this claim to be real citizens?

The facts are that nobody is calling for a confiscation of firearms; not the government, no rational citizens, not the "liberal media", nobody. Yet here these gun rights folks are shaking in their boots about losing their precious security toys. In fairness, Adams lists several of the proposals the Obama administration suggests as acceptable, but warns that the AK magazines will be very hard to find. Gosh. Everyone should find a box of 30 round AK magazines under the tree every year.

One of the mantras of the gun rights people is that the citizens have the right to defend themselves against government tyranny. I admit that history shows us that the U.S. government has acted tyrannically against labor unrest, the "Hoovervilles" in Washington, D.C. and other isolated incidents such as herding Japanese-Americans into concentration camps during WW II. But the causes and reactions for these actions have been solved by the necessary LAW changes in order to prevent unnecessary bloodshed between our own people. I think that is included in the phrase in the Constitution that deals with the "general welfare" of the citizens. It is also about governing.

The real tyranny is the tyranny of fear in the hearts and minds of the fearful. Those who think an inanimate object designed to kill other human beings, foreign or domestic, are their security blankets are missing the whole point of living in a free society. Why is it, for these people that the gun has to be the center of their security? What are they afraid of? They are much more likely to lose their jobs, their homes and their health insurance to the club of laughing billionaires than to actually have to draw a bead on a bad guy. Shouldn't the ballot box be the better weapon to eliminate fear, rather than the gun being the tool of terminal justice?

It should be noted that in 2002, the Bush administration fostered a law that protected gun manufacturers from being held liable for any misdeeds the owners of such guns perpetrated. Families of victims still try to sue gun makers for the deaths of their loved ones, but the ruling by a California Federal judge that no connection between the gun maker and the shooter is viable still stands.

Finally, I am not advocating gun confiscation, nor doing anything with the Second Amendment, except maybe clarifying its meaning. Either one of these actions would spark another civil war – as Mike Adams suggests. The fear of the gun worshiper in the United States is so uncontrollable that they would cast their fate with the thing they trust the most: their guns. Their fear is their real tyranny because it consumes them, destroys their ability to reason and makes violence and killing their top priority.

Fear will not make this country a better place in which to live nor is it a true representation of the "home of the brave".

Chapter 45:   Who Are We?

Americans assume to be the best and most sophisticated humans on Earth, yet we mindlessly commit one shooting tragedy after another by yet other mindless individuals who mindfully manage to obtain thousands of dollars worth of firearms, SWAT equipment and ammunition. Some of us who look at these continuing events from a longer view are left to ponder who and what we are as a nation. Of course, there are those who pay no attention at all, and just keep yelling about our Second Amendment rights being violated. Is anyone coming forth to voice, with equal stridency that a victim's right to live as been *permanently* violated by being killed by a deranged gunman?

After WW I we contracted and reduced our military and militarism to the point of absurdity compared to the rest of the world. We also couched our national philosophy as strict isolationist: "No more foreign wars," we said. When the Weimar Republic was overthrown by the National Socialists and Japan insisted on taking the mineral resources from China, we were not at all prepared (nor did we care to) to police the world as we do today. We had a minimal military budget until the winds of war blew its waves upon our shores and those of our best trading partners.

Before Harry Truman was picked as FDR's last vice-President, he chaired a Senate committee that rooted out corporate corruption and bureaucratic bungling while we were actually fighting WW II. Even during wartime our corporate moguls were finding ways to cut corners and fiddle contracts to increase profits. It didn't matter to them that they were sending inadequate, shoddy and faulty equipment to our fighting men overseas. Truman sorted them out and production volume and quality soared sufficiently that we overwhelmed our enemies and created the greatest industrial base in the history of the world. Everybody made lots of money the right way.

The prophetic warnings from President Dwight D. Eisenhower, the major hero of the European Theater in WW II, about the military-industrial complex becoming the political force in the United States were insufficient to quell the mindless militarism of the Cold War and the subsequent fears we live with today.

Our politics have become exactly what Ike warned us about and FDR said we weren't. We are in fact a nation of fear. The people own 300 million guns in the home of the brave. I was teaching 8th grade science on April 20, 1999 when two spoiled, enabled and deranged teens shot up Columbine High School killing 15 people, including themselves. By killing themselves after their heinous crimes they illustrated how fear and hate morph into cowardice. Since then, we have recorded over 1 million deaths by gun in our country from all causes. When Barack Obama was elected President, gun and ammunition sales stripped the shelves of every store that sold them. Why? Fear, that's why. People were told that somebody was coming after their guns and they believed them. They also listened to the echoes of our past slavery times and the fears of an uprising by the oppressed. Now, black

172

and brown people represent those cloying fears from our great national bleeding, the 19th century and the Civil War.

Any person smart enough to sip coffee knows that nobody is coming after anyone's guns. They might get shot, after all, from a fearful gun owner. I do not enter into arguments with others about the 2nd Amendment and its perverted interpretations because it will have no positive outcome. Fear undermines logic every time. True believers can look at facts and ignore them for the sake of their fears.

Everyone should do what they want. After all, guns and weapons of war are about all we make in this country. Buying guns is good for business and puts people to work. That's who we are, isn't it?

Part VI

Resetting the American Idea

Behind the ostensible government sits enthroned an invisible government owing no allegiance and acknowledging no responsibility to the people. To destroy this invisible government, to befoul the unholy alliance between corrupt business and corrupt politicians is the first task of the statesmanship of the day.

- Theodore Roosevelt, 19 April 1906

Liberalism is inherently nonpartisan. It means freedom for all, or it means nothing at all. It maintains that everyone benefits from everyone's freedom and that all are diminished whenever one individual or group is not free.

This precept can contort liberals into the uncomfortable posture known as tolerance. Some think that tolerance means treating all opinions as equally deserving of respect, but the point of liberalism is not that views are equally valid. It is that society has no reliable way to evaluate opinions other than to let everybody freely express and criticize them – and, if they gain sufficient support, to try them out.

174

· Timothy Ferris

.

Chapter 46:   Understanding Ourselves

The human condition is much less grand than people are led to believe by civic leaders, churches, businessmen and educators. They ignore our past, our frailties and our chronic self-absorption. Who can blame them; it's how they lead, exploit, teach and promote their brands. We have evolved biologically, as a species, rather slowly compared to our technological and social advances, yet a visible history of the steps along the way are evident when we examine social structure, community and economics around the world. Neolithic communities persist in remote jungles, Iron Age societies exist in areas of Earth where no or little resource exploitation is possible; these people are mostly left alone by the maw of modern business and industry and allowed to practice the lifestyles with which they are comfortable and successful. Rituals and rites of passage for societies range from the brutal (in modern, Western terms) to the quaint to the exotic.

Herein lies the conundrum of modern man. The species is confounded by its own logic of worshipping life and reproduction behavior to the detriment of its own survival, its systematic killing of its own individuals, its necessity for community while it arms itself to the teeth in fear of others in that same community. The species worships abstractions like deities they've never seen or things they invented (money) from and for their own needs and successes. They attempt to govern themselves by preaching egalitarianism while creating massive policing entities to quell lawbreakers. This begs the question, Why have societies of laws if so many members of that society are so eager to break them? There must be something else at work here.

The disconnect between organized societies of all types and our primitive nature that promotes hoarding, defense of home, hearth and resources is profound and visible when constant conflict for land and mineral resources creates highly destructive and constant warring. War, after all, is *normal* to the human condition of both the past and the present even as much as the "civilized" members decry it. Recorded human history is filled with constant war and conflict. We must assume, therefore, that human tribes fought each other before the written word. Even our closest relatives in the animal kingdom, the chimpanzees, organize raids on other tribes of their kind for the sake of food, territory and reproductive necessities. Our common ancestor must have been this aggressive in order to establish its survival. There is nothing glorious in life on Earth. Life is competition among every species in its own environment. Life is amazing to watch for an intellectual mind, like that of man's, but for everything else it's just another day on the prairie.

So why are we so caught up in our own wonderfulness, when in fact we are just another cog in the great machine of life on planet Earth? Perhaps Bertrand Russell captured some part of an explanation when he said,

There is something feeble and a little contemptible about a man who cannot face the perils of life without the help of comfortable myths. Almost inevitably some part of him is aware that they ARE myths and the he believes them only because they are comforting.

But he dares not face this thought! Moreover, since he is aware, however dimly, that his opinions are not rational, he becomes furious when they are disputed.

One of those myths, and one of the major themes of this book, is taking of the abstraction known as *money* and turning it into THE most important part of survival in modern human societies. Rebecca Costa discusses these money memes in her book, *The Watchman's Rattle*. One of them directs humans to only pursue activities that result in profit irrespective of that action being beneficial or harmful to the society in general. The recent attacks on the U.S. Postal Service by so-called conservatives, comes to mind, as representing the foolishness of one of the money memes. The U.S. Constitution *requires* the Congress to provide for postal services, yet a "conservative" Congress deemed that its financial obligation shall include ensuring that its employee retirement system be funded *up front* thus creating a phantom cash flow burden. The "conservatives" are therefore trying to privatize the postal service and disband the government control over it. In view of how well private, for-profit enterprise does with public services in the United States, I can only imagine how this paradigm shift will affect normal posting of mail. Remember, beginning with the Reagan administration, the Sherman Anti-trust Act ceased being enforced.

The public good is not about profit, it's about quality of life. So-called conservatives insist that everything should be privatized and turned into a profit center. Educating and healing our citizens are the two most crucial "services" on the table for these people. Money has overturned the concept of citizens' rights from its government for educating their children and providing excellent health care for everyone. THOSE are the notions that make a great nation great, make its people happy and productive and enhance the cohesiveness of its many factions.

But no... We have allowed the corporation to become our law, the bank our master. Thomas Jefferson predicted an unhappy future should this situation occur:

The end of democracy and the defeat of the American Revolution will occur when government falls into the hands of lending institutions and moneyed incorporations. No wonder conservative state school boards want to get Jefferson out of history books.

Ron Shalach, the founder of Panera Bread Parade said, in 2012:

My message to corporate leaders is this: Unless we take care of the society we live in there won't be any society left to support our businesses. A recent poll of small businesses shows that about 70% of the owners are very concerned that their customers don't have enough money to spend and allow the business to stay viable.

This kind of logic is basic and simple, but the money meme is so entrenched in the corporate mindset as to render it moot. Marx warned us about unregulated capitalism. Jefferson warned us about corporations and banks ruining our good thing, democracy. Eisenhower warned us about the military-industrial complex making policy decisions by bribing government. John Kenneth Galbraith said:

The modern conservative is engaged in one of man's oldest exercises in moral philosophy; that is, the search for a superior moral justification for selfishness.

Garrison Keillor of *Prairie Home Companion* fame is also in on the discovery of our race to destruction:

The party of Lincoln and liberty has transmogrified into the party of hairy-backed swamp developers and corporate shills, faith-based economists, fundamentalist bullies with Bibles, Christians of convenience, freelance racists, misanthropic frat boys, shrieking midgets of AM radio, tax cheats, nihilists in golf pants, brown shirts in pinstripes, sweatshop tycoons: Republicans: The number one reason the rest of the world thinks we're deaf, dumb and dangerous.

This covers the highlights of those things that need changing if our great experiment in democracy is to persist and thrive. The current corporate/capitalist mindset ignores everything except profit. It insists on consuming resources and people at an increasing rate to keep on the profit growth curve thus making its stockholders happy. Blind are they to the inherent and assured exhaustion of those resources and the people making them ever richer. This blindness will end up being the lever that tips the United States of America onto the slide to oblivion. Worse, the resultant pollution of the Earth that feeds us will eliminate our abilities to survive our own mindlessness. Franklin Delano Roosevelt saw this too when he addressed the growing inequality in the world that is the prelude to the coming Dark Ages II. His second Bill of Rights appeared in his final State of the Union Speech in 1945. His subsequent death and the end of the World War II muted this message of equanimity and fairness for all in work, play, education, health care and lifestyle.

Chapter 47:   The Wages of Disagreement

In the spring of 1960 my best high school buddy received many football scholarship offers from the major colleges east of the Mississippi. My friend came from western Virginia, though our school was in Ohio. His nickname was "Hillbilly".

He chose to attend a southern university. I asked him why there and not Ohio State? Without blinking he said it was because in the southern athletic conferences he didn't have to play with any..... (of those people). It didn't register with me then what he really meant.

We kept in touch for a few years, but eventually went our separate ways. We re-connected again around 2003 and discussed a variety of things not the least of which was our invasion of Iraq. He still lived in Florida and sent me all sorts of material via internet supporting the weapons of mass destruction "theory". During one of our telephone conversations he warned me that we probably differed on most things. I naively dismissed his warning because I didn't think *my pal* could be anything but my pal. I was wrong. After I pointed out to him that the stuff he was sending me was in error and part of a big lie and cover-up he wrote me back to tell me we were done as friends. It was then that I understood what he meant in 1960. Our paths were diverging, but I refused to accept that.

A couple years later I reconnected with an old roommate from my days in San Diego. He worked as a civilian contractor for the Navy in Maryland. After some newsy updates he started in on the hate Obama rhetoric that I've come to see as the main theme for right wing extremism, aka the Tea Party. It was immediately clear that we and the times had changed. I terminated our communication.

These anecdotes are typical of what the instant communications environment and highly charged political debate seen 24/7 on all our media, including e-mail, has done to some of my relationships; many friends and relatives say the same. E-mail gives people the chance to tell somebody off in language that they wouldn't ordinarily use face-to-face. I'm guilty of doing that and am not proud of it. When the passions of belief and partisanship are high, common sense, grace and intelligent discourse seem to dissipate with each keystroke or word.

Beginning with the 2008 election cycle my political activism increased and my ability to hold old friends who felt differently decreased. I've made many, many new friends who are similarly active, but have lost many old friends who don't want to hear the other side or are just tired of it. Karl Rove must be thrilled with this outcome.

I think the loss of friendships, civil discourse, bipartisanship, compromise and the ability to understand the pure and absolute truth about anything are the wages of disagreement that today's mind-flooding "communication/information" environment creates. We're all prisoners of our own emotions, what we think is right and are loathe to give any of it up.

Where do we go from here? Is this divisiveness part of some great plan to separate "us" from "them" in order to win elections, obtain money from corporations and exercise irresponsible power? Almost everything we do in today's society seems to indicate that we are headed for another wrenching separation from one another rather than pursuing the path of "binding up our wounds" and working together to save democracy.

Chapter 48: Where Are We Headed?

I read conservative and progressive articles to gain balanced insight into social and political issues. I avoid certain right wing ideologues because they, like so many pundits on the left, spout company line after company line. It gets boring and predictable. A recent column by my favorite conservative columnist, David Brooks, is worth mentioning.

Brooks discussed the long-held dream of most Americans: *upward mobility*. He mentions two kinds of inequality: BLUE inequality, the type separating the higher salary earners and everybody else in and around big cities. RED inequality is that gap between college graduates and everybody else in smaller towns and cities. In "blue" areas, 69% of the top 1% earners operate some sort of financial business. The other 31% are the doctors, lawyers, athletes and engineers. Notice that there is no mention of manufacturing industry here.

Brooks notes that in 1979 the average college graduate made 38% more than the average high school graduate. Today, that number is 75% more. More importantly, perhaps, is that today's college graduates have a much better chance of passing their legacy down to their children than those who do not go to college. In 1970, college and high school graduates had more similar lifestyles. Today, the differences in divorce rates, smoking, longevity, obesity, friendship networks and community activism is much greater between the two groups, with the high school graduates being on the downside.

Most of the garnered attention the "Occupy" movements related to the "blue" inequalities, but the "red" inequalities may be more important to how we extract ourselves from this economically difficult time. Tens of millions of Americans have and are dropping out of college and high school for many reasons, mostly financial. This is a huge problem because it involves so many citizens. Add to that, 40% of our children are born to unwed mothers, and our workforce of skilled and semi-skilled labor is languishing in dormancy for lack of meaningful job opportunities. The key word here is "opportunity".

We might be disgusted at the "blue" inequality of CEO and star athlete salaries compared to everybody else, but the "red" inequality is being saddled with the specter of having no hope. Studies show that poor people have virtually no chance of upward mobility irrespective of their education. The middle classes are showing a steep drop in upward mobility. Subsequent generations do worse than previous ones. Only the educated people coming from already wealthy families are showing any upward trend in socio-economic mobility. The dream of working one's way to the top or out of poverty is dimming rapidly for most Americans.

While corporate America hastily sent our jobs to other countries, there was no attempt to replace them with anything but service sector employment. While we've let our infrastructure crumble, we've also cut our school vocational programs thus depriving our society of skilled labor resources. We have dumbed-down our school curricula for the sake of passing unfunded, but mandated testing regimes that serve no purpose other than political expediency. The children become bored and disinterested and drop out to do any number of things not all of which are legal or productive to society.

I hate to say it, but these trends look an awful lot like what describes a second world nation. Is that what we are, or where we're headed? While the elites scurry to their gated, *McMansion* communities, the vast majority of the working class, the poor and the underclass scrape for a dream of some sort to which they can aspire even as their opportunities dwindle. People talk of the incentives of capitalism, but we seem to be avoiding the preparation of upcoming generations to be incentivized. An increasing number of Americans see the *Great American Dream* as the *Great American Lie.*

There are countless slogans decrying the state we're in and how we've lost our national compass. It was the strong middle class that made this country great. They spent the money and became the engine of our economy. Today, 50 million people live in poverty to varying degrees. They spur nothing. Today, the middle class's job quality and rewards have degraded to a point where they no longer spur the economy either. What incentives do they have besides the avoidance of starvation?

Is this where we are headed? If so, how do the elites expect to keep raking in their millions when nobody is making or buying anything other than subsistence? The money meme is exacerbated by the continuing lust for resource consumption (oil and gas fracking), the search for lowest wages possible and the expectations that both physical and human resources are inexhaustible. There is NO plan B for environmental exhaustion, the harmful end game of climate change or for when all the cheap labor is not cheap anymore or too sick to work.

We're supposed to be the most intelligent species on earth. Those of us not hoarding money should be able to reverse the downward spiral to oblivion while creating a positive paradigm for life on Earth.

Chapter 49:   What's Really Important? Hint: It isn't Ultra-Conservatism

The history of capitalism shows painful and turbulent evolution. The turbulence comes from the relationship between labor and the hierarchy of businessmen who exert influence on national policy, the interpretation of law and demands on the government.

After the Civil War, a resurgence of capitalism created huge labor and product markets – especially in the North. The South's industrial infrastructure was in shambles, and freed slaves streamed North to readily available jobs. At first glance, one might think that this was good for everyone. It was not.

Northern white workers coming home from the war needed to work to support their families who had had to suffer economic hardships similar to, but not as horrible as their Southern counterparts. Businesses, however, only cared about how little they could pay for labor. The blacks, of course, took jobs for fractions of what white workers would ask. The inevitable friction between the races in the North was exacerbated by white labor disaffection with the business and industry leaders who did what any capitalist does.

Over the next decades, the Populist movement was replaced by the Socialist movement that led up to and included the First World War. These two eras had commonality in that working conditions for labor were utterly dreadful by today's standards. No laws existed to protect workers from employer whimsy and abuse. No laws existed to protect workers from unsafe working environments. No laws existed that defined a limited work day or week. The wages were draconian in their parsimony.

Imagine, for example, sending your 12 year old son to work in a sweatshop of the late 19th century. He would have to work 60-70 hour weeks for less than a dollar a day. Factory women were treated about the same for about the same wages. Woe unto the employee who got sick or was late for work. If they weren't fired outright, they were often whipped by foremen. This is another way to define slavery in "modern" times.

Meanwhile, corporations and businesses were reaping record profits and all the while trying to expand markets. The Spanish-American War, for example was fought primarily to gain control over more resources and larger markets for the surplus of goods being produced by human and mechanical labor. Islands across the Pacific, including the Philippines, were needed for coaling stations for the merchant fleet's ships. The drive for profit was limitless and relentless. American Imperialism was necessary to slake the thirst of American capitalism's expansion during this time.

When labor organized and revolted, the conservatives' position was almost exclusively repressive. The first amendment right to assembly was ignored as hired militia and mercenaries were sent in to disrupt and disperse organized labor meetings. The result, of course, was violence. Hundreds of men, women and children were gunned down in our streets and fields because they didn't want to be indentured servants to the company store. The conservative state and Federal governments actually allowed Federal troops to go to the rescue of businesses as the revolts and strikes grew more frequent and more intense.

As America lurched toward anarchy and violent, open class warfare, conservative administrations began the painful process of reform. They saw that without reform there would indeed be another revolution. One of the salient events that spurred this move was the Ludlow Massacre in Colorado in 1914. Dozens of men, women and children were shot and burned to death because they wanted to be paid in U.S. currency and have safe working conditions for themselves and their children. Instead, the Rockefeller Trust paid the salaries of the Colorado National Guard to break the strike by any means possible. Killing strikers became a normal occurrence sponsored by corporate/banking America. This was one of the few times in our history when government actually worked to curb the excesses of capitalism's quest for power over people.

This history reflects but a sample of what "conservative", capitalist philosophy did in the name of profit. Today, the conservatives want to overturn many of the laws of the reforms that so many people died for. Ultra-conservatives want to return to the time when government did not interfere at all with how businesses were run. There is even a movement in Missouri to allow school children to skip school so they can go to work.

Ultra-conservative movements are clearly out of date and fail to understand that certain kinds of bells cannot be un-rung. The bell of fairness and caring about our fellow citizens cannot and will not be un-rung by the people who think they want to "take their country back."

Chapter 50:   The Echo Chamber

We've all heard or said, "He just likes to listen to the sound of his own voice." We've all known people who fit this statement perfectly. The thing is, the only time a person hears the sound of his own voice is when it is played back to him or her from a recording. Then the speaker hears what his/her audience hears. Otherwise, he/she is hearing a voice filtered through bones and tissue that alter the actual timbre and volume of that voice.

Adjunct to this concept is the obvious fact that in our social and political discourse we like to hear other voices that we think sound like ours. It is natural to want agreement and reassurance from others. Over the last 20 years, or so, that I've been paying attention to our history, national politics and social conversations, I better understand how this phenomenon of the echo chamber has ruined the elegant concept of debate. There are people out there in the media getting paid obscene amounts of money to be an echo to an audience that wants to hear nothing except what they think or think they understand. Anything else except the pure echo becomes a cacophony of disinterest, ridicule or hostility.

Place *GUILTY* around my neck regarding this desire to crave agreement. Since I began writing for public consumption I've been shocked by how many people don't agree with me or I with them. I had spent most of my life surrounding myself with friends and acquaintances who agreed with most of my thoughts and words. This was especially egregious behavior for me since I had fancied myself a scientist and teacher who fostered discussion and demanded proof. I professed to question everything and require substantiation for theories and hypotheses. I am guilty of denying my own teachings and tenets of logic and communication. If you've ever been to a scientific symposium where manuscripts are presented you'd know what I mean. Scientists are ruthless with one another when it comes to analyzing reports and summaries.

I began asking: How did I let myself work against my own teachings? It started by asking someone who disagreed with me to prove their point with facts. If they couldn't, I pounced...and kept pouncing on those who either repeated somebody else's echo chamber rhetoric or created their own original script; no proof, no echo from me. The really bad news is that many parts of the discussion where some agreements or seeds for resolution were possible, they were swept away in the whirlwind of dissonance and blind egoism.

Multiply my example of wanting to be echoed or be somebody else's echo millions of times and we have what may be described as a dissonant, dysfunctional and gridlocked national conversation that extends into our government. Both sides say they want to honor and follow the guidelines of our Constitution. Yet one side will create a platform for doing just the opposite of governing; they desire to *command* the people rather than govern them. The other side wants to maintain certain social programs and enhance others to actually work toward *the general welfare* of the citizenry. The opposition (conservatives) to this latter position ridicules and hurls claims of irresponsible monetary policy while supporting endless war, taxpayer subsidies to highly profitable corporations, allowing taxable income and profits to be hidden in foreign banks and the dismantling of education and infrastructure that built the very country they honor.

Both sides surround themselves with experts and pundits that echo their particular view and disparage the opposition. Cacophony; pure white noise is the net result. Gridlock. Dysfunctional government writ large, very large. A divided citizenry.

Our political environment has become two echo chambers completely insulated from one another and playing to their own audiences. For each Sean Hannity there is the opposing Chris Matthews. Their guest lists are echo generators and woe unto the "guest" who disagrees with the host. The media sound machine host will do its best to hatchet that disharmonic guest for as long as THEY hear the echoes of approval from their echo-craving audience.

There are architects for this divide in the laboratory of debate and few of us have been exempt from seeing and hearing the results. Karl Rove, Lee Atwater, Roger Ailes and Rupert Murdoch created the thickness of the wall now dividing the echo chambers of national discourse with Fox News. The airwaves are too full of echoes to count or mention in this short piece, but you don't have to punch too many TV remote buttons to find your echo or the echo of the "other" chamber.

We have always had bitter political disputes over many, many issues in our U.S. history: The Civil War was the result of our citizens and governments ignoring the necessities of compromise. The current episode of lost compromise began in ernest the moment Barack Obama's lifted his hand off the Bible on January 20, 2009.

Seeking the comforting echo is a parallel need to blaming somebody else. We spend so much time blaming the "other side" for all the ills of the world. Blaming wastes our time because it is an echo too. It achieves nothing except to thicken the walls in our chambers of self. Until we step out of our personal echo chambers and find the threads of elegant debate once again, no deals will be made, no solutions will be found and no harmony will come to this nation. We will succumb to our own collective stupidity and to the way of the Mayans, Rome, Egypt and a host of other great societies that failed to fix their problems. Instead they just listened to the sounds of their own, self-righteous voices and let greatness slip away into the uncaring dust of history.

Chapter 51: Forgetting Democracy

In the hurly-burly of our political environment we often lose sight and forget how things really work – or at least are supposed to work. As I've written before, the President gets too much credit when things are going well and too much blame when things aren't going so well. For example: When gasoline prices decline, the Republicans tout free-market enterprise. When gasoline prices rise, they blame President Obama. Neither of these statements is correct. Oil prices are set by oil commodities speculators around the world based on the price of oil they assign. An oil tanker may have its cargo value change 3 times between the Persian Gulf and the refinery. The gasoline price at the pumps is set by refineries and the accountants at the various oil companies that sponsor retail outlets.

Every dollar that a President can spend must be appropriated by the Congress. Every authority to act has been given to the President by the Congress. Even executive actions are allowed under the law as long as they don't conflict with other laws or Constitutional strictures. Our system of government is built on the idea that Congress *pro*poses and the President *dis*poses. The Founders wanted the President and Congress to be partners, not antagonists, in the governing process. At the core of that partnership was the principle of compromise; in America, nobody gets it their way all the time but everyone gets some of their way most of the time.

Republicans continue to say that this President does not have a plan to deal with unemployment. The fact is that President Obama asked Congress to pass a bill that would create and save over a million jobs in all sectors. Congressman Paul Ryan rejected the plan in committee so in never came up for debate in the House. In spite of that, as of February, 2015, we have experienced job growth of over 200,000 for 12 straight months and positive job growth for almost 60 months. This is the largest job growth since the Clinton administration.

The problem is not that the President has no plan, he has no partner! There are too few members of Congress willing to work with him and too many willing to use working class Americans as pawns in partisan politics. Nothing speaks to this more than Mitch McConnell's egregious commitment of the Republican Party to make their first priority the defeat of Barack Obama. This commitment has been in practice since 2009 and has stalled anything beneficial to the people of the country and our national economic health.

What sort of people think this is good? How can elected officials thumb their noses at 310 million citizens in order to regain political power? What is their motive? It is beyond craven, it is anti-social and anti-American.

Compromise is a most cherished American value. The Republican Party has declared it will not honor that value.

So, in coming elections, we won't be so much about electing one man or another to be President, it will be about who we elect to Congress. This Congress achieved the dubious honor of having the lowest approval rating of any in history: 9%. That's only slightly higher than friends, relatives and staff of the Congress people. No wonder voters don't register and/or stay home on voting day. Worse, the people perceive that they don't select candidates, because they are picked to run by the major parties who are primarily funded by corporations and banks.

We the people must put in office those who are not corrupted by corporate money and/or political poison. If we are to retain our vigor as a nation, we must elect those who represent US, the 310 million who desire a government that works in our best interests, not exclusively the corporations'.

UPDATE: The 2014 mid-term election showed the world how a failing democracy works when 30% of those eligible to vote remain unregistered and 2/3 of the electorate doesn't vote at all. As a result of this pathetic performance by the American populace, the backward-thinking regressive politicians were "elected" and re-elected by those who do vote. With the average margin of "victory" being around 20 percent, the actual percentage of eligible voters who picked the "winners" was around 17%. Some voice of democracy that... Furthermore, progressive ballot issues like gun registry and background checks passed overwhelmingly.

It just shows us that the general public has tired of the professional politician and only the ideologues and true believers living in echo chambers vote. This is how democracy will be eaten and destroyed by its own hand.

Chapter 52:   The Assault on Women

During the election cycles of 2012 we learned how the backward-thinking legislature of Virginia and its highly ambitious Republican governor dealt with the law allowing abortions. Bob McDonnell – now a convicted felon for bribery and other crimes – and his compliant legislature floated a bill that would *require* a physician to perform an invasive procedure known as *trans-vaginal insertion* of and ultrasound probe into a woman's reproductive system *before* an abortion could be performed. Every obstetrician and gynecologist not quacking said this procedure was absolutely not necessary.

The "defense" for this requirement from the Republicans included statements that suggested that this penetration was a good as the next one that would produce the abortion and that most abortions are performed for "lifestyle convenience". What they don't say is that this invasion of a woman's body is designed to show the woman pictures of the embryo/fetus in the hopes of discouraging the abortion decision. The media finally exposed these "keep-government-our-of-our-lives" hypocrites and the bill was shelved until 2013. The bill has not resurfaced since.   Then there were the "hearings" held by the California hatchet, Darrell Issa, the richest man in Congress, "discussing" the free contraception mandate in the Affordable Care Act. Not only did this theater of the absurd use the separation of church and state as its basis, the first panel of witnesses did not include a female. When Sharon Fluke was finally allowed to speak, her testimony was brushed aside by the committee and sordidly derided by the sewer Rush Limbaugh calls a mouth. The only thing worth mentioning from this exercise in political cesspool dredging was the disgrace of the Republican brand.

There's more: The nearly brain-dead Senatorial candidate from Missouri, Todd Akin, exhibited his callous ignorance of women, their rights and the law by venturing into the physiology of human reproduction and the concept of "legitimate rape". On both topics, this sorrowful lackey of corporate America missed badly in both accuracy and common decency.

A little research turned up a 1996 report from the *Journal of Obstetrics and Gynecology* that noted there were over 32,000 pregnancies per year as a result of rape. It represented 5% of the victims raped between ages of 12-45. This data extrapolates to over 640,000 reported rapes. We are 18 years passed that study wherein a more courageous female population reports rapes more often rather than hiding the facts. Rape is an expression of violence, not sex, according to psychologists.

Do we really have that many frustrated, angry and violent men walking around abusing women only because they can? What about the subjugation of women in other societies like those of the Muslim faith? Are women born to be second-class citizens, breeding mares and housekeepers? Who decided that and when? I suspect that religion and ancient cultures are responsible for this conflict against equal rights for women and the men in charge are loath to change anything about it because they fear a loss of manhood…I guess. Even in the United States, with all its relative egalitarianism, women were not allowed to vote until 1920. How did we miss that in the 18th and 19th centuries? Wyoming, of all places, was the first state to allow women the vote before 1920. Why not other states? Oppressors usually oppress those they fear. Have men always feared women?

From the information I find, the rate of violence against women is about the same today as in 1996, yet the GOP has recently voted against the *Violence Against Women Act* proposed by the Obama administration. Instead, the Republicans want to eliminate all abortions irrespective of cause, limit or eliminate birth control for women and destroy *Planned Parenthood*, who performs proactive (non-abortion) female reproductive health care in 95% of its work. That said, it is notable that men's erectile dysfunction drugs are not addressed by politicians and are paid for in most health care insurance policies while birth control pills for women are not covered.

Why, then, do Republicans want to end *Planned Parenthood* for women, especially poor women? In sum, the GOP memes say: "You must have that baby, but once you do, you and it are on your own; no welfare, no food stamps, no Medicaid". That policy sounds a lot like an assault to me.

The syndicated columnist for the *Washington Post,* Maureen Dowd may say it best when addressing the assault on women and who is leading that assault.

She points out what the RNC is saying and doing: *"…by reiterating language in their platform call for a no-exceptions Constitutional amendment outlawing abortion, even in cases of rape, incest and threat of life to the mother.*

"Paul Ryan, who teamed up with Akin in the House to sponsor harsh anti-abortion bills, may look young and hip and new generation, with his iPod full of heavy metal jams and his cute kids. But he's just a fresh face on a Taliban creed – the evermore antediluvian, anti-women, anti-immigrant, ant-gay conservative core."

This assault on women is fueled by extremists from evangelical churches and mainstream Republican males of every stripe. There must be some inherent insecurity in these men that they feel so compelled to control women's reproductive rights. Instead, they hide behind the man-made shields of religion. Perhaps they should look into themselves for answers to

191

their fears before emulating the attitudes toward women similar to those of Saudi Arabia.

Eliminating rape and violence against women is a good starting place for the debate. Rape is a violent act of power by males against physically weaker females. If we accede to this barbarity, we are admitting we are barbarians. If we allow full-term pregnancies from rape and/or incest, we are admitting that these crimes against women are O.K. They are not! Any first-year genetics student or civilized person can explain why, especially for incest rape.

I don't like the concept of abortion; I prefer prevention of pregnancy. Our current laws allow some legally sanctioned abortions. Roe v. Wade was not approved by the Supreme Court on a whim or a message from God. It was made to allow women freedom over their bodies. Men don't get pregnant nor give birth. They should not be solely responsible for making laws that prevent women from expressing that personal freedom.

A poll in 2012 showed that Caucasian males in the U.S. favored Mitt Romney by about 29%. In view of the subject of this essay, I wonder what percentage of voting age females favor anything Republican. In the 2012 elections, women voted for Democrats by an overwhelming margin. With GOP attacks and fear mongering against people not in their "base", it follows that all women and those who are not in a "favored" group will be compelled to vote out and against those who are working against their best interests. The GOP remains the party of exclusion.

NOTE: In the 2014 elections, the U.S. voter turnout was the lowest since 1942. Over 2/3 of the eligible voters stayed home; only the white males voted in numbers representative of their group.

My questions are: How could anyone with any respect for women and their hard-earned rights even consider voting for an agenda that condones rescinding those rights as well as rejecting a law intended to squelch violence against women?

Chapter 53:   Changing Minds and Habits

Someone asked me recently if I thought my writing was changing anybody's mind about their politics or how they view government at any level. My answer was, "I don't know." Frankly, I don't see any of my articles or books as mind or habit changing entities. They are what they are: Words cobbled together that try to make sense of an increasingly discordant society, the U.S.A.

I'm not alone in the not-changing-any-minds category. There are plenty of self-ordained pundits telling us how our President isn't touting enough American exceptionalism and instead is apologizing around the world for our mistakes. The truth is the rest of the world is sick and tired of hearing about our exceptionalism and is most grateful that somebody had the grace to apologize for grievous errors of the past. In these pundits' world apologizing is a sissy thing to do, even though it is the correct thing to do. I wonder how the Iraqis feel about our exceptionalism after we invaded and destroyed their country based on lies. Not all pundits have a memory that isn't yesterday.

Then there are comments about how exceptional our military personnel are and how we should honor and respect them. I agree. We should. But we also shouldn't waste them, along with hundreds of billions of dollars on fruitless military campaigns and projects either, especially those based on lies. Now that's honor! That's respect for our troops, the builders of their hardware and the taxpayers who fund it: Be frugal with their lives and equipment.

Finally there was the conservative pundits' "glory" moment when our multiculturalism and decades of illegal immigration was blamed for ALL our problems. Since these pundits live on the right wing, I wondered why they didn't blame President Obama for that too. Then I realized that all of us in this country are a product of some blend of cultures...except those descendants of the original inhabitants of this and the southern continent. Our Euro-American ancestors took this land away from the originals, didn't they?

Why, even our military is heavily sprinkled with multicultural and multiethnic personnel some of whom (gasp) are even sons and daughters of illegal immigrants. I guess that was too obvious a point to be made in one little column.

It might be noted that if any of us traced our ancestry back further enough we'd find that we all have a common ancestor, and she's African. All the rest of our genealogy is a blend of mixed "races" over hundreds of thousands of years. The meme of racial purity favored by racists is absolutely a *non sequitur.*

Studies show that true believers are almost never swayed from their positions by opposing facts and validated information. In fact, they tend to become even more entrenched in them.

This kind of entrenched opinion by convenience is not going to be changed by anyone or anything. It is locked in for any number of reasons. But there is also the straight party ticket button in the voting booth. How convenient. I think we've all seen that not every Republican nor every Democrat is necessarily the best choice for a vote, so why vote for those who don't measure up? Are we too lazy as voters to actually research our candidates? In 2010 92% of Republican voters voted straight ticket in Texas while only 28% of the Democrats did that. It would seem that Democratic voters at least try to discriminate and pick the most acceptable candidate instead of just pressing "ALL". The public schools in Texas know how well that turned out every day.

Chapter 54:   The Koch Archipelago

There are parallels to the famous *Gulag Archipelago* written by Alexander Solzhenitsyn in today's right wing efforts to control the lives of the majority of humans by an oligarchy of the few and powerful men who aspire to world domination. It may sound like what fascists do (Hitler, Mussolini, et. al.), but today the Koch brothers, Charles and David, sponsor organizations that actively try to institute those controls over free men and women.

A little historical research took me back to the founding of the infamous John Birch Society in 1958 by Robert W. Welsh in Indianapolis, IN. Lo and behold, a co-founder of this extremist, paranoid organization was none other than Fred Koch, the daddy of Charles and David. After reviewing the tenets and activities of the JBS, I was struck by the similarities I see in today's propaganda mills around the country. Virtually every state has a *"Public Policy Foundation"* that "studies" and promotes virtually the entire JBS agenda. Libertarianism seems to have hitched its wagon to this star. When one looks at the financiers of these organizations, one finds not only Koch Industries, but several other multi-national corporations, their CEOs and a host of local Republicans all singing from the JBS song book.

John Birch, a Baptist missionary and WW II military intelligence officer was killed by Chinese communists in 1945, thus establishing, in Welsh's mind, the horrors of communism, socialism and anything else that didn't meet his criteria for absolute free market enterprise as the sole operator of American capitalism. He opposed anything that smacked of cooperating with the rest of the world in politics (U.S. out of the U.N.), economics (no regulation of businesses) and social issues (the workers are there to serve business). I guess the practice of those principles that caused the Great Depression didn't register on his memory. A delicious irony and hypocrisy here is that Welsh declared that the society he founded be based on Christian principles. That said, one wonders why they are against the Civil Rights laws, equal voting rights, financial and material aid for the poor, worker safety regulations and a host of other people-friendly parts of our society all the while being all about making the rich richer.

The JBS tried hard to get ultra-conservative politicians elected to office by funding their campaigns from virtually the day it came into being. In some cases they succeeded (with the ultimate paranoiac, Joseph McCarthy being the cherry on top) and others failed. They even attacked President Eisenhower as possibly being a power monger and a communist who wanted to create a whole world government. I'm not making this up.

Well, today we have the American Legislative Exchange Council (ALEC) which acts as a dating service for right wing politicians to meet corporate America and their fellow ideologues to write legislation that promotes the agenda of conservative politics. ALEC is a secretive organization that will not disclose its membership or donation sources. Yet, they are responsible for writing heinous legislation like voter ID laws, stand your ground laws, show your papers laws, anti-abortion laws and laws trying to punish insurers who participate in the Affordable Care Act insurance exchanges on the *Healthcare.gov* website.

We now see the formation of this archipelago of mind control "foundations" leading to governmental control by modern oligarchs: the ghosts of the John Birch Society, the Koch brothers and their fellow hypocrites of freedom. Take a look at your state *Public Policy Foundation* via a web search and read their mission statements, the resumes of their organization, the departments for "research" and what they intend to do with their "education" initiatives. To me, it sounded just like the tenets of Robert Welsh pushed through a sophisticated propaganda practice that would make Joseph Goebbels blush. Then look up the *National Center for Public Policy Research* and you'll know for sure that the extremism, power madness, paranoia and the seeds for society's destruction are sown within.

We have the relative luxury to see first-hand what these people are doing and still have the ability to stop them from destroying what so many died to preserve and worked so hard to build. We still have the opportunity to educate ourselves, get off our butts and vote for those we know and trust. If we don't do that, we will be subject to a 1984 style takeover from the oligarchs.

That situation will eventually sow the seeds for a second revolution/Civil War. In view of the general public possessing over 300 million guns plus ammo, the fight against the police/military indentured to the oligarchs will be a bloody fight indeed. Police departments across the country haven't acquired all that military hardware for nothing.

Chapter 55:   The Outrage of the Corporatocracy

It may sound weird to have a retired biology teacher and engineer write about the doings of corporate America when he should be tending his garden or putting stroke. I feel obliged, however, to describe the outrageous behavior that our corporations are foisting upon the moral, ethical and scruples compasses of our economy and business world. For those who read this, know that your hard work and faith is being undercut by those very entities that built this country into the economic giant it is.

In 1952 corporate America paid over 30% of the Federal tax bill to keep our highways in repair, our military strong, national parks in great shape and our overall infrastructure second to none in the world. Today, corporate America pays only 9% of the nation's tax dollars while the majority of the tax burden falls on the declining middle classes and the poor. Oh, the rich will trumpet that they pay 58% of the tax bill, and they are correct. But the rich are generally taxed at a lower rate than the middle classes while the poor pay virtually no Federal taxes because they don't earn enough. The rich have purchased enough law to allow them to only pay 15% on capital gains and transferred interest, the loopholes that allow the wealthy to avoid their fair share of taxes.

Meanwhile, corporations have purchased enough law such that they can bank their overseas profits without paying any U.S. taxes on them. The rich also shift huge sums of money to offshore banks and thus avoid paying ANY U.S. taxes at all. Our seven largest corporations pay NO corporate taxes via these and other tax avoidance schemes.   They still yell that the 35% corporate tax rate is what is driving them to get the laws changed so they can avoid paying taxes altogether. The last figures I read showed that over $30 trillion in untaxed U.S. capital lay in offshore banks - waiting for the ultimate rainy day, I suppose.

It wasn't enough for corporate America to fiddle tax codes to their favor. No, they had to get the Supreme Court to declare that they were people and that they could donate unlimited amounts of private, secret money to any political candidate they wanted. Well, if corporations are people, they should be barred from buying and selling each other; the 14th Amendment forbids it.

Furthermore, the corporations have been using American ingenuity, labor, resources and infrastructure for over 200 years to build the economic behemoths we've become that provides a potentially comfortable life for all our citizens. Now they want to pull an "inversion" and re-incorporate in another nation so they can avoid even more U.S. taxes. Walgreen's™ had the good sense to feel shame from its customers who threatened to boycott should they go through with incorporating in Ireland. It just doesn't get much more craven than this. Burger King recently moved to Canada and bought the Tim Horton restaurant chain.

Our lawmakers, however, willingly accept the lobbying benefits and allow corporate America to abandon the American people. If you want to know what an abandoned industrial society looks like, visit inner-city Detroit or Camden. Added to the vast slums and destruction zones is violence between the people left behind. Detroit is now, by far, the most violent city in the United States. Poverty and hopelessness will do that to the fiber of communities. All the major industrial cities with abandoned factories and dwellings are being systematically stripped of their metal and sold to foreign countries as scrap.

In a sickening irony, our failing nation is providing the basic materials for the emerging economies around the world; the countries from which we buy our junk. The word "scrap" is an ominously poignant word here.

The final question remains: How much corporate profit is enough? The answer from corporate America is that it's never enough. Profit is more important to the stockholders than the health of the nation in which they reside. Profit at the expense of the infrastructure that the vast majority of the people depend on is the theme for corporate America. Growth in profits isn't enough, if you read the papers. It's rapid growth of profits that matter most on Wall St. Corporations have purchased enough influence to all but destroy labor unions, but in spite of that, they shipped millions of jobs overseas to even cheaper labor markets. That's what NAFTA is all about. Future trade pacts currently being discussed in Congress and the White House further the opportunities of corporate America to degrade the American work force.

The value of corporate stock has more than doubled since 2009, but the earning power of the middle class and poor has declined. How does increasing growth philosophy jibe with a consumer class less able to support it? Corporate America is still all about cutting its tax burden and labor costs. These actions, of course, leave less money for the governments to maintain that wonderful infrastructure we all appreciate unless taxes on those who can least afford them are raised. Corporate America is doing its best to fulfill Marx's prediction of capitalism destroying itself from within.

Chapter 56:   War and Veterans

In my childhood I met many of my father's friends who fought in World War II. Some walked with a limp. Some had scars on their bodies. All of them had scars in their minds. As a curious kid I asked them about their war experiences and they were very patient to tell me stories, but were not too graphic. I discovered the truth later.

A very good friend of my parents had been a Marine on Pelilieu. He managed to survive, but earned a Purple Heart and a chest full of other medals in the process. Eugene Sledge, writing about that battle many years later, mentioned this Marine by name in his book and I almost jumped out of my chair. I had no idea that Pelilieu and Okinawa were such horror shows. This Marine friend never went into the details with me.

But another Marine from that era DID get into details. He was married to a nurse at the defense plant where my father worked. This Marine spent the entire war in the South Pacific with raider groups like today's Recon outfits. His stories were brutal and horrible leaving a kid like me in tears and trembling. I had the bad dreams that night. This Marine suffered for years after the war with what we now call Post Traumatic Stress Disorder. He would wake up screaming and throw his wife around the room. They had to sleep separately until his dreams diminished. Nobody knew how many of our troops suffered so from this kind of debilitation.

The guy who helped my father coach my Little League team was also a Marine and served on a destroyer during the battle of Okinawa. He showed us a piece of the Japanese airplane that crashed into his ship and gave him HIS Purple Heart. Yet another Marine who walked with great difficulty told me how he broke his back crashing his shot-up Corsair onto the deck of a carrier.

To an easily influenced kid these guys were my instant heroes. I'd seen all the John Wayne movies of the era and I bought the glory of the fighting man Hollywood so eagerly sold us. Every one of the men mentioned above took me by the lapels, figuratively, and told me otherwise. They despised Hollywood for cheapening their duty and glorifying their experiences. Even the heroes didn't feel like heroes. They just wanted to stop killing. They just wanted the war to end. Five years later after World War II ended we got Korea.

The ultimate point of this piece is not to just heap still more appreciation on men and women who have sacrificed up to and including their lives in the line of duty, but to question why we have so many veterans and why so many have the Combat Infantry Badge on their tunics?

The Korean conflict was an extension of World War II in that the northern Korean political environment compelled those in charge to invade South Korea to gain favor from China after the Soviet Union shunned their plans to unite the divided country. The United States was the only Western country with enough military capability to hold off this "communist invasion" at that time. Our reaction, in view of the advent of the cold war, was to fight the communist invasion. It is true that Joseph Stalin was more interested in spreading his rule than world peace and with the enormous military machine he built to defeat Germany, he announced his presence with authority everywhere he could in Europe.

Harry Truman was our President in 1950 when the North Koreans crossed the 38th parallel to invade the South. In the winter of 1940, Senator Harry Truman (D-Missouri), acting on complaints from his constituents, discovered gross waste and neglect among contractors building facilities and weapons for the government. In 1941 he formed and chaired *The Special Committee to Investigate the National Defense Program.* By 1944, this watchdog group saved over $15 billion in wasted effort and rooted out defective products in order to help the war effort become more streamlined and honest.

Big business got very, very rich from the war. Seventy-one percent of the government contracts went to the top 100 businesses in the country while smaller businesses had to scramble to become at least sub-contractors. The infamous "cost-plus" contract arrangement allowed businesses to inflate the cost of building something while tacking on the automatic profit of their choosing. The Truman Committee eliminated the worst of those abuses and policed the contractors.

The merry-go-round between wars and industry is what President Eisenhower warned us about in 1960, but we've ignored the warning. The military-industrial complex DOES influence policy. We as a nation seem to exist for war. The Middle East claimed American troops' lives in every decade of my life. Viet Nam cost us almost 60,000 troop deaths and hundreds of thousands more injuries. Iraq and Afghanistan have been our most recent and longest adventures in military action against enemies resembling ancient tribes with modern weapons instead of traditional combat units. Another 6,000 deaths and tens of thousands more injured and maimed combatants are the results to date. The war on terror has as many shadowy enemies as there are people who hate the perception of American imperialism.

Wasn't it interesting to watch the Republicans in Congress cut veterans' benefits and health care during the Bush years? They also fought President Obama on every benefit he attempted to reinstate. In 2014 the

200

Congress is once again going after military and veteran benefits for individuals and their families. Many military families depend on SNAP (Food stamps) to supplement their food costs. Republicans have cut SNAP benefits while continuing subsidies for big agriculture.

Communism was never going to be a political influence here, so why did we fear it so? Perhaps the capitalist moguls were afraid of the influence that populace-based philosophy would have on the working classes irrespective of its political influence while they were trying to cut labor costs. This fear is obvious when our President and anyone who agrees with him on any topic is immediately called a communist by the right wing extremism that continues to lack a viable and proactive message.

Why do we spend more money than the next 20-something industrialized nations combined on defense and security? We aren't being invaded so our sovereignty isn't being threatened. We still own the world's most dominant economy. But that economy needs resources, most importantly oil. The oil we want and need is under the ground of countries where the people have been fighting Western hegemony for over 1,000 years. There's the rub.

If our business people were so good at striking deals, why don't they negotiate deals for resources without having wars? Why don't we make the Afghans an offer they can't refuse for their iron, lithium and copper? Why is blood part of the bargain? Is it cheaper than negotiation? Then again, our self-righteousness, nihilism and hubris continues to direct us to eliminate religious persecution, as we view it, by backward sects like the Taliban. I cannot find a document yet that says that is our job.

The concept of having fewer veterans of combat to celebrate is more appealing to me than having more of them. Then, I'm a selfish, jingoistic American who happens to like his fellow countrymen and wants them to lead peaceful, productive lives so that we, as a nation, can drive the future for the betterment of all mankind and the environment that supports it. Silly me...

Chapter 57:   Rediscovering the Art of Governance

After the 2012 election cycle wherein the Republicans were badly beaten by the Electoral College vote, Bobby Jindal, the Republican governor of Louisiana published an essay wherein he suggests several ways the Republican Party could change and become a party of governance instead of one trying to create a beauty contest every year with no beauties. He begins his essay with the usual canards we've come to know as false:

"Government spending still does not grow our economy. American weakness on the world stage still does not lead to peace. Higher taxes still does not create prosperity for all. And, more government still does not grow jobs."

So, after flashing his GOP credentials he gets down to reality. Jindal's comments are italicized.

"We need to modernize, not moderate. Here are seven lessons Republicans should learn in order to move forward."

1. **Stop looking backward.** *We have to boldly show what the future can look like with the free market policies that we believe in.* I think the 1920s and the 2000s showed us how well this worked out. Free market policies DO look backward. They didn't work then and they won't work now. Supply-Side economics has failed twice in the U.S. and several times in Latin America and Europe. Regulated markets are necessary in a global marketplace or chaos will ensue. See Europe.

2. **Compete for every single vote.** *The 47% and the 53%. And any other combination of numbers that adds up to 100 percent. President Barack Obama and the Democrats can continue trying to divide America into groups of warring communities with competing interests, but we will have none of it. We are going after every vote as we try to unite all Americans.* This is a real news flash considering that Karl Rove and all the GOP operatives have been creating an *us v. them* country for 30 years or more. Which communities are warring for competing interests? The unemployed? The poor? Who? Did the Democrats invent the Tea Party?

3. **Reject identity politics.** *The old notion that ours should be a colorblind society is the right one, and we should pursue that with vigor. Identity politics is corrosive to the great American melting pot and we reject it. We will treat all people as individuals rather than as members of special interest groups.* Here is his first major break with the GOP dogma operating since 1972. Holy cow! We are a diverse nation! But this doesn't explain the destruction of the *Voting Rights Act* by the SCOTUS, nor the race to

conservative states' voter ID laws which clearly disenfranchise voters who tend to vote Democrat.

4. ***Stop being the stupid party.*** *It's time for a new Republican party that talks like adults. It's time for us to articulate our plans and visions for America in real terms. We had a number of Republicans damage the brand this year with offensive and bizarre comments. Enough of that.* No kidding. This means divorcing themselves from the evangelical right wing extremists, et. al., that push a tax-free religious agenda as well as disconnecting from the Tea Party craziness.

5. ***Stop insulting the intelligence of voters.*** *We need to trust the smarts of the American people. We have to stop dumbing down our ideas and stop reducing everything to mindless slogans and tag lines for 30-second ads. We must be willing to provide details in describing our views.* Gosh. I hope it's not about supply-side economics or unregulated free markets. The silence will be deafening. He's right about insulting the voters' intelligence, though. The Tea Party shows us all what stupid and crazy really means. By dumping the GOP sloganeering and admen, unemployment will jump a tenth of a point. As of this writing, we're still waiting for some pro-active GOP ideas that benefit the general public.

6. ***Quit "big."*** *We are not the party of big business, big banks, big Wall Street bailouts, big corporate loopholes, or big anything.* Actually, you are, Bobby. *We must not be the party that simply protects the well off so they can keep their toys. We have to be the party that shows all Americans how they can thrive. We are the party whose ideas will help the middle class, and help more folks join the middle class. We are a populist party and need to make that clear.* I can't help but hear the dulcet tones of Franklin Roosevelt here. Is Jindal trying to create a second coming of **New Deal** populism? This sure sounds like it. What a strange coincidence that in 2014, none of this came out as part of the GOP campaigns.

7. ***Focus on people, not government.*** *We must stop competing with Democrats for the job of "Government Manager," and come up with ideas that can unleash the dynamic abilities of the American people. We need to lead the way with policies that can create prosperity. We believe in organic solutions, not big government solutions. We need a bottom-up government that fits the digital age. Right now we have an outdated centralized government trying to manage a decentralized economy.* I remember Barack Obama talking about a bottom-up government during the campaign. Jindal is reversing $6 billion worth of campaign hype and rhetoric. Losing will do that, I suppose. The trick here, of course, is to get the "organics" motivated enough to participate in pushing their representatives to "unleash the dynamic abilities of the

203

American people". Perhaps voting for a JOBS BILL or two would be a good start.

So, here is one of the "bright" stars of the Republican Party trying to straddle both ideals of pure conservatism and the necessities to make our nation work. Right now, those ideals are still going in opposite directions, but the Democrats seem reenergized to hold firm and show that just giving in is not compromise just as saying "NO" to everything is not governing.

As the old man of 2014 wanders toward the swaddling babe of 2015, we will see how much respect our elected officials have for their constituents. Will bi-partisanship arise within a GOP controlled Congress, or will gridlock and ineffectiveness once again plunge us into economic and social turmoil? With the Democrats running away from the President and the positive accomplishments from the last six years, it's no wonder that two-thirds of the electorate stayed home and didn't vote. The Democrats made themselves look like they ALSO were the whores of Wall Street to the voters. No wonder they lost so many Senate and House seats.

If the social/economic cliff is our destiny then it is clear that we have yet to rediscover the art of governance and our Congress will continue to experience single-digit approval ratings from the people AND the world. As Jindal suggests, unless we rediscover our senses and put away the divisive nonsense created by Rove, Ailes, Atwater, Norquist and their ilk, we may never be able to effectively govern ourselves and will end up as another great civilization that failed by its own hand. Rediscovering the art of compromise as a replacement for rancor and partisanship for all things political might just blow the dust off the intentions of our founders when they wrote the Constitution, warts and all.

Chapter 58:   The Trap of Unlimited Progress

In order for us to grasp solutions to complex problems, problems that have been building since our ancestors first learned to chip spear points and arrowheads, we must first come to understand how the problems came into being. Our biological evolution directed us toward having a brain somewhat larger than our ape ancestors who also gave rise to chimpanzees, bonobos and, to a more distant extent, orangutans. The growth of those brain structures allowed us to reason, solve increasingly complex problems, speak in complex language and, in sum, become able to survive as tribal organisms that learned to share tasks and specialize in them.

As with any highly evolved organism, we retained certain brain operations that contributed to our survival over the millennia that ended up defining our species as human. Among those survival traits was competing for resources and hoarding of food and materials to sustain life when times were tough and to ensure that the tribe would be able to reproduce. The latter trait is, of course, central to all living things.

The model for today's world's industrialized economy is based on consumption of goods and services with little attention given to the necessities that serve that philosophy. In the financial milieu of today, profit is the prince while growing profit through ever-expanding consumption is the king. I don't think the question is so much how well we're doing, but how we're doing it and how long it will last. We may be trapping ourselves in our own, ancient instincts, instincts that may lead to our own destruction and extinction.

The documentary, *Surviving Progress* reminded us that "modern" humans have been around for only 50,000 years, or so. There is, however, plenty of hard evidence indicating that humans and their ancient ancestors have been inventing tools and weapons for a million years or so. Further evidence shows that the species, *Homo sapiens*, has walked the planet for almost 200,000 years. All the while, our species developed new and better technology by which it survived rapid climate, habitat and food source changes. The film suggests that one of the major reasons we adapted more rapidly than any other multi-celled organism is that a small, modern portion of our brains has the ability to ask, "Why"?

By asking that question about everything our lives encounter we are able to work out alternate solutions to problems real or imagined. The film uses the example of success being its own trap. Humans invented weapons and tactics to subdue large mammals, like the wooly mammoth elephant, for food, clothing, tools and building materials for their shelters. Recent evidence points to humans developing tactics that herded elephants over cliffs thus avoiding the dangerous "combat" required to kill one for the tribe. By stampeding the elephants off the cliff, humans were able to develop a surfeit of materials and food. In fact, they created a surplus, most of which they couldn't use. That overkill is attributed to the extinction of a highly successful animal, the wooly mammoth. There is no other plausible explanation for their extinction except for the over-hunting by their only predator, man. Sound familiar? Our hunter/gatherer relatives were too successful at killing their food source and caused it to become extinct.

If we use the 50,000 year timeline for modern man, all but about 10,000 of those years were as a hunter/gatherer and tribal organism. Written chronicles are more recent than 10,000 years. Less than 0.2% of our existence on Earth is attributed to "civilization" and only in most very recent times has the majority of the population been deemed to be civilized. The point here is that we are maintaining civilization software (our consciousness) in a 200,000 year old hardware structure (our brains). This civilization thing is very, very new and we're still working it out. The question is, "Will we have time to sort it out before we go beyond our means to do so?"

Our ability to ask "why" also suggests that we have the ability to look to the future and to the consequences of our actions. That is, however, also a relatively new phenomenon and our brains are still not quite used to it. It is plausible to assume that there were two directions early humans traveled in this thought/survival process development.

One direction was that of the gatherer who hoarded as much as possible for lean times. Those who experienced and understood that whatever they gathered for food was either seasonal or climatological and they in fact stashed what they could when times were good. The other direction, most likely followed by the hunters, was to kill and eat as much as they could for as long as they could. If, however, the food sources became too difficult to catch or too scarce to feed the tribe due to seasonality or climate changes, great suffering and die offs would result. It must have been that the gathering philosophy merged with the hunting philosophy to find ways to prepare for lean times and assure the survival of the tribe. After all, here we are today, 7 billion strong….and counting.

From this unique mental platform of asking why, humans learned to experiment with the limits of their observational abilities to explain observable phenomena. This intellectual breakthrough could be said to be the birth of science. If using rock "A" while knapping spear points produced a point that was inferior to the people using rock "B", the "A" people started using the "B" rock to keep up and improve the technology. Still, here we are today in a modern technological world that is about 200 years old (think: the industrial revolution) with a 50,000 year old mindset that is now the storehouse of ancient survival skills as well as the accumulation of great technological advancement in a very, very short time.

In her book, *The Watchman's Rattle*, Rebecca Costa summed this up by saying that social evolution has far outstripped biological evolution for the human being. The ancient humans were subjected to natural laws while modern humans rewrote those laws and invented a few new ones to boot; like economics and medicine. Will these modern inventions and laws be our own epitaph? Let's look at some of our successes to help make that conclusion.

The most serious and dangerous "success" humans have experienced is the ability to reproduce at rates that are now exceeding the planet's ability to sustain that life. How did this happen? From the time of Rome's fall to the time Columbus set sail for North America, 13 centuries passed and the human population of Earth increased by perhaps 200 million individuals. Now, we make 200 million new human additions to Earth every 3 years, or one United Kingdom's worth of people per year!

Agricultural industry and science, medicine, including the invention of antibiotics, religion and labor-saving machinery have all contributed to assuring that more humans, irrespective of their genetic package, will have increased opportunities to reproduce. The constant fight against disease shows its success with a spike in human population growth following the discovery of antibiotics and vaccines. This spike came right around the start of the 20th century, only just over 100 years ago. When I was in 7th grade (1954) I heard my teachers tell me that the world's human population was just over 3 billion. When I taught AP biology in 2000, I told my students that the population just topped 6 billion. In just another 14 years we have surpassed 7 billion humans on Earth. The demand for resources, food and care are exploding right along with the population growth. This is where we find ourselves in serious trouble with our planet being able to support us and everything else. Still, our capitalists fight like crazy to avoid regulations or altered/new technologies that would stop the pollution of our oceans, atmosphere, fresh water sources and soils. They fight against controlling the waste products of our industry that is causing an unnatural warming phenomenon that will eventually alter the climate to the point where millions of humans will be at risk of starvation, poisoning and environment loss.

There is an attitude found in some religions that whatever we humans do to the earth is O.K. because "God will provide". The scientists and philosophers in the documentary, *Surviving Success* suggest otherwise. In great detail they describe how the Earth is a resource bank from which early humans enjoyed living off the interest. There was abundant soil, water, air and opportunity to grow and develop our own food and shelter that the "capital" of the Earth's resources were not at risk. That was when we had a population of less than 3 billion and the fossil fuel engines had yet to become the dominant tool of our existence.

The ecological impact of our marriage to fossil fuels cannot be understated. The *unlimited progress* trap assumes that resources will last forever and that the Earth is infinitely large to assume our increasing growth. Key data and thresholds are ignored by the business of business to the point where we are creating a climate not seen since the Cenozoic, 65 million years ago. Furthermore, our addiction to fossil fuels coupled with the pursuit of maximum, ever-growing profits creates ecological disasters in the coal fields of Appalachia, the gas fields everywhere, the tar sands in Alberta and our oceans around the world.

This looming disaster is progressing apace such that the oceans are becoming sufficiently acidic as to destroy life-giving, oxygen-producing plankton and fish. The seas can only absorb so much carbon dioxide before they become toxic to life. The fossil record shows that this has happened before during periods of extensive volcanism with major die-offs following. The streams and rivers of Appalachia – and everywhere else where unlimited coal harvesting occurs – are so polluted as to be undrinkable by humans and unlivable for fish and other creatures. The slurry above small towns are not only polluting the ground water and creating pockets of cancers, but are held back by earthen dams that have broken and will break creating massive sludge inundations and killing scores of people.

Most of the people at risk are poor. Businesses fight like hell to keep regulations away even though the citizens that make them wealthy are at extreme risk of dying miserably one way or another. The coal industry's legal battle with the victims of black lung disease is a prime example of how corporate America disregards the human element in their balance sheets: The workers who make them rich are expendable. The poor are seen as the cost of doing business in the world of stockholder demands for continuous financial growth. Indeed, some corporations deem it less expensive to pay law suit settlements than to fix the things that cause the injuries or sickness. This is the height of cravenness, but also reflects the mindset of the corporation in particular and unregulated capitalism in general.

The Earth is at risk too, but there are no lawyers strong enough to defend its sanctity for providing an environment for life. The Earth will respond to our irresponsible stewardship by destroying our ability to feed ourselves, have safe drinking water and to resist epidemic diseases. We have already seen how the economics of pharmacy works regarding AIDS and now Ebola diseases: the rich countries get the most attention while the poor countries are given little care, hope or resources. Add to that the corruption within the poor countries, and any great benefits are siphoned off by the local politicians or gangsters. These phenomena are not new and are the primitive responses from a population of humans in desperate want for their perceived survival.

The "trap" of ever-growing economics, the resistance by the rich to give up some of their wealth (redistribution) for the benefit of the greater good and our marriage to the memes of money first is closing around us while we run away from its jaws only to accelerate their closure upon us all.

Chapter 59:   Let Freedom Ring

There has been much talk about our freedoms as a people in the United States and how many or how few of them are being usurped, threatened or damaged by some decision made by some agency, politician or court ruling. All facets of the political spectrum seem to have some opinion about this subject so near and dear to the hearts of all red, white and blue citizens.

Take the Patriot Act...please. The 4th Amendment specifically states that any intrusion by government shall not be permitted without just cause or a warrant. The "emergency" legislation that produced this large governmental boot, the Patriot Act, was ginned up before 11 September 2001 by a justice department headed by some guy who lost an election for state attorney general in Missouri to a dead man and became the attorney general for the whole United States. The opportunity to foist this invasion of our privacy by government resulted in the multi-billion dollar boondoggle bureaucracy known as Homeland Security. The Bush administration scared Congress into giving it *carte blanche* to staff this outfit to the tune of over 40,000 new government employees, dozens of new buildings and great publicity that have produced the illusion of security. No attacks by crazed terrorists must mean, to those who fostered this fear response, that it all this worked. The 4th Amendment was the price.

So, how do you feel about having your telephone monitored, your e-mail read and your location checked every day? Are you a risk to our nation? Where are the warrants? Do we trust homeland security to be ever so diligent and fair?

Instead of just directing better coordination of our intelligence communities that already exist, Cheney and the fear mongers created a whole new government agency and stomped on the 4th Amendment.

We have laws that give women the freedom and rights to choose their reproductive decisions. The First Amendment guarantees each of us the freedom of and from religion. It also guarantees us the right to assemble peacefully, to speak our minds and have our grievances heard. Why, then, were police using all the force necessary to break up the peaceful Occupy gatherings? The media have the freedom to print anything they like, but the people have the freedom to decide whether the publications are real or claptrap. Sadly, the press/media are owned by businesses who struggle with the ethical dilemma of printing and influencing information that may be opposite to the ownership's view. Most, but not all media, practice high ethical standards. The real question with the media is whether or not they are being complete in their investigations or just complicit with political pressure.

The conservative side of American politics keeps saying that the other guys are trying to destroy our freedoms. The more conservative the voice, the more freedoms are said to be in jeopardy. Yet conservatives keep saying a Judeo-Christian agenda is the basis for our Constitution, that our fears justify our phones being tapped without a warrant, that a woman does NOT have the right to choose her own reproductive behavior; they want to legislate who can marry who and say that the mostly peaceful gatherings of the "Occupy" movement are illegal and harmful. Conservative media blasts every other media as liars and exhibiting irresponsible bias.

I don't hear those freedoms being threatened by progressives or liberals. I hear: Let Freedom Ring!

The problem with having a conservative-dominated Supreme Court is that the bias toward political expediency influences their decisions and warps the letter and intent of the Constitution itself. There is no "fair and balanced" view from the media and the court is performing as a social/political judiciary rather than interpreters of the law. Perhaps limiting the tenure of Justices to 20 years instead of the life terms they are currently sentenced to would bring more honesty to the bench.

Chapter 60:   Let's Try to Accentuate the Positive

The best-selling author, Steven Johnson, wrote a piece that offered an alternative to the "gloom and doom" of current punditry. He begins by asking us to take the quiz about our how we feel we're doing compared to four years ago and then toward a longer look back.

He uses criteria covering the last 20 years for *social health, high school dropouts, college enrollment, juvenile crime, drunken driving, traffic deaths, infant mortality, life expectancy, per capita gasoline consumption, workplace injuries, air pollution, divorce, wage equality between genders, charitable giving, voter turnout, per capita GDP and teen pregnancy.*

Mr. Johnson tells us that our overall "social wellness" has improved by more than 20% citing modern medicine, anti-depressants, insulin pumps and coronary bypass surgery improvements. I think he really meant to say "physical wellness" here. The social issues like crime trends and stable families/communities are improved over the last 20 years, but only crime trends get the publicity.

Johnson reminds us that most Americans think ½ of our marriages end in divorce, but points out that this number has declined by almost 1/3 since the early 1980s. He does not mention how and why the divorce rate declines, but it is known that the marriage rate is also declining for people in the same age group from 20 years ago. Maybe marriage in a "modern" society requires more maturity than the high school sweetheart condition offers.

More: "...though the world's population has more than doubled over the past 50 years, the percentage living in poverty has declined by 50% over that period. Infant mortality and life expectancy have improved by more than 40% in Latin America since the early 1990s. No country in history has improved its average standard of living faster than China has over the past two decades." That's nice to know, but what about the United States where our poverty rate continues to rise (50 million people in poverty from the latest reports) while we rank near the bottom of the top 10 in infant mortality? Coincident with our increase in poverty and poor infant mortality is the growing gap between the rich, the middle class and poor, now at levels equivalent to the 1920s.

Life expectancy improvements in Latin America must be attributable to improved medical services, drugs and more caregivers. That worked for us, so it should work for them. Also, they had a long way to go from where they were; the data indicates a *relative* improvement. Safe drinking water is still a challenge in most of Latin America.

Good for China. They had a long, long way to go too. During World War II, hundreds of thousands of Chinese laborers built airfields for Allied bombers and fighters by HAND. Obtaining the gasoline and diesel-powered devices to improve labor conditions since then may have helped construction efficiency while Western capitalist democracies sent all sorts of unskilled, then skilled jobs to China. The Chinese are very industrious people, so it should be no surprise that they would rapidly grow into the Western-style economies and improve on the concept of capitalistic productivity. The main attraction of China's labor force by Western businesses is that it is both abundant and cheap.

Unemployment in the United States remains stubbornly around 6% while our politicians dither over how to fix our economy. U.S. household debt has soared over the last two decades – similar to the 1920s when people were buying stocks on margin. The recent recession and financial crisis has slowed this problem, but the rules haven't changed for investment banking to prevent a recurrence of the latest orgy of greed. The two most dramatic economic downturns in the last 100 years in the United States mirror each other regarding their causes: Unregulated banking/investing, government austerity as it pertains to the public sector and the absent-mindedness of the moneyed elite. They proved that those who forget or ignore history are doomed to repeat it, just as Santayana said they would.

Global warming and climate change stories keep increasing in the media and the warnings from real science keep coming true. Yet, our species is so wed to fossil fuel energy that we refuse to see the error of our ways and develop real, sustainable fuels and energy sources that won't threaten the planet's ability to provide living opportunities for us and everything else.

We hear much more about the negative trends than the positive ones for two main reasons, according to Johnson.

The media, who are influenced by big business, lead us to believe that our private sector developed technology will solve all problems and provide ever-growing improvements in our lives. One has to wonder how another version of the iPod will cause more food to grow on overused soil. The positive trends in our social health, however, come from more complex sources that include government investment, public service, demographic changes, increases in shared knowledge and rising affluence. The private sector only participates actively when there is profit immediately available. In the United States there is little long-term planning for new technologies as long as old ones keep selling. Moreover, the media is the main sales vehicle for most products.

During the last decade, the concept of *geo-engineering* has entered the conversation as ways to reverse the global warming trend. This "movement" is actively discussing ways to shield sunlight such that warming will be abated. They want to create a similar effect to volcanic activity in the upper atmosphere. Instead of attacking the problem of low atmosphere pollution, the "engineers" want to pollute the upper atmosphere. If anything screams out more to the enabling of fossil fuel users and consumers freedom from the responsibility of planet destruction, I'm not aware of it. Naomi Klein's newest book, *This Changes Everything* discusses this alarming, corporate sponsored "investigation" in frightening detail; people are actually serious about spraying sulfur dioxide into the stratosphere to deflect the sun's energy instead of *harnessing* that energy to avoid fossil fuel addiction. Amazing.

The public sector (government), meanwhile, doesn't spend billions of dollars on marketing campaigns that trumpet its successes. If a multinational corporation, for example, invents a slightly better detergent, it will spend a fortune to alert the world that the product is now "new and improved." The government agencies don't take out prime-time ads to tout the remarkable decrease in air pollution from technology and regulations over the last 20 years, even though that success story is far more important than a trivial improvement in laundry soap. Is it any wonder that so many Americans are clueless about what their government is doing, both good and bad?

Our national blind spot on this fact is compounded by our short attention span for stories of incremental progress. The public is more attuned to tabloid journalism or huge leaps in progress that directly affect their immediate needs. They are also more inclined, like motorists passing a highway wreck, to be fascinated with the negative opinions of certain pundits. The celebration of slow, steady progress doesn't happen until certain success points are reached. It's about the sale of entertainment that has created this need to be constantly entertained no matter what the issue.

The second half of the 1990s was a period in which both economic and social trends were decisively upbeat. The stock market was surging, and the inequality between classes was declining. Coincidentally crime, drug use, welfare dependence and poverty were all trending in an encouraging direction.

With Bill Clinton, a Democrat, in the White House, you might assume the op-ed pages of the left-of-center *Washington Post* would be bursting with pride over the state of the nation. That was not the case. During 1997, in the middle of the greatest peacetime economic boom in U.S. history (and before the Monica Lewinsky scandal), 71% of all editorials published in the Post expressing opinions about the country's current state focused on negative trends. Less than 5% of the total number of editorials concentrated on a positive development. The *If it bleeds it leads* philosophy still ran the show.

Johnson goes on to speculate that the media bias ignoring incremental progress will be more damaging than any bias toward any political party; the bias being *toward* extreme events and the more negative the event, the deeper the bias. Mr. Johnson points out that neuroscience and psychology show that the human mind is more inclined toward negative information than the positive...as much as some of us clamor for it. All one has to do is look at the Fox News tapes after Sgt. Bergdahl was released from terrorist captivity to see how some good news can morph into politically-charged rancor.

One positive social trend that did generate a significant amount of media coverage, but was mostly ignored by the public was the extraordinary drop in the U.S. crime rate since the mid-'90s. The violent crime rate dropped from 51 to 15 per thousand people between 1995 and 2010. Yet according to a series of Gallup polls conducted over the past 10 years, more than two-thirds of Americans believe that crime has been getting worse, year after year. Perhaps the gun lobby is behind this so that the gun makers can keep raking in record profits.

Two major points conclude this subject: (1) We underestimate the incremental progress occurring everywhere around us. (2) We misunderstand where that progress arises. The lesson for all of us here is that we, one of the most educated nations on Earth must do more objective homework in appreciating our progress while examining the veracity of the negative aspects of our society. We should do what the human toolmaker is supposed to do: fix the problem. If we aspire to low goals, we will not fix the complex problems. If we aspire to continued social development we are *compelled* to fix them. The latter is the positive, progressive direction we all should take in our daily lives. It may help us elect more representative government instead of more professional politicians.

Chapter 61:   Outside of the Box

Democracy is at risk of being undermined by the oil and gas industries. Towns are being sued by the energy industry for voting against having holes drilled in their property for the sake of extracting oil/gas. Recent shocking news and documentaries have shown private residences with exploding and burning water coming from their water taps and garden hoses and earthquake swarms after fracking began in their area. The pollution potential has yet to be fully understood or quantified. You might recall when this attack against the private ownership of the land began.

It happened during George W. Bush's first term when Dick Cheney and friends, including the felonious Kenneth Lay of Enron infamy, convened a secret series of meetings that gutted the EPA, OSHA and other regulatory agencies that would oversee the technology and the drilling for environmental and human safety purposes. They rammed virtually unlimited drilling and exploration through to laws or Presidential decree. An article (1/17/2013) by David Sirota shocked readers by exposing the naked attacks on the citizens of America by the oil/gas companies insisting that what lies beneath is theirs to exploit. The title of the article is *Can Capitalism and Democracy Coexist?* I think that question is more poignant now than ever.

In view of the complexity of our national problems, most of which involve money, jobs, our environment, the poor, education and health care, let's step outside the box and try something new, you know, like using existing technology to create new industries, employ millions and solve short-term problems for the long term. We've done it before. Remember, we went from the experimental rockets of World War II to the moon in 12 years.

Some engineers at NASA who, having had their budgets reduced and thus with time on their hands, conjured up some new ideas for space exploitation. They thought we could assemble those solar panels used to operate satellites and our international space station in a large array such that it could generate enough electricity to supply cities and towns on Earth. The transmitter attached to this array sends the electrical energy to receivers on Earth much like we receive TV signals from communication satellites. When they proposed this idea to our Department of Energy, they were told to go mind their rockets and nozzles. Our intrepid engineers then went to Canada's energy people who fell over themselves with excitement and are currently developing this idea.

We must keep in mind the massive project necessary for electrifying the Earth from space-gathered sunlight. The arrays would likely have to be the size of Rhode Island. So what? They'd be hundreds of miles above the

Earth's surface, on the job 24/7 and everyone would be thrilled to see them in the night sky. We do have the technology to build it. Do we have the political will?

Would this project be expensive? Oh yes! We may even resurrect the space shuttles from the museums to kick it off until we build something even smarter, like reusable robotic rockets that launch and deposit sub-assemblies for space-based workers or robots to assemble. The cost recovery, savings and avoidance are difficult to assess, but intriguing in light of dwindling carbon-based energy fuels and the pollution they create. The new technologies needed would rival our original space exploration efforts.

Could we do this alone? Probably. After all, we have 20 million unemployed people in country who would be excited about finding work. Who would pay for this project? We would. All of us on Earth who use electricity. The vast wealth of the current oil/gas business would be used to fund some portion of the project of the sun and they would reap huge profits for time immemorial. Additionally, the $30-some trillion sitting in offshore banks would adequately kick-off this massive project. Here's how.

With unlimited, constant electricity for everyone on Earth, everyone would be obliged to pay for it. Every dwelling, camper, vehicle, business that used this power would pay just like we pay for satellite radio or TV. The world is the subscriber to guaranteed energy for as long as the sun shines. Current estimates say the sun is good for another 3 billion years or so.

Now, the payback.... Coal-fired power plants go away, and with that the rape of Appalachia goes away too. Coal mining will be greatly reduced and could revert to a much more environmentally friendly process than just blowing the tops off of mountains and poisoning the water tables. We will still need oil for the interim until the new electrical grid starts to come on line. We'll just need much less of it. In fact, some of our petroleum refinement capacity could be converted to coal tar refinement. Nuclear power plants will no longer be necessary. Use the fuel for other things that are safer. Cutting up all those unnecessary oil tankers provides a bonanza of scrap metal for just about everything else to say nothing of the reduction in diesel fuel use. Dismantling power lines provides another metallic bonanza, in this case, copper. Think of how much quieter we will become when most of our vehicles are electric powered with never a need for refueling...as long as they don't let their subscriptions expire. These conductive metals would be used in liquid metal batteries that show promise in providing great sources of usable, local electricity.

We won't need to spend our money on fuel transporting our oil from the exotic and wonderful places on Earth where the citizens love us so to refineries. We can channel our current petroleum reserves to people-positive

218

items for cheaper commodities...like antibiotics, drugs and containers for them. This would also tend to keep the tar balls out of the oceans.

Of course, we'd have to educate an entire generation of citizens to understand this undertaking, build it, design and build the spin-off products and solve one of the most onerous of looming problems mankind faces. Since most of the Western world has lost/forgotten the capabilities for sustenance economics and the ability to live in a peaceful country, this chance to liberate ourselves from the basic modern need for energy might just allow democracy to regain its control over capitalism and thus preventing the United States from becoming a plutocratic dictatorship run by such lovely beings as the Koch brothers. That prospect alone is enough to motivate me to try.

Chapter 62: Grid Level Electron Storage

While working on this book I came across a topic that managed to light up my science geek lights. I watched a documentary film that exposed the downsides to using giant wind farms in proximity to people as alternative electricity sources.

These wind generators are enormous. They are over 400 feet tall, have a rotor that weighs 7 tons and spins at close to 200 mph speed at the tips. This action creates a boundary layer of air along the leading edge of the blade that smacks into the pylon and makes a *whoosh, whoosh, whoosh* noise audible for half a mile or so. When the sun is low the blades create a pulsing shadow/light phenomenon that drives people nuts, in addition to killing bats and birds. Furthermore, the companies trying to market this technology create all sorts of community strife while buying their way into poor, rural areas that have lots of wind.

A little research shows that there are over 83 countries using wind power to generate as much as 25% of their national electricity. We are at something below 5%. But due to intermittence of the wind, there has to be a gap-filler in the electrical grid to keep the lights on. That means that coal, oil, gas and nuclear power plants can't go away. The same logic applies to solar electrical generation.

It costs about the same to generate a wind farm that produces enough electricity to replace a coal or gas facility supplying the same number of customers, but you still need the fossil fuel plant for the problems stated above. So, this pathway to energy independence takes us to a new paradigm: *Grid Level Electron Storage.*

An MIT professor, Donald Sadoway, has worked with graduate students to develop a device that provides sufficient electricity when the sun isn't shining or the wind isn't blowing. It is called the *liquid metal battery.* It uses the very basics of the original battery invented by Mr. Volta himself: two different metals and a salty electrolyte to conduct electrons. The following website shows Professor Sadoway's introduction to this technology (http://www.ted.com/talks/lang/en/donald_sadoway_the_missing_link_to_rene wable_energy.html).

The really interesting part is that this battery stores enough electricity for a practical usage scale and is cheap to produce at the start, not by the one millionth unit. The battery requires electrical input to keep the electrons circulating and that's where the solar and/or wind devices play a supportive role, not a primary role in providing electricity. Oh, and the excess heat generated by the chemical reactions inside the battery may be used to heat homes or make steam.

As of March, 2012, Sadoway and his team of scientists, funded by both private companies and government agencies, produced a 4 KwH battery that is smaller than a medium coffee table. Four KwH is enough to power a small cottage. Their newly formed company, LMBC, Inc., is working on a shipping container sized battery that can provide 2 MEGAWAT hours of electricity, enough to supply 200 homes. The metals used are not rare, plentiful and found in this country.

In the previous essay you read about building a space-based solar array that beamed electrical energy to Earth. It might have a use for other things, but this battery is available now and it's much, much cheaper that anything we'd put in space. I can be swayed by facts and practicality too.

The point is we cannot drill or bomb our way out of our energy difficulties. The wind will keep blowing somewhere on Earth all the time. The sun is good to go on lighting us up for another 3 billion years, or so. Cheap, reliable electrical power readily available to everyone and anyone gets ours and every other nation dependent on Middle Eastern oil off of that nipple. I can't imagine that there are any reasons coming from sane people who can disagree with this premise.

None of these alternate suggestions mean that wind is a minor player. With the new materials available we can build huge sails for ocean-going ships thus easing their total dependency on oil as their fuel for sailing goods from one country to the next. Plus, with liquid metal batteries and plenty of wind and sun at sea, they can seriously augment or replace their diesel fuel use with the combination of propulsion energy systems.

I hope some entrepreneur gets onto this and markets the daylights out of these simple devices to indeed remove people from the grip of energy companies not motivated to employ new technologies. As long as there is plenty of oil, coal and gas, they won't do a thing. Once again, *We the People* must stand up and demand the new technologies, invest in them and make the changes toward an oil-free future.

We'll get there one way or another, sooner or later. Wouldn't it be nice if we prepared for that day and did it sooner?

Chapter 63:   The Twenty-eighth Amendment

For a few years, people have been passing around different versions of what a twenty-eighth Amendment to our Constitution should include. Frankly, my research and stringing together of history and facts leads me to think that it may take more than just one more Amendment to fix the problems of our form of democracy and avoid another revolution and/or civil war. The items appear in no particular order and are not couched in legalese for which all of us are grateful.

1. Make all elections publicly funded. This should apply to all Federal and state elected offices.   A petition process shall be necessary such that a threshold of valid signatures be collected be sufficient to render a candidate eligible to run for office and receive government funding for the elections.

2. The election "season" shall be limited to six months before the election date, where active campaigning can occur. Another six months prior to the season is allowed for petitioning and candidate validation.

3. The *Citizens United v. Federal Election Commission* decision shall be vacated since no private money whatsoever will be allowed into the electoral process.

4. Once a candidate is fairly elected to a Federal office, he/she will not be permitted, at the end of their term, to seek employment with any organization, company or firm that deals with U.S. or state government projects or contracts.

5. The term limits for U.S. Senator will be limited to two, six-year terms. The term limits for U.S. House of Representatives will be limited to four, two-year terms. Supreme Court Justices will be limited to terms not exceeding 20 years.

6. Election days will be declared a national holiday.

7. Voter registration will be mandatory for every U.S. citizen seeking a driver's license from any state, armed forces enlistment, social welfare services and Social Security Agency registration.

8. Lobbying elected government officials where gifts or money of any value exchanges hands will be interpreted as a felony of bribery and both parties will serve mandatory prison terms as determined by the courts.

9. Abolish the Electoral College and declare election winners by simple majorities of popular votes.

10. Close tax loopholes that allow money earned to be sheltered off-shore. Require that income earned by American companies in foreign lands be brought home and taxed fairly. Eliminate the flat corporate tax of 35% and reduce it to 10% on these earnings.

Some of these suggestions may be difficult to implement, but it will take political willpower and citizen participation such as we haven't seen since World War II to accomplish any of them. The basic problem with trying to get some or all of these items through the existing Congress and to the states for ratification is that the professional politicians are not going to change laws that put them at risk of not getting reelected or threatens them with pulling them off the teat of lobbying and campaign money.

Even though a twenty-eighth Amendment attempts to return government to the citizens through their direct representatives who are working for and listening to THEM, it is more unlikely that something like this will make it to the floor of Congress any time soon. The trick is going to be getting it ratified in time BEFORE anarchy enters the picture, and enough social fabric is frayed that the system of laws breaks down for want of fair distribution of food, shelter and other basics of modern society that keep people from reverting to savagery.

I don't think there is an "ism" yet invented that is perfect for this experiment in a democratic republic. There are things that must be preserved like direct voting for representatives. But to make this work, very high participation by the electorate is necessary. Our culture must have a shift toward revering our vote as being as valuable as our job. The "my vote doesn't count" meme must be replaced by "my vote is essential to my quality of life".

Capitalism must be strongly regulated to prevent abuses, graft and abuse of workers and the environment. We must reinstate the Glass-Steagall Act to prevent greedy speculators for losing depositor money on "creative" schemes that only enrich the few. Vulture capitalism must be stopped to prevent the catastrophe of having our industrial bases moved to cheap labor markets. Health care and public education must be seen as *rights*, not profit centers. Labor unions must be allowed, once again, to flourish, but not to the point where holding companies for ransom is allowed. In short, these additional suggestions are a kind of un-Reagan, a momentum shift by everything we do back to a center where equal opportunity is a reality, educational achievement without drudgery and debt are rewarded with expanding opportunities in new businesses and technologies that are not strictly motivated by short-term profit, but include the successful model of venture capital trial and error.

Afterword

My biggest challenge writing this book was to avoid hyperbole where the writer's "voice" becomes a stentorian scream at silent walls with the hope that someone on the other side of the wall is listening. I know they are not. My voice, strong and opinionated, tries to teach and cajole and encourage change for the better in almost every aspect of our society. Since the task is enormous, I've tried to hit sufficiently on those topics which I think have the greatest impact if pursued by active people. But sometimes, the sarcasm just comes spilling out. An anonymous quote comes to mind: *Sarcasm is what one does instead of kicking the living shit out of somebody. That's illegal.*

Political activism is not for everyone, but community activism should be required by all. It is the community's combined effort that creates responsible representation in government when the vast majority of its members are participating. This is a basic, but necessary definition of a community organism such as we humans are. We are a little smarter than ants, but ants know how to do community. We are not ants and our communities are a little more complex, but some of the principles of utilization, caring, sharing and teaching and seeking are important specialties we share with them.

My final words are for you to be encouraged by your power and your voice. Use them. If you aren't participating, don't complain about the outcomes. It doesn't hurt you at all to be active in your community in a capacity that does something good for you and for someone else. My volunteer teaching of science at a local women's prison certainly woke me up to that fact. My political activism and writing for newspapers was nice and very enjoyable, but it was somewhat abstract compared to actually working with the women whose lives are a shambles but still are resilient enough to try to improve themselves. They are heroes to me.

I'm all in with things like that. I can use your help.

Acknowledged Sources

Birnbaum, Michael

Bracey, Gerald

Britt, Dr, Lawrence

Brooks, David

Bucheit, Paul

Carey, Ray

Costa, Rebecca

Dionne, E. J.

Dowd, Maureen

Edsall, Thomas

Fraser, Steve

Freeman, Joshua

Friedman, Milton

Hartmann, Thom

Hedges, Chris

Helyar, John

Jindal, Bobby

Johnson, Steven

Keynes, John Maynard

Klein, Gene

Klein, Naomi

Meyerson, Harold

Ravitch, Diane

Sadoway, Donald

Summer, Mark

Stern, Andy

Zinn, Howard

www.ingramcontent.com/pod-product-compliance
Lightning Source LLC
Chambersburg PA
CBHW081414270326
41931CB00015B/3274